Assisted Dying

This book provides an in-depth critique of the arguments surrounding legislative control of assisted dying, with particular emphasis on the regulatory role of the state. In the classical tradition of libertarianism, the state is generally presumed to have a remit to intervene where an individual's actions threaten another rather than harm the individuals themselves. This arguably leaves a question mark over the state's determined intervention, in the United Kingdom and elsewhere, into the private and highly personal choices of individuals to die rather than live.

This book will argue that the state's interests are and should be second to the interests that people themselves have in choosing their own death. The book evaluates the arguments for and against legalisation of assisted dying primarily within the context of the United Kingdom and concludes that the case against assisted dying is not made. It also concedes that the arguments in favour of legalisation lead inexorably to the position that the gate-keeping role of healthcare professionals, which is typical in those countries which have legalised assisted dying, cannot be defended.

Sheila A. M. McLean is International Bar Association Professor of Law Ethics in Medicine at the University of Glasgow and Director of the Institute of Law Ethics in Medicine.

D1382427

Biomedical Law and Ethics Library
Series Editor: Sheila A. M. McLean

Scientific and clinical advances, social and political developments and the impact of healthcare on our lives raise profound ethical and legal questions. Medical law and ethics have become central to our understanding of these problems, and are important tools for the analysis and resolution of problems – real or imagined.

In this series, scholars at the forefront of biomedical law and ethics contribute to the debates in this area, with accessible, thought-provoking and sometimes controversial ideas. Each book in the series develops an independent hypothesis and argues cogently for a particular position. One of the major contributions of this series is the extent to which both law and ethics are utilised in the content of the books, and the shape of the series itself.

The books in this series are analytical, with a key target audience of lawyers, doctors, nurses and the intelligent lay public.

Available titles:

Human Fertilisation and Embryology (2007)
Reproducing Regulation
Kirsty Horsey and Hazel Biggs

Intention and Causation in Medical Non-Killing (2006)
The Impact of Criminal Law Concepts on Euthanasia and Assisted Suicide
Glenys Williams

Impairment and Disability (2007)
Law and Ethics at the Beginning and End of Life
Sheila McLean and Sheila Williamson

Bioethics and the Humanities (2007)
Attitudes and Perceptions
Robin Downie and Jane Macnaughton

Defending the Genetic Supermarket (2007)
The Law and Ethics of Selecting the Next Generation
Colin Gavaghan

The Harm Paradox (2007)
Tort Law and the Unwanted Child in an Era of Choice
Nicolette Priaulx

Assisted Dying
Reflections on the need for law reform
Sheila A. M. McLean

Forthcoming titles include:

Medicine, Malpractice and Misapprehensions
Vivienne Harpwood

Best Interests of the Child in Healthcare
Sarah Elliston

Euthanasia, Ethics and the Law
From Conflict to Compromise?
Richard Huxtable

Values in Medicine
The realities of clinical practice
Donald Evans

Medicine, Law and the Public Interest
Communitarian Perspectives on Medical Law
J Kenyon Mason and Graeme Laurie

Healthcare Research Ethics and Law
Regulation, Review and Responsibility
Hazel Biggs

The Body in Bioethics
Alastair Campbell

About the Series Editor

Professor Sheila McLean is International Bar Association Professor of Law and Ethics in Medicine and Director of the Institute of Law and Ethics in Medicine at the University of Glasgow.

Assisted Dying

Reflections on the need for law reform

Sheila A. M. McLean

Routledge·Cavendish
Taylor & Francis Group

First published 2007 by Routledge-Cavendish
2 Park Square, Milton Park, Abingdon, Oxon OX14 4RN

Simultaneously published in the USA and Canada
by Routledge-Cavendish
270 Madison Ave, New York, NY 10016

Routledge-Cavendish is an imprint of the Taylor & Francis Group, an informa business

© 2007 Sheila A. M. McLean

Typeset in Times by
Florence Production Ltd, Stoodleigh, Devon
Printed and bound in Great Britain by
Antony Rowe Ltd, Chippenham, Wiltshire

British Library Cataloguing in Publication Data
A catalogue record for this book is available from the British Library

Library of Congress Cataloging in Publication Data
McLean, Sheila.
   Assisted dying: reflections on the need for law reform/Sheila A. M. McLean.
      p. cm.
   Includes bibliographical references and index.
      1. Euthanasia – Law and legislation – Great Britain.   2. Right to die –
   Law and legislation – Great Britain.   I. Title.
   KD3410.E88M35 2007
   344.4104'197 – dc22   2007020938

ISBN10: 1–84472–055–1 (hbk)
ISBN10: 1–84472–054–3 (pbk)
ISBN10: 0–203–94047–7 (ebk)

ISBN13: 978–1–84472–055–2 (hbk)
ISBN13: 978–1–84472–054–5 (pbk)
ISBN13: 978–0–203–94047–1 (ebk)

Contents

Introduction

It is scarcely surprising that there is a huge volume of literature about assisted dying. The way in which we die is obviously of great significance to us, as is the life we lead and the way we live it. We are now living longer, often with chronic but manageable conditions. Indeed, even conditions which would previously have been terminal can be handled in such a way that we may survive with them longer now than ever before. Paradoxically, however, it has been said that '[t]he most striking result of the success of medical technology is the very strong trend toward the combination of longer lives and worsening health'.[1]

For some people confronting the end of their lives will be a peaceful, even defining, moment. For others, however, the possibility of a drawn-out death, characterised by loss of control and suffering, deforms the final stages of life. Modern medicine raises the possibility – doubtless welcomed by some – of extending lifespan, with or without perceived quality. For others, these same capacities are more like a threat. Thus:

> The . . . possibility of being maintained on life support for months and in some cases for years, has engendered anxiety among elderly and non-elderly patients. Accordingly, patients and their families are more and more willing to take part in the medical decisions at the end of life.[2]

In some cases, this search for engagement, for involvement in end-of-life decisions will take the form of wanting to control our deaths as we wish to shape our lives. Although longevity is increasing, and is actively encouraged by the advice on lifestyle, which can help us live longer, and the medicines and therapies, which can help achieve this, not everyone values quantity

1   Callahan, D, *The Troubled Dream of Life: In Search of a Peaceful Death*, 2000, Washington, DC: Georgetown University Press, at pp 43–44.
2   Frileux, S, Lelievre, C, Nunoz Sastre, M T, Mullet, E and Sorum, P C, 'When is physician assisted suicide or euthanasia acceptable?', (2003) 29 *Journal Medical Ethics* 330–336, at p 330.

over quality of life. Although life with quality can be ensured for many by a combination of modern medicine and people's own life choices, such a happy outcome is not always possible. Some deaths come 'not as the peaceful conclusion to a life, but as a violent and cruel destroyer'.[3] Moreover, there are also some conditions which cannot be alleviated – for example, some of the neurodegenerative illnesses – and which lead inevitably to a prolonged, unhappy dying process. Thus, some people experience 'growing concern about the prospect of protracted deaths marked by incapacitation, intolerable pain and indignity, and invasion by machines and tubing'.[4] In fact, even where treatment is available, some people may prefer not to accept it, choosing rather to die on their own terms. For some this will mean taking their own life by suicide. However, for others, that option is not available for emotional, physical or situational reasons. In these cases, people may seek help to ensure that their lives can be ended when they want and in a painless way.

Underpinning this debate are the relative values to be given to the ethical and legal principles which demarcate the line between lawful and unlawful conduct as well as between what is deemed ethical and what is not. Identifying these principles and calculating the weight to be given to them are difficult but important tasks on which wide differences of opinion are both possible and real. Deeply held and fervent argument rages as to whether or not the apparent desire of some people to grab control of their deaths as well as their lives should be facilitated by law. An important question, then, is:

> Can an advanced society steeped in the medical doctrine of death as defeat end prolonged suffering without compromising its ethical underpinnings? And can suffering people be given the help they crave without bestowing on physicians a power that is intimidating, both in its magnitude and in its potential for abuse?[5]

In some societies, this particular nettle has been grasped by the legalisation of assisted dying (in the form of voluntary euthanasia or assisted suicide). However, there is significant debate about whether or not in those countries where legalisation has already taken place the result has been abuse or liberation. It is important that this debate is informed and clear, yet all too often both opponents and proponents of legalisation of assisted dying seem to muddy the waters by protesting loudly that their position is the right one, to the detriment of rational argumentation. Each claims that their position is correct based on

---

3   Woodman, S, *Last Rights: The Struggle over the Right to Die*, 1998, New York and London: Plenum Trade, at p 25.
4   Thomasma, D C, 'An analysis of arguments for and against euthanasia and assisted suicide: Part one', (1996) 5 *Cambridge Quarterly of Healthcare Ethics*, 62–76, at p 62.
5   Woodman, S, at p 73.

ideology or empirical evidence which is often interpreted with a particular perspective in mind. Like virtually everyone else, I come to this question with already established views about how best we can measure the arguments and reach a satisfactory conclusion. As I will explain in more depth in what follows, I start from the position that the legitimacy of state control over private choices is not to be taken for granted unless it can be shown that failure of the state to intervene results in harm to others. I will, therefore, evaluate the debate against a Millian value system. It is, of course, quite possible to address assisted dying from other perspectives, but I have chosen this one as it underpins the legal, philosophical and political framework of most – if not all – western democracies, to a greater or lesser extent.

Even though people differ in their views about end-of-life decisions, arguably most will concede (albeit possibly in different situations) that life is not always preferable to death. Thus, even the most fervent opponents of legalisation of assisted dying will accept that in some circumstances it is permissible not to strive to maintain or save life, accepting therefore that it may be permissible to withhold or withdraw life-saving or life-sustaining treatment where, for example, it can be described as futile or 'extraordinary'. However, these same people would also argue that it is never right actively to assist someone to die. On the other hand, proponents of assisted dying will want to suggest that there is no real difference, ethically, between actively helping someone to die and merely omitting to save them. The gulf between these positions is both significant and subtle. It rests at first sight most fundamentally on respect for the sanctity of all life, but in fact is informed by a much more complex set of values and interpretations of principle. In fact, one of the great paradoxes of this entire debate is the extent to which both sides essentially use the same language in their apparently irreconcilable arguments; importantly, however, they mean different things by the same concepts. For example, as we will see later, everyone can surely agree on the value of the sanctity of life, but whether we adopt a secular or religious version of it will have a significant impact on what we then conclude in respect of assisted dying.

It is probably true that there has never been a better opportunity than now to reconsider the arguments for and against assisted dying in the United Kingdom, in large part because of recent parliamentary activity which has thrust the issue back into the public domain. The efforts by Lord Joffe to gain Parliamentary approval of his Assisted Dying for the Terminally Ill Bill resulted in a sustained debate in the House of Lords and the establishment of a Select Committee to consider and report on the Bill.[6] Although the Bill failed to be endorsed in the House of Lords, Lord Joffe has indicated his intention

6   House of Lords Select Committee on the Assisted Dying for the Terminally Ill Bill, *Report of the House of Lords Select Committee on the Assisted Dying for the Terminally Ill Bill* HL Paper 86-1 (2005).

to reintroduce it. Meantime, British people are travelling to other countries – most notably Switzerland – to have an assisted death.

At the same time, doctors seem ambivalent about their possible role. Their previous firmly held opposition to legalisation of assisted dying has seemingly undergone change, although at best their professional organisations are neutral rather than overtly supportive. Since it is generally assumed that doctors would have ultimate responsibility for assisting in end-of-life decisions, it is perhaps scarcely surprising that they should have strong, albeit far from uniform, views on this subject and indeed that their views are given considerable weight. Yet some would argue that too much weight is given to doctors and the role they play. Katz, for example, suggests:

> It cannot be accidental that the principles of medical ethics have never commanded physicians and their patients to get to know and understand one another so that they can make decisions jointly. We need to enquire why physicians have been so insistent in their demand that all authority be vested in one party – the doctor.[7]

We need, therefore, also to interrogate the question as to whether or not the views of this group (which is of course by no means homogeneous) should be permitted to dominate a debate which is, at base, about the balance to be struck between rights-based claims on the one hand and concerns about slippery slopes on the other. For doctors, the question is as follows:

> Respect for autonomy, privacy, and dignity on the one hand, and avoiding harm to third parties, prohibiting suicide, and respect for biological life on the other, inform the debate over how, if at all, medicine may sanction and participate in the hastening of death.[8]

Despite the differences between opponents and proponents, or perhaps because of them, on one thing they will likely agree. This is not a debate that will go away in a hurry. Irrespective of the legal position in the United Kingdom, people will continue to hold strong views about assisted dying and those who are driven to find assistance will continue to seek, and sometimes obtain, assisted deaths, triggering legal and social debate. Even if the United Kingdom Parliament chooses never to legalise assisted dying, therefore, people in the United Kingdom will continue to have an interest in the subject and will continue to seek to choose their own deaths. For this reason, if for no other, we need to continue to review the debate. Moreover, as life expectancy grows

---

7   Katz, J, *The Silent World of Doctor and Patient*, 1984, New York: The Free Press, at p xvii.
8   Hilliard, B, *The US Supreme Court and Medical Ethics*, 2004, St Paul, MN: Paragon, at p 324.

the 'new epidemiology'[9] of the way we die will vest increased significance in whether we, doctors, the state or others actually have control over it. This pits powerful ideologies against each other; for example, respect for autonomy versus the (often faith based) doctrine of the sanctity of life.

In what follows, I will attempt to evaluate these issues and explore the values which shape our conclusion as to the ethics of assisted dying. It will, of course, also be necessary to consider what role, if any, the law can or should play in translating any conclusions into reality. Ultimately, as Devlin says, '... the question is not how a person is to ascertain the morality which he adopts and follows, but how the law is to ascertain the morality which it enforces'.[10]

---

9 Battin, M P, *The Least Worst Death: Essays in Bioethics on the End of Life*, 1994, Oxford University Press, at p 9.
10 Devlin, P, *The Enforcement of Morals*, 1965, Oxford University Press, at p x.

Chapter 1

An outline of the debate

'Dying woman seeks backing to hasten death'[1]

This is just one of the seemingly endless headlines concerning UK citizens who want to obtain an assisted death at a time of their own choosing and irrespective of the views of others. As Donnison and Bryson noted,

> until recently, people have usually seemed content to leave decisions about death and dying to doctors. In the last few years, however, death and the medical decisions bearing upon it have rarely been out of the headlines or off the television screens for long.[2]

While the law in the United Kingdom stands resolutely (for the moment at least) against facilitating requests for assisted dying, individuals continue to resist and even ignore it, arguing that this is a matter of personal conscience. Some even travel overseas (usually to Switzerland) to achieve the death they so desire. Of course, these people are a relatively small minority; most people die 'naturally', albeit sometimes with medical assistance (within the terms of the law). Nonetheless, we cannot dismiss the importance of this debate simply because for the moment so few people try to circumvent the law. Not only does this tell us nothing about how many people might choose an assisted death were it legally available to them, but numbers are not measures of morality.

The subject of assisted dying is one which generates considerable controversy because 'it arouses questions about the morality of killing, the effectiveness of consent, the duties of physicians, and equity in the distribution of resources. . . .'.[3] Volumes have been written arguing both for and against legalisation, yet those engaged in the argument seem unable to convince the opposing

1 Dyer, C, *BMJ*, Vol 334 (17 February 2007), p 329.
2 Donnison, D and Bryson, C, 'Matters of life and death: attitudes to euthanasia', in Jowell, R, Curtice, J, Park, A, Brook, L and Thomson, K, (eds), *British Social Attitudes: the 13th Report*, 1996, Aldershot: Dartmouth, pp 161–183, at p 163.
3 Battin, M P, *The Least Worst Death: Essays in Bioethics on the End of Life*, 1994, Oxford University Press, at p 101.

side of the value or rightness of their position or even to imagine a way of accommodating the other position. Feelings, and ideological commitments, run deep and drive different conclusions. As Kuhse says:

> People who approach ethics from different moral, cultural or religious perspectives will often arrive at different answers to morally controversial questions. These answers have their source in particular value systems and can therefore not be shown to be true or false, in the ordinary sense of those terms.[4]

This is undoubtedly true and makes resolution of the problem that is the assisted dying debate exceptionally difficult. Yet the debate will continue. At most, each side in the debate can hope to influence or persuade those whose ethical position lies somewhere between the two extremes. Thomasma, for example, suggests that since

> . . . philosophical arguments for and against physician aid in dying line up rather equally on either side. . . . Philosophical analysis alone seems unable to tap these deeper concerns well enough, or articulate them well enough, to be persuasive enough to win one side to another.[5]

Thus, negotiating a path between the various sides in this debate is essentially deeply problematic. The bases from which arguments begin often seem miles apart and those who hold to certain views tend to be intransigent about them. Both opponents and proponents of legalised assisted dying, however, share one primary characteristic; that is they both 'assume that there is an objective standard in morality, while disagreeing on what the ultimate standard of that morality might be'.[6]

Not only are the arguments complex, but the antagonists in this discussion also cannot be categorised simplistically. While many people who hold firmly to a religious faith might be expected to oppose legalisation of assisted dying, this will not universally be true. Equally, there will be some people with no faith who also oppose it. In the recently published British Social Attitudes Survey, for example, it was found that

> . . . how often someone attends a religious service proves to be the single most important variable in our analysis. It may be that a high

4   Kuhse, H, 'Voluntary euthanasia and other medical end-of-life decisions: Doctors should be permitted to give death a helping hand', in Charlesworth, M, (ed), *Bioethics in a Liberal Society*, 1993, Cambridge University Press, pp 247–258, at p 254.

5   Thomasma, D C, 'Assessing the arguments for and against euthanasia and assisted suicide: Part two', *Cambridge Quarterly of Healthcare Ethics* (1998), 7, 388–401, at p 388.

6   Ibid., at p 391.

level of attendance reflects a prior commitment to a faith and acceptance of its approach to issues of life and death.[7]

However, the authors also noted that

even though we have taken into account a respondent's religious background, a belief in the sanctity of life is still independently associated with attitudes to dying. Those who oppose suicide, capital punishment and abortion are all significantly more likely to oppose assisted dying.[8]

Ideologies other than faith can also affect attitudes to assisted dying. For example, it has been argued that social and political considerations can have a profound impact on people's views about the kind of event that an assisted death actually is. If seen as a threat to the social order it may lead those who can be described as 'more "communitarian" in outlook' to oppose legalisation because support for assisted dying is seen as 'atomistic in its philosophy, an affirmation of individual moral freedom in a world lacking moral absolutes'.[9] It would be a mistake, then, to think that we can easily presume to describe and categorise the kinds of people who will and will not support assisted dying or that their attitudes can be easily typecast even if we can identify some common characteristics. We must avoid, therefore, making simplistic assumptions about the kind of debate in which we are engaged.

The factors which underpin people's opinions in this area are important and will likely be crucial to any resolution of the debate. Laws are made, after all, by people, and while recent opinion evidence suggests that around 80 per cent of those sampled in the United Kingdom would support assisted dying where a person was suffering from an incurable, painful and terminal illness, this support reduced when different variations were presented to them.[10] For example, the percentage in favour of assisted dying was lowered to 33 per cent when the person suffered from an incurable and painful illness which was not terminal.[11] The British Social Attitudes Survey research reinforces findings from an earlier US study which concluded that '. . . poll numbers in the United States are deceptive. Americans endorse a generalized and abstract right to die, but when pollsters ask questions relating to specific medical

---

7 Clery, E, McLean, S, Phillips, M, 'Quickening death: the euthanasia debate' in Park, A, Curtice, J, Thomson, K, Phillips, M and Johnson, M, eds), *British Social Attitudes: the 23rd Report – Perspectives on a changing society*, 2007, London: Sage, pp 35–54.
8 Ibid.
9 Magnusson, R S, *Angels of Death: Exploring the Euthanasia Underground*, 2002, Yale University Press, at p 37.
10 Clery, McLean and Phillips, op. cit. at p 39.
11 Ibid.

situations, public support declines'.[12] Thus, even positions adopted in favour (or against) a particular proposition are more nuanced than is often reported or recognised.

Assisted dying introduced

There can be few matters more sensitive and challenging than those which concern the deliberate and knowing ending of another person's life, whether by providing them with the means to commit suicide (generally referred to as assisted suicide) or by actively taking steps to end it on their request (voluntary euthanasia). In 1994, the House of Lords Select Committee on Medical Ethics stated:

> That prohibition [of intentional killing] is the cornerstone of law and of social relationships. It protects each of us impartially, embodying the belief that all are equal. . . . We acknowledge that there are individual cases in which euthanasia may be seen by some to be appropriate. But individual cases cannot reasonably establish the foundation of a policy which would have such serious and widespread repercussions.[13]

On the other hand, Woodman points to the actual experience of many modern deaths as a reason for seeking control over one's own death, saying:

> . . . it is not surprising that so many of us fear being rushed into an intensive care ward, placed on life-support equipment, and made to linger in a state of semiexistence against our will. This particular fear seems to have grown in direct proportion to our physicians' abilities to perform these life-prolonging feats. The very measures that we once viewed as miracles of modern medicine can now be seen in a more critical light. Now we know that machines designed to prolong life can sometimes do nothing more than prolong the dying process. Many who once considered death too unpalatable to contemplate are beginning to realise that living can be worse than dying. As a result, more and more suffering people are asking their physicians to help them die, not keep them alive.[14]

---

12 Dowbiggin, I, *A Merciful End: The Euthanasia Movement in Modern America*, 2003, Oxford University Press, at p 175.
13 House of Lords Select Committee on Medical Ethics, *Report of the House of Lords Select Committee on Medical Ethics* HL Paper 21-1, 1994, para 237.
14 Woodman, S, *Last Rights: The Struggle over the Right to Die*, 1998, New York and London: Plenum Trade, at p 19.

What Illich calls 'cultural iatrogenisis',[15] results, he claims in 'intransitive activities', such as dying and suffering, being 'claimed by technocracy as new areas of policy-making and . . . treated as malfunctions from which populations ought to be institutionally relieved'.[16] Thus, we are controlled by, rather than in control of, the ways in which we manage important markers in our lives, including our deaths. Despite what the House of Lords said about the importance of prohibiting killing, and while many would accept their position entirely when it comes to the involuntary or unwanted taking of life, the principle to which they appeal has less resonance when the decision is taken *by the individual him or her self*. We may also question just what are the 'serious and widespread repercussions' to which the House of Lords refers. While the undesirable consequences of not outlawing the random and non-consensual taking of a life are self-evident, it is moot whether these same (or similar) consequences would flow from respecting a competent choice for assistance to bring about the end of one's own life. Although apparently comfortable with eliding the two scenarios, the House of Lords surely errs in doing so. For example, we can reasonably approve of voluntary sterilisation while at the same time entirely disapprove of non-consensual sterilisation. Although the outcome in this example is less serious, the important characteristic of the two examples is that they are rendered neutral, or at least not objectionable, by the willing involvement of the individual him or her self in the choice.

People's desire to control their lives extends, for some at least, to control of their deaths. At the same time, we are dying in different ways. No longer is life 'nasty, brutish and short'. People can expect to live for longer than their three score years and ten, and may well die from diseases related to the natural break-down of the human body. Battin believes that it is because we 'now typically die late in life of deteriorative disease'[17] that we are so exercised about the way in which we die. The extent to which our desire to gain control over our dying is permitted in law will – at least for those who wish to have such a choice available – affect not only how we die, but also how we live.

This book is primarily concerned with the choices of competent people; competent in terms of legal status and capacity. However, it is not possible entirely to omit consideration of others such as children, people in a permanent vegetative state and so on, since these situations provide an interesting comparative model. Accordingly, some time will be devoted in what follows to those whose deaths are brought about without their direct authority.

The arguments for and against legalisation will take up much of what follows in this book. For the moment, the complexities of this area and the

---

15 Illich, I, *Limits to Medicine. Medical Nemesis: The Expropriation of Health*, 1975 (reprinted in 1976, 1977, 1995, 2001, 2002), London and New York: Marion Boyers, at pp 33–4.
16 Illich, op. cit. at p 132.
17 Battin, M P, at p 9.

sensitivities surrounding the debate make it necessary to define the terms of this enquiry. For convenience, and as will become clear for philosophical reasons, throughout this book I will use the term 'assisted dying' to encapsulate events which might otherwise be described as either (physician) assisted suicide or voluntary euthanasia. Where a difference needs to be noted between these two this will be highlighted, but – although mechanically they differ – at the heart of each of them is the positive choice for death. It is decision-making control, or choice, that drives each of them, so that – although they are given effect to differently – they are facets of the same decision and will be supported or refuted by essentially the same arguments.

The current law in the UK

That said, there are some legal differences which merit brief consideration here. In common with most – but not all – legal systems throughout the world, commitment to upholding and reinforcing the sanctity of human life, whose importance is not in dispute, means that the United Kingdom currently outlaws the deliberate killing of another person (except in very limited situations), although suicide is not in itself a crime. Killing is covered by the law of murder, or in some situations the law of manslaughter or culpable homicide,[18] and '[t]he criminal law does not recognise euthanasia as a special category of homicide'.[19] Throughout the United Kingdom an act of voluntary euthanasia would be criminalised by common law. In other words, either a murder or a manslaughter/culpable homicide charge would be competent where someone deliberately takes the life of another even with that person's consent. Consent is irrelevant to the criminal law except in crimes such as rape where consent (or rather its absence) is an essential component of the crime itself.

In terms of assisted suicide, in Scotland the rules are derived from the common law in which suicide was probably never a crime. Although there is little doubt that a person assisting a suicide would be guilty of a criminal offence, either murder or culpable homicide (most probably the latter), Mason and Laurie note that 'it is difficult to imagine a common law offence of aiding an act which is not, itself, a crime'.[20] In England and Wales, however, there is a specific legislative prohibition on assisted suicide contained in the Suicide Act 1961.[21] This piece of legislation decriminalised suicide, but specifically created the crime of assisting in suicide; doubtless, a direct attempt to reinforce the sanctity of life doctrine. While prosecuting a failed suicide was perhaps

---

18 This is the Scottish equivalent of manslaughter.

19 Otlowski, M F A, *Voluntary Euthanasia and the Common Law*, 1997, Clarendon Press: Oxford, at p 13.

20 Mason, J K and Laurie, G T, *Mason and McCall Smith's Law and Medical Ethics*, 7th edn, 2006, Oxford University Press, at p 611, para 17.30.

21 Suicide Act 1961, s 2(1).

seen as serving little, if any, social purpose, there may have seemed to be reasons for prosecuting those who help someone else to die.

The sanctity of life principle works to prevent the unauthorised or unwanted removal of life, and is breached permissibly only in certain situations, such as acts of self-defence, in war or in states where judicial killing is permitted. In the past, its tenets were also imposed on those who took their own lives, as we have seen, but this is now legally irrelevant. What is critical is the idea that people should have their lives protected, as they are, for example, by the terms of Article 2 of the European Convention on Human Rights, which was incorporated into UK law by the passing of the Human Rights Act 1998 and which states:

1   Everyone's right to life shall be protected by law. No one shall be deprived of his life intentionally save in the execution of a sentence of a court following his conviction of a crime for which this penalty is provided by law.

It is obvious, therefore, that the modern statement of sanctity of life at least in this international statement is subject to some caveats. These are as follows:

2   Deprivation of life shall not be regarded as inflicted in contravention of this Article when it results from the use of force which is no more than absolutely necessary:

(a) in defence of any person from unlawful violence;
(b) in order to effect a lawful arrest or to prevent the escape of a person lawfully detained;
(c) in action lawfully taken for the purpose of quelling a riot or insurrection.

It will be noted that 'consent' or 'autonomy' feature nowhere in the justifications for killing contained in Article 2. This, however, does not mean that consensual killing could not be accommodated by the terms of the Convention. In the case of *Pretty v United Kingdom*,[22] for example, the European Court of Human Rights, which adjudicates on the Convention rights, accepted that assisted dying had been legalised in some Council of Europe Member States. This did not mean that they were in breach of their Convention obligations and subject to censure. The jurisprudence of the Court of Human Rights respects the rights of individual states to act according to their collective conscience (of course, within limits). Thus, Mrs Pretty's argument that the United Kingdom was in breach of its Convention obligations by *not* legalising assisted dying given

22 (2002) 66 BMLR 147.

that other states had done so was dismissed using this 'margin of appreciation' doctrine. The Court agreed with Lord Bingham[23] when he said:

> It is not enough for Mrs Pretty to show that the United Kingdom would not be acting inconsistently with the Convention if it were to permit assisted suicide; she must go further and establish that the United Kingdom is in breach of the Convention by failing to permit it or would be in breach of the Convention if it did not permit it. Such a contention is in my opinion untenable. . . .[24]

In this discussion, I will consider a range of arguments about assisted dying from the perspective of the United Kingdom and its society. Although assisted dying has been legalised in some jurisdictions in one form or another, this book will not repeat at length the wealth of literature that has arisen around this. The way forward, it is argued, is not continually to rehearse statistical information about what has happened elsewhere, particularly when the same set of figures is given such a wide range of interpretations depending on the perspective of the person interpreting them. However, the debate generated by these various interpretations is important and this will necessitate some reference to other jurisdictions.

Primarily, this discussion will seek to identify whether or not there are principled reasons either for or against legalisation of assisted dying. Once identified, these principles will be interrogated against the role of the law. Arguably, even if we could find arguments which firmly support legalisation of assisted dying, it is necessary to ask whether or not these can or should become the legal as well as the ethical position. We do not always incorporate moral positions into law – for example, we might disapprove of women who do not make behavioural changes in the course of their pregnancies to protect the developing foetus, but we do not (any longer) translate this into legal restrictions on their choices.[25] The primary question in this part of the discussion, therefore, is whether or not it is possible to abhor killing yet support assisted dying. In other words, what principles (if any) might allay the fears of opponents of legalisation and yet satisfy those who would legalise assisted dying?

It is self-evident that this is a highly emotive area. Those who object to legalisation of assisted dying can, and do, point to the possibility that allowing assisted dying will generate considerable fear for those in our society who

---

23   *R (on the application of Pretty) v Director of Public Prosecutions and Secretary of State for the Home Department* [2001] UKHL 61.

24   At p 159.

25   For discussion of this issue, see McLean, S A M and Ramsey, J, 'Human rights, reproductive freedom, medicine and the law', (2002) *Medical Law International*, Vol 5, No 4, 239–258.

might be, or feel themselves to be, vulnerable. There is reason to be concerned about the way in which some groups, such as the elderly or people with disabilities, are treated and the concern that they might become victims of, rather than participants in, legalisation of assisted dying. This concern cannot be lightly dismissed and will be considered in more depth later. However, Campbell argues that:

> The absence of the euthanasia option undoubtedly results in a great deal of unnecessary suffering, which in some cases is simply horrendous ('undignified' is too weak a term) and, in other cases, deprives people of their preferred mode of exiting this life before their quality of life deteriorates to a level they find unacceptable.[26]

The challenge is to work out whether or not the suffering of either group is capable of resolution by prohibition or legalisation. There are social, political, religious, human rights and many other reasons why societies are reluctant to move down the legalisation path, some of them more principled than others. For example, some politicians have been reluctant to endorse moves towards law reform, perhaps in part based on their fear of losing the support of some of their electorate. Members of Parliament with constituencies in which certain religious and ethnic groups are strongly represented may fear that supporting the rights of people to make their own end of life choices will be a fast and easy route to unemployment. Whatever their reasons, the democratic deficit that results from a failure to adequately debate these issues (which has been rectified to some extent in England and Wales recently[27]) results in disempowering the voices of those who wish to take control over their own dying (and, arguably, living). The consequences of this, however, are that

> increasingly, thoughtful people, especially those with distressing experiences of seeing others go through the process of dying, fear that they themselves may have to go through a terminal illness or process of mental and physical deterioration within a health system in which the combination of economic and legal limits can lead to unnecessary suffering and dreadful neglect of their wishes and interests.[28]

At the heart of objections to legalisation of assisted dying, however, is the concept of the sanctity of life. This is an essential component of civilisation and offers protection to those individuals who are otherwise vulnerable to abuse. It would be a morally bankrupt society that did not take this commitment

---

26 Campbell, T, 'Euthanasia as a human right', in McLean, S A M, (ed), *First Do No Harm: Law, Ethics and Healthcare*, 2006, Aldershot: Ashgate, pp 447–460, at p 448.

27 For further discussion, see Chapter 5.

28 Campbell, op. cit. at p 449.

seriously. Whether it is an overwhelming argument against legalisation is, however, moot and will be considered in more depth in what follows. It is, of course, not only the law of the United Kingdom that purports to prioritise the sanctity of life. Indeed, in those countries where assisted dying has been legalised, citizens and Parliamentarians alike would doubtless robustly defend the importance of this principle. These countries, for example, still have crimes such as murder; they would, however, differentiate taking life from those who wish to live it from taking it at the request of the individual who competently decides that life is no longer wanted. Moreover, international agreements on civil and political rights and on human rights also adopt the sanctity of life as a central plank of their agenda. This 'sanctity' argument hinges on the concept of the 'right to life' itself. This is, of course, absolutely critical to the enjoyment of any other rights that are specified in these international and national agreements. Without life, we cannot enjoy freedom of speech, freedom of religion or freedom of association, for example. Equally, given that most of the significant international treaties still depended on today were developed in the aftermath of the Holocaust and the systematic slaughter of millions of people throughout Europe, it is scarcely surprising that this right is given such priority. It remains, however, debatable whether our contemporary commitment to the sanctity of life – which is in part historically based on the fear of a repetition of wholesale slaughter or abuse – is strictly relevant to the question of chosen death.

Times and contexts change, and we are now more likely to die from disease than from genocide – at least in most Western democracies. The fact that about one in three of us will experience cancer at some stage in our lives is at least in part a result of the fact that – in the developed world at least – we generally will live longer. Some cancers simply result from the breakdown of the body and its inability to survive intact for as long as we now live. It is likely also that the increased longevity in the developed world has led to an increased interest in the subject of choosing death. Many people will now die in hospitals, subject to invasive and sometimes undignified interventions, long beyond the time at which some of them believe their own lives to have value. Indeed, it has been suggested that the suicide rate in the elderly among the United States has been growing over the years because they fear being inappropriately kept alive past the stage at which they would wish to live, in part at least because of the legal position in which their caregivers find themselves.[29]

We may, therefore, choose to avoid the suffering which sometimes accompanies modern death. Of course, suffering (which is broader than just pain) can be, and often is, alleviated so that arguably people need not fear the end of their lives. In addition, there are ways of bringing about death earlier

---

29   Angell, M 'Prisoners of technology: the case of Nancy Cruzan', (1990) 322 (17) *New England Journal of Medicine*, 1226–1228, at p 1228.

than it would otherwise occur which, as we will see, are currently tolerated by the law. For example, acting within the law, doctors may place a 'do not resuscitate' order on a patient's chart when it is felt that resuscitation would be futile (sometimes it appears without consultation with the patient) or take the decision to withhold or withdraw treatments even when existence could be maintained were the treatment to be offered or continued. Patients are entitled to refuse even life-sustaining treatment, and doctors are legally obliged to respect that refusal even when it breaches their own professional or personal position.[30] However, the prohibition on assisted dying leaves people who positively *wish* their lives to be ended as the group most likely to endure a drawn-out – even undignified – dying process. Those who can reject assisted nutrition and hydration or mechanical ventilation can competently refuse to be so treated. But those unable to speak for themselves may find their apparent plight alleviated by using such devices as the principle of double effect or the alleged distinction between acts and omissions. Perhaps paradoxically, only one group is denied assistance in their dying; those who are competent, but have no life-sustaining treatment to refuse. For proponents of legalisation, this is a cruel and unjustified restriction; for opponents, it merely reflects the differences they wish to draw between killing and letting die.

Indeed, most opponents of legalised assisted dying do not find the examples where death is brought about passively exceptionable – albeit that they foreseeably result in death. They would seek to make a distinction based either on intention or on the grounds that these are clinical decisions which engage with the symptoms, not the individual. It is nonetheless clear that such decisions are made with the foresight – perhaps even the intention – that the outcome will be death. In other words, as we will see later, decisions about some deaths are routinely made not by patients themselves but by third parties and, as we will also see, these decisions require the involvement of these third parties (even if the action is to remove or withhold treatment). Yet, the competent adult person who wishes to take that control from third parties and into their own hands is currently denied the ability to do so unless they are in a situation where they have life-sustaining treatment which they can refuse. Perhaps particularly for those with degenerative conditions for which there is no treatment, the inability to avoid the suffering and the indignity that accompanies the progress of their illness must surely be a cause for concern, if not downright anger.

Moreover, it will be important to ask just what is the critical difference between 'killing' and 'letting die' that might justify the law's current approach. As Beauchamp and Childress note, '[r]ightness and wrongness depend on the merit of the justification underlying the action, not on the type of action it

---

30 See, e.g. the case of *Re B (Adult: Refusal of Treatment)* [2002] EWHC 429 (Fam); (2002) 65 BMLR 149.

is'.[31] Thus, it is important that the legal response to acts (and omissions) that result in death actually takes account of what is real, as opposed to cosmetic, about the alleged differences between them. This matters not just because it exposes the true nature of the debate, but also because – unlike the current legal position – it seems more likely to bring about some consistency. Consistency is an aspirational value for legal systems and its importance should not be underestimated. It is consistency that serves to offer certainty; the knowledge that we will be treated as equals under the law. If we can detect inconsistency, we have reason for concern that this equality is absent. There is also a more esoteric reason for aspiring to consistency in our value systems, parts of which are shaped or protected/intruded on by law. While we might be satisfied that where there are differences between situations it is permissible – legally and morally – to treat them in different ways, these differences must be real, not imagined or artificially constructed. During this discussion, therefore, I will adopt a position for which I have argued elsewhere; namely that

> [i]t is vital that the similarities of the cases, rather than their differences, are focused on if we are to build or develop a coherent set of standards which will satisfy our legitimate demand for transparency and clarity, for equality of treatment and for certainty of outcome.[32]

In other words, while judges, legislators and others try to find ways of differentiating choices for death from each other in order to permit some and prohibit others, they ignore the possibility that the intention (in a non-legal as well as a legal sense) and the outcome are the same irrespective of how we describe or categorise the events. This lies at the heart of my discussion of this issue. If there are indeed relevant distinctions between, for example killing and letting die, then it is right and proper that they should inform the social and legal response to assisted dying. However, the claim that such differences exist is highly contentious. Some will see the differences as being entirely clear; for others it is disingenuous, if not downright dishonest, to attempt to differentiate between them. As an example of the latter, the pro-assisted suicide group, Dignity in Dying, points out that:

> ... on the one hand, a doctor who, at the patient's request, supplies life-ending medication is criminalised, despite the fact that it is the patient's intention and action that brings about death. On the other, a doctor who shortens a patient's life by administering high does of opioids

---

31   Beauchamp, T L and Childress, J F, *Principles of Biomedical Ethics*, 5th edn, Oxford University Press, at p 142.
32   McLean, S A M, 'Law at the end of life: what next?', in McLean, S A M, (ed), *Death, Dying and the Law*, Aldershot: Dartmouth, 1996, 49–66, at p 52.

– regardless of the patient's wishes – may be justified under the principle of double effect, even if he foresaw that death would occur.[33]

This, they say, shows that the law is unacceptably inconsistent; it fails to treat like with like as well as disvaluing the competent decision of the individual who wants to choose assisted dying. On the other hand, others are perfectly satisfied that these two situations can be clearly distinguished and that it is right and proper that the legal position on each of them is different. Moreover, they would doubtless agree with Callahan's critique of the pro-assisted dying lobby. He says:

> This is a dangerous direction to go in the search for a peaceful death. It rests on the illusion that a society can safely put in the private hands of physicians the power directly and deliberately to take life. It threatens to add to an already sorry human history of giving one person the liberty to take the life of another still a further sad chapter. It perpetuates and pushes to an extreme the very ideology of control, the goal of mastering life and death, that created the problems of modern medicine in the first place. Instead of changing the medicine generating the problem of an intolerable death, it simply treats the symptoms, all the while reinforcing, and driving us more deeply into, an ideology of control.[34]

Quite why an 'ideology of control' is necessarily a bad thing is not clear. Equally, it is debatable whether or not the possibility of safely regulating assisted dying really is merely an 'illusion'. These and other issues will be considered in what follows, as will the alleged inconsistencies of the law.

Given the clear differences between the positions of opponents and proponents, both honestly held, it is necessary to return to the principles on which this discussion will rest. While opponents seek to use the Nazi atrocities, for example, to show why we should *never* permit killing in any form, in fact reflecting on these very atrocities may lead to a different conclusion. The primary argument in favour of legalisation tends to depend on respect for the autonomy of the individuals; manifestly this was no part of the Nazi philosophy. Indeed, the reaction of the international community to the atrocities of the Nazi regime's murderous assaults on Jews, homosexuals and the disabled was to develop a sphere of privacy around the individual in order to protect them from rogue states. In this way, a corrupt state would find it more difficult to invade the freedoms, liberties and rights of its citizens. However, respect for the individual *qua* individual militates *in favour of* and not *against* respect for their autonomous choices. Of course, whether or not decisions for death are

---

33 *Dignity in Dying: The Report*, London: Dignity in Dying, February 2006, at p 8.
34 Callahan, D, *The Troubled Dream of Life*, 2000, Washington, DC: Georgetown University Press, at p 93.

truly autonomous is also an important question which will be discussed in more depth later. Further, the libertarian position adopted in this discussion will need to tackle the question of whether or not, in the classic words of John Stuart Mill, decisions to seek assisted dying are truly within the sphere of behaviour which can be described as 'private'. For Mill, the legitimacy of state control does not extend to private choices, unless there is evidence of harm to others. Thus, it will also be necessary to consider whether or not legalising assisted dying would directly or indirectly cause harm to third parties.

It is perhaps valuable at this point to repeat what Mill said:

> ... the sole purpose for which power can be rightfully exercised over any member of a civilised community, against his will, is to prevent harm to others. The only part of the conduct of any one, of which he is amenable to society, is that which concerns others. In the part which merely concerns himself, his independence is, of right, absolute. Over his own body and mind, the individual is sovereign.[35]

Of course, some would argue that choosing assistance in dying is by no means only a private choice; in fact, they may say, it is *never* a private choice. The House of Lords Select Committee on Medical Ethics, for example, emphasised that 'dying is not only a personal or individual affair. The death of a person affects the lives of others, often in ways and to an extent which cannot be foreseen'.[36] Certainly, it is the case that all deaths affect more than the person who dies (assuming, of course, that they have a social network of some kind). However, two things need to be said about this. First, that this in and of itself does not make the decision a matter of public interest or concern. The fact that a decision has an effect on the public is not the same as arguing or concluding that it is therefore subject or subservient to the concerns, interests or private morals of third parties – even of society itself. Second, *every* death has a public effect. Accordingly, those who choose to commit suicide (which is not illegal), those who competently refuse life-sustaining treatment (which is lawful), those who choose novel or experimental treatment with an inherent risk of causing death (which may be regarded as laudable) and those who die naturally (which is inevitable) will have an impact on society. We do not (and in some cases cannot) prevent this, even when the deaths are the subject of a direct choice rather than the result of the natural progression to the end of a life.

Mill's position is also adopted because it provides a remarkably contemporary account (despite its age) of the priorities accepted as important in most developed countries. The separation of the state from the private lives of its citizens is, for example, protected in almost exact Millian terms by Article 8

---

35 Mill, J S, *On Liberty*, 1859, London, at p 75.
36 *Report of the House of Lords Select Committee on Medical Ethics*, op. cit. at para 237.

of the European Convention on Human Rights by which the United Kingdom is bound since its incorporation into domestic law by the Human Rights Act 1998. This Article first says:

1   Everyone has the right to respect for his private and family life, his home and his correspondence.

This right is, however, qualified as follows:

2   There shall be no interference by a public authority with the exercise of this right except such as is in accordance with the law and is necessary in a democratic society in the interests of national security, public safety or the economic well-being of the country, for the prevention of disorder or crime, for the protection of health or morals, or for the protection of the rights and freedoms of others.

Thus, the onus is on the state to show why it is somehow in the interests of others that the right of the individual to private life can be breached, very much in line with Mill's position. My discussion, therefore, starts from the assumption that Mill's approach is a legitimate way of addressing this issue. For the moment, it is also important to note that the primary argument developed here will begin by adopting the default position that voluntariness, like competence, should be presumed where there is no evidence to the contrary.

I have already indicated that the arguments both for and against assisted dying are intense and often highly polarised. There is, however, one difference between them that must be taken account of up front. That is, those who would adopt a libertarian position – who would support a patient's right to make such choices – run no risk of imposing their views on others. As with all rights, there is no obligation on individuals to seek to assert them. A law which permitted assisted dying would likely, therefore, be used only by those who approved of it (questions about the autonomy of the choice will be examined in more depth later). Conversely, people who wish to see the prohibition on assisted dying retained in those jurisdictions where that is currently the law, force others to live with the consequences; namely, that their ability to act on their own moral position is discounted by the morality of others. Certainly, opponents of assisted dying might reasonably be uncomfortable living in a jurisdiction which permitted it. Their discomfort however might plausibly be described as less significant than that experienced by those whose morality points in a different direction and who are denied the opportunity to make a decision they truly value and believe in. As was said in one American case:

> Those who believe strongly that death must come without physician assistance are free to follow that creed, be they doctors or patients. They are not free, however, to force their views, their religious convictions, or

their philosophies on all other members of a democratic society, and to compel those whose values differ from theirs to die painful, protracted, and agonizing deaths.[37]

This will be discussed in more depth in the conclusion to the book, but it forms an important plank of my argument and therefore needs to be clearly stated up front. However valid or firmly held the arguments on either side, it is not unreasonable to suggest that the current legal position gives disproportionate weight to the position of opponents.

There are several strands to this narrative. First, that although there are strongly held and important arguments against legalising assisted dying, on their face they can be refuted. Second, that it is incumbent on the law to offer certainty, logic and consistency in this important area; and finally that we should prefer a society which intervenes in private choices only when harm to others results from a failure to do so. If – as is the case – there are some circumstances in which we already can choose death, and if – as is the case – sometimes others may choose it for us, the justification for preventing competent people from receiving assistance in their death requires to be robustly defined and defended. Nor is my argument dependent on the fact that often the current law on assisted dying is ignored or in practice disregarded. Pretty well every law is broken by someone at some time, and this is no justification in and of itself for making a change to the law. Other justifications need to be found for change and it will be argued here that they are readily available.

Although I have no interest in defending majoritarianism, it seems that significant numbers of the (surveyed) public agree that the law needs to be reformed. This, of course, begs a number of questions. First, polls do not register the views of those who were not surveyed. Second, such surveys can unintentionally skew the outcome based on the way in which questions are framed and put to the interviewee. For these reasons, I have some sympathy with the views of the House of Lords Select Committee on the Assisted Dying for the Terminally Ill Bill, which cautioned against too ready an acceptance of the results claimed by at least some opinion evidence.[38] In presenting the report to Parliament, Lord Mackay of Clashfern suggested that 'there is a need to look behind the results of opinion polls in order to ascertain the extent to which the views expressed are based on informed opinion . . .'.[39]

On the other hand, while opinion surveys need to be analysed carefully and cannot be taken as definitive of serious ethical issues, it could be argued

---

37 *Compassion in Dying v State of Washington* 79 F 3d 790 (9th Cir 1996) 810, at p 839.
38 House of Lords Select Committee on the Assisted Dying for the Terminally Ill Bill, *Report of the House of Lords Select Committee on the Assisted Dying for the Terminally Ill Bill*, HL Paper 86-1, April 2005.
39 House of Lords, *Hansard*, Vol 674, Col 15 (10 October 2005), available at http://www.publications.parliament.uk/pa/ld199900/ldhansrd/pdvn/lds05/text/51010-04.htm.

that there is sufficient congruence in the results to render them of more than merely anecdotal interest. However, the criticism of opinion evidence by the Select Committee should be borne in mind. This works the other way as well, of course. I indicated earlier that I will not 'play the numbers game' and this is equally applicable to those who would want to argue that their opposition to legalisation represents the mainstream view. Either may be true, but if we cannot deduce from opinion evidence which consistently shows support for legalisation that the majority favour law reform, we equally cannot deduce that the views of those who were not involved in the survey are uniformly opposed. In any case, arguments about, or primarily based on, numbers are inherently futile. As Harris has said:

> The community's true morality is not to be discovered by taking opinion polls about particular moral issues. It is to be discovered by asking what answer to a particular issue would fit consistently with abstract rights to which the community has already committed itself in its constitution and international practices – such as rights to liberty, dignity, equality and respect.[40]

Thus, even if we could conclusively prove that a majority fell on one side or the other of the debate, that would tell us nothing other than that bare fact, even if we were certain that the questions had been properly phrased and perfectly interpreted. Sheer weight of numbers is no basis from which to reach ethical positions – whichever way they point. Equally, the tyranny of majority is anti-democratic. Perhaps this was best explained by Hart who said:

> It seems fatally easy to believe that democratic principles entail accept-ance of what may be termed moral populism: the view that the majority have a moral right to dictate how all should live. . . . The central mistake is a failure to distinguish the acceptable principle that political power is best entrusted to the majority from the unacceptable claim that what the majority do with that power is beyond criticism and must never be resisted. No one can be a democrat who does not accept the first of these, but no democrat need accept the second.[41]

Conclusion

In the long run, we must ask why we are so reluctant to allow people to make their own decisions about the timing and manner of their deaths. Is it some misplaced interest in the lives of others, or a legitimate effort to protect them

---

40 Harris, J W, *Legal Philosophies*, 1980, London: Butterworths, at pp 177–178.
41 Hart, H L A, *Law, Liberty and Morality*, 1963, Oxford University Press, at p 79.

from unwise and, in this case, permanent decisions? In another context, Lee has suggested that '[c]hange tends to be viewed in a very one-sided way, as something that is likely to bring about harm'.[42] Certainly, changing the law to permit assisted suicide would require a shift in attitude, and many fear that the inevitable consequence of this would be somehow to damage the very fabric of our society; to render those who are already vulnerable subject to increased likelihood of danger and to destroy the bedrock of our law.

On the other hand, respect for the law is an important part of liberal, western democratic society and although laws are not always observed, '[l]aws that attempt to ban what people want to have or to find out about are, generally, honoured only in their breach'.[43] There is ample evidence that healthcare professionals already break the laws prohibiting assisted dying. Magnusson, for example, argues that:

> When doctors kill, they usually do so quietly and discreetly. Euthanasia bubbles away beneath the surface, erupting into the public arena only when doctors (or others) are 'caught' transgressing key legal boundaries, or when they grow tired of the deception, and go public in a blaze of martyrdom. Euthanasia is not an isolated breakdown in medical self-discipline; it is a widespread phenomenon, at least in western democracies where technology can prolong both dying and the pain of living, and where the ethics of libertarianism gives moral substance to patient demands for swift release.[44]

However, I do not propose this as an argument for changing the law. People are raped, murdered and robbed yet nobody would seriously propose that the fact that this is in breach of the law should lead us to decriminalise that behaviour. Rather, I prefer to identify principles beyond this which will survive even in the face of alternative values and principles. Changing law in this area is also likely to be subject to the 'yuk factor' as we reconsider the shape of our society, and this too is problematic. As The President's Council on Bioethics (US) has said, many of our responses to new possibilities are essentially rooted in 'initial revulsions' which 'are hard to translate into sound moral arguments'.[45] Yet sound arguments are needed if we are to find a way through the moral maze and towards a societal and/or legal reflection of a principled approach to end-of-life decisions.

42   Lee, E, 'Debating "designer babies"', available from Spiked-Science (http://www.spiked-online.com (accessed on 11/10/05)).
43   Brown, B, 'Human cloning and genetic engineering: the case for proceeding cautiously', *Albany Law Review*, Vol 65, 649–650, p 650.
44   Magnusson, R S, op. cit. at p 34.
45   *Beyond Therapy: Biotechnology and the Pursuit of Happiness*, The President's Council on Bioethics, Washington, DC, 2003, available at http://www.bioethics.gov, at p 284.

Finally, while some might argue that the onus to provide such robust arguments rests on those who wish to change the law, in my conception of the argument this is not the case if we can establish that the existing position rests on an unsound basis. The liberal tradition requires that 'the liberty of citizens should not be abridged unless good and sufficient cause can be shown as to why this is required'.[46] This view has profound implications for this debate, and in particular for the kind of society we wish to see in the future. Although there is realistically no point in trying to convince people to change their mind on this subject, especially given that both opponents and proponents of legalisation hold their opinions strongly and in good faith, we must ask how we can resolve the issue for society as a whole, respecting these views as much as possible and minimising, if not removing, any possible negative consequences. McCarthy suggests that:

> An ongoing, and perhaps permanent, feature of free societies is that reasonable people disagree on basic values. In such conditions, there are really only two choices. One is to have a society in which whichever interest group happens to achieve the balance of power gets to force its values on others who can reasonably disagree with those values. The other is to have a society in which value disputes are resolved in a way in which no one can reasonably reject.[47]

Adopting a liberal position is more likely to achieve the latter – arguably more desirable – outcome than is the former. As Charlesworth has said, '[t]he essence of liberalism is the moral conviction that, because they are autonomous moral agents or persons, people must as far as possible be free to choose for themselves, even if their choices are, objectively speaking, mistaken'.[48] It will be necessary at the end of this argument to explain how we might achieve the kind of resolution that McCarthy postulates. As he says, '[i]n a pluralistic democratic society built on the ideals of free and equal citizenry, there is always a presumption in favour of liberty. The burden of proof is always on those who want to restrict the liberty of others'.[49] In the next chapters, we will see whether or not the burden of proof can be met by either side in this debate.

---

46 Harris, J, 'No sex selection please, we're British' (2005) 31 *Journal of Medical Ethics*, 286–288, at p 287.

47 McCarthy, D, 'Why sex selection should be legal', *Journal of Medical Ethics* 2001; 27: 302–7, at p 302.

48 Charlesworth, M, *Bioethics in a Liberal Society*, Cambridge University Press, 1993, at p 4.

49 McCarthy, op. cit. at p 306.

Chapter 2

An evaluation of the arguments for and against legalisation

Although it is common to deal with the arguments for and against legalisation under separate headings, I intend to deal with them together in the same (and therefore rather long) chapter. To split them from each other is to decontextualise them; to treat them as if they only stand or fall alone or exist in a vacuum. In fact, ideologically and pragmatically they are intensely inter-twined and very often cannot be accepted, rejected or properly evaluated without reference to the other(s). In addition, to treat them as distinct is merely to reinforce the polarisation that often characterises this debate and which seems doomed to leave us permanently divided, with no real prospect of ethical resolution. Of course, it might be argued that resolution is in itself not desirable; that if we were able to accommodate each side of the argument we would merely achieve a lowest common denominator account of an unusually important issue. This will be returned to in the final chapter of this book. It is important to note at the moment, however, that treating the arguments together is not undertaken for the purpose of finding a compromise but rather so that their richness, and particularly the richness of the conflicts between them, can be clearly observed.

The gulf between opponents and proponents of legalising assisted dying is captured in the following two quotations. Woodman says:

> For too many people, death comes, not as the peaceful conclusion to a life, but as a violent and cruel destroyer. What it destroys, along with the life in question, is the possibility for release among those left behind. People say that for a long time afterwards, the memory of a painful death-struggle obliterates the much more precious images that they want to preserve.[1]

Those who wish to see assisted dying legalised would point to this as one of the classic descriptors of why people might want to make their own choice

---

1   Woodman, S, *Last Rights: The Struggle over the Right to Die*, 1998, New York and London: Plenum Trade, at p 25.

to die with the assistance of someone else where this is needed. Somerville, on the other hand, argues that '[t]o legalize euthanasia would damage important, foundational societal values and symbols that uphold respect for human life. With euthanasia, how we die cannot just be a private matter of self-determination and personal beliefs . . .'.[2] Thus, she says:

> How a society treats its weakest, most in need, most vulnerable members tests its moral and ethical tone. To set a present and future moral tone that protects individuals in general and society, upholds the funda-mental value of respect for life, and promotes rather than destroys our capacities and opportunities to search for meaning in life, we must reject euthanasia.[3]

Of course, her argument presupposes that a society which allows the 'weak' and the 'vulnerable' respect for their own decisions is incompatible with a good 'moral and ethical tone'. We can respect life while acknowledging that our respect does not have the necessary effect of denying that others may have different views about their own lives. I do not disrespect your life (nor indeed mine) by competently deciding that its end should be brought about, whether or not I need assistance to achieve that end.

Each of the arguments for and against legalisation is powerful, and each appeals to different individuals and groups within society. Equally, as can probably be deduced from the mere fact that this is so, each is open to debate. In what follows, I have grouped the arguments under broad headings. The order in which they appear is relatively random and should not be taken to imply a hierarchy.

Sanctity of life

Despite the fact that I have not attempted to arrange the arguments in hierarchical order, it is probably true to say that the argument from the sanctity of life features as a fundamental underpinning of all of the other arguments in this area. Steinbock suggests that the historical source of this principle derives from 'religious doctrine, for example, the claim that only God has the right to determine when a person will die, or that committing suicide is a blasphemous rejection of God's gift of life'.[4] It is also, of course, based on the idea that:

---

2 Somerville, M, 'The case against euthanasia and physician-assisted suicide', Spring 2003, 33–34, available at http://www.secularhumanism.org, at p 33.
3 Ibid. at p 34.
4 Steinbock, B, 'The case for physician assisted suicide: not (yet) proven', (2005) 31 *Journal of Medical Ethics* 2005: 31: 235–241, at p 236.

> The value placed by law on every innocent human life is such that its intentional destruction is the greatest crime, an expression of the law's acceptance that every innocent person has a right to the integrity of his/her life: that is that they not be intentionally killed.[5]

While the law, as developed over the centuries, was undoubtedly heavily influenced by the doctrines of religion and cannot entirely be disconnected from them, as we will see later not only are there other constructions of the sanctity of life principle, but the law does not always prioritise the absolute sanctity of life in its modern incarnation.

As we have seen, in its religious and original form the sanctity of life argument depends on the belief that life is a gift from God and that only God can decide when that life should end. It is therefore illicit and impermissible for individuals to make a decision outside of what God prescribes for them. This argument, therefore, would also preclude regarding suicide as a legitimate act of self-deliverance. For those who would adopt this position, rejecting the gift of life for whatever reason is in a very real sense an insult to the Creator. Even if that life is tainted or dominated by suffering – physical or mental – this is nonetheless part of God's plan, which we are not entitled to second guess and should not attempt to escape from. Indeed, in some faiths, suffering is in and of itself seen as an important part of our spiritual journey and has benefits (as well as the obvious burdens) associated with it.

On this argument, whatever God provides for us is what we should accept, even if it involves suffering. Obviously, if one approaches life (and death) from this perspective it is essentially an irrefutable argument. Faith is a personal as well as a cultural force that is not defeasible by non-faith based arguments. As Steinbock says, however, '[w]hatever the force of such arguments for believers, these arguments do not justify restricting the liberty of individuals in a secular society'.[6] In any case, as Thomasma says:

> Because those who resist terminating life must defend an increasingly unpopular view, some have resurrected the notion of 'the value of suffering,' or of 'accepting what God has chosen for you'. Perhaps at one time, when almost all persons died suddenly of an accident or illness, this mostly theological conception had some merit. Today, however, human interventions prolong the suffering as a necessary trade-off for gaining additional months or years of life.[7]

---

5   Pollard, B J, 'Can euthanasia be safely legalized?', *Palliative Medicine* 2001: 15: 61–65, at p 61.
6   Steinbock, (2005), op. cit. at p 236.
7   Thomasma, D C, 'An analysis of arguments for and against euthanasia and assisted suicide: Part one', *Cambridge Quarterly of Healthcare Ethics*, (1996), 5, 62–76, at p 68.

Thus, if we believe that life is a non-returnable gift from God and/or that suffering has inherent value, then it is likely that no argument for legalisation will trump this position. There are no doubt many people for whom these arguments have profound resonance, but it is also clear that in a society whose values are pluralistic and increasingly not intimately connected to faith they are likely to carry little weight. Indeed, in such a society, it is not unrealistic to question whether or not views which are almost certainly held by a minority should be permitted to dominate. I have already accepted that the weight (or lightness) of numbers for and against a particular position is not a proper basis for evaluating its worth, but if it can be resisted by strong, independent arguments then it casts doubt on the importance to be given to it.

It has already been noted that not all opponents of legalisation derive their position from a religious perspective although religious or quasi-religious arguments often do play a significant role in their views. There are non-faith based arguments against legalising assisted dying, which may be social, ethical, personal and political. Somerville, for example, suggests that 'there are secular reasons – moral, rational, and medical – for respecting the sanctity of life and rejecting euthanasia . . .'[8] and these will be considered in more depth in what follows. For the moment, however, it is important to examine to what extent the sanctity of life argument still represents the basis of modern law and ethics.

The more secular version of the sanctity of life argument, which is the one most commonly reflected in modern legal systems, can lead to a conclusion with which Somerville almost certainly would not agree. While the law is at pains, particularly through the judiciary, to assert the significance of the sanctity of all human life, it has also been prepared to concede that the sanctity of life principle can be superseded by the need to respect autonomy. In a number of cases, as we will see later, the law has simultaneously restated the importance of the sanctity of human life while at the same time respecting the decisions made by people to reject that life by according dominance to the principle of respect for autonomy. If the secular version of this principle is accepted, therefore, the sanctity of life is not in itself an argument that successfully defeats the claims of the proponents of legalisation of assisted dying. Rather, it acts as a brake on treating human life in a casual way, and of course it protects people from having their lives unwillingly removed. As Harris says, 'I suggest that there is only one thing wrong with dying and that is doing it when you don't want to. . . . There is nothing wrong with doing it when you want to.'[9] In fact, '[m]edical technology and laws to protect

8   Somerville, M, *Death Talk: The Case Against Euthanasia and Physician-Assisted Suicide*, 2001, Montreal and Kingston: McGill-Queen's University Press, at p 82.
9   Harris, J, 'Consent and end of life decisions', *Journal of Medical Ethics* 2003: 29: 10–15, at p 13.

sanctity of life may unintentionally prolong life regardless of the costs or the patient's wishes'.[10]

What is important in the sanctity of life debate is that, in the religious version, the wishes of the individual take second place at best; the secular version, however, is capable of accommodating the notion of individual choice or self-determination. The importance of self-determination leads inevitably to consideration of a second major argument, generally used by proponents of legalisation; namely, that of respect for autonomy.

Autonomy

Autonomy has become the central and dominant biomedical ethics principle of the modern era, and is routinely protected by law whenever possible. Indeed, autonomy and the right to make self-determining choices are also championed at European and international levels by a number of human rights codes and declarations. Since we are by and large free to make self-regarding decisions about our lives, by analogy the argument runs, we should be free to make similar choices about our deaths. Given the ultimate inevitability of death, proponents of legalisation see it as being merely another part of one's life that we can avoid the kind of death we do not want by choosing the kind we prefer. Dworkin, for example, says that, among the reasons for supporting legalised assisted dying is 'the interest of patients in determining the time and manner of their death. Autonomy and relief of suffering are values that we can all agree to be important'.[11] Even the House of Lords Select Committee on Medical Ethics, while declining to support the legalisation of assisted dying, conceded the importance of autonomy:

> The increased importance attached to individual autonomy, or the freedom to make decisions for oneself, has meant that relationships between state and citizen, between doctor and patient, teacher and pupil, parent and child, have all become less paternalistic. Most individuals wish to take more responsibility for the course of their lives, and this applies equally to decisions about medical treatment.[12]

Such decisions, unsurprisingly, will – for some people – include decisions in the healthcare setting (and beyond it) about whether or not their own lives

---

10 Valente, S M, 'End-of-life challenges: honoring autonomy', *Cancer Nursing*, 2004, Vol 27, No 4, 314–319, at p 315.

11 Dworkin, G 'Introduction', in Dworkin, G, Frey, R G and Bok, S, *Euthanasia and Physician-Assisted Suicide: For and Against*, Cambridge University Press, 1998, 3–5 at p 3.

12 *House of Lords Select Committee on Medical Ethics, Report of the House of Lords Select Committee on Medical Ethics* HL Paper 21-1, 1994, at p 7, para 4.

are worth living. From the age at which we are competent, we strive for some form of control over our environment and our life plan. If death is simply one – albeit unusually important – aspect of life, then it makes sense that we seek control over our death also. Of course, it could be said that we have such control already since suicide is no longer a crime. If, therefore, we wish to take charge of our own deaths, it can be argued we have always the option of committing suicide. Changing the law to allow others to kill us is, on this account, unnecessary, not to say dangerous.

However, for many people, this is an inadequate protection of the right to exercise autonomy, given that many who might seek assistance in their dying would be physically, contextually or emotionally disbarred from committing suicide. Suicide is also not always the best way to control our death. For example, for those who fear a drawn-out death with significant impairment the option of suicide is only available when they are still physically able to act for themselves. The suicide option, then, may need to be acted upon before rather than after life ceases to have value for them, thus depriving them of a number of months or years of valued life.[13] This is surely a perverse outcome. It is, therefore, imperative on this argument that if people are to be granted control of their death, they can act in a self-determining manner even if they require assistance. The lawfulness of suicide, even were we all capable of utilising that option, does nothing for those who wish to live until life is too full of suffering to be bearable for them and to a time when suicide is no longer a practical physical option.

What is autonomy?

It is important that we are clear on what we mean by autonomy and the circumstances in which it amounts to a viable basis for demanding that our choices are respected. Autonomy plays an important role in most philosophies, and even many opponents of assisted dying would concede the importance of self-governance. However, they will generally do so with a number of caveats. First, they might argue, autonomy – while an important value – is not the only or the primary concern that we should take account of here. Choices for death, they would suggest, cannot be totally vindicated by autonomy-based justifications because these are not only private choices, otherwise protected by the principles of liberalism, but rather have public effects and a social impact. Thus, the fact that I want to do something cannot be given unfettered support because it does not only affect me; in the case of choosing death, my family and friends, workmates, even the entire society, are engaged with it.

---

13   Angell, M, 'Prisoners of technology: the case of Nancy Cruzan', (17) 322 *New England Journal of Medicine*, 1990, 1226–1228, at p 1228.

As Donne said 'No man is an island', or to put it another way, '[p]rivate moral choices have public consequences'.[14] Meisel also argues that 'the patient's interests are not the sole interests involved. Others also have an interest in the patient's well-being and an interest in defining what counts as well-being'.[15] This may be so, but it does not inevitably militate against permitting patient choice at the end of life. Every death affects someone else (assuming the individual to have a social network of some sort) yet, as we will see, in a significant number of cases choices that are designed to bring about death – even sometimes by third parties –are tolerated, even facilitated, by society and the law. Many of them are even endorsed by the philosophy of those most opposed to the legalisation of assisted dying.

Although autonomy has become the dominant concept in modern bioethics, it is not a concept that is always uncritically accepted, nor interpreted in the same way. Feminists, for example, have long argued that the modern concept of autonomy is essentially masculine in nature; that is, that it emphasises the atomisation of the individual from the community/relationships which make up the fabric of our lives, and that it is insensitive to the subtleties of the context within which we live. Donchin, for example, says:

> Western philosophy . . . has been captivated by a paradigm of personal agency that incorporates two dubious assumptions: that individuals are isolated ahistorical monads and that the choices available to them are extracted from a fixed and immutable set of options. According to the conception of personal autonomy implicit in this model of agency, individuals are separated from one another by sharp boundaries that can be justifiably breached only by the consent of self-determining subjects.[16]

Thus, even if we value autonomy, it should be a relational rather than an atomising version to which we subscribe. In this way, we can avoid the appearance of selfishness which the more 'masculine' interpretation is argued to support. On this basis, autonomy cannot 'require that human agents and choosers act and choose in an eerie vacuum. The self that is self-governing in any workable and attractive model of autonomy has to be a self that acknowledges and even celebrates its social formation'.[17] To what extent, if at all, then, can the autonomy claims of those who wish to avail themselves

14 Cohen, C B, 'Unmanaged care: the need to regulate new reproductive technologies in the United States', (1997), *Bioethics*, Vol 11, No 3, 349–365, at pp 364–365.
15 Meisel, A, 'Ethics and law: physician-assisted dying', *Journal of Palliative Medicine*, Vol 8, No 3, 2005, 609–621, at p 610.
16 Donchin, A, 'Autonomy, interdependence, and assisted suicide: respecting boundaries/ crossing lines', (2000) *Bioethics*, Vol 14, No 23, 187–204, at pp 187–188.
17 Mills, C, 'The ethics of reproductive control', *The Philosophical Forum*, Vol XXX, No 1, March 1999, 43–57, at p 44.

of assisted dying be seen as compatible with what, to this writer at least, is a more attractive version of the autonomy principle?

I have already suggested that it is likely that every death – however it is brought about – has implications for the community of which the person has been a part. But the social and relational consequences of denying choice also have personal and social consequences. There are costs – even harms – caused to those whose wish to be spared suffering when this is not available to them; indeed, there may be additional costs associated with living life knowing that an assisted dying will not be available, however much it is seen as a good option.[18] Costs may also be social but the important issue is that we must reflect on the extent to which it is 'relationally appropriate' to insist that autonomy is always and inevitably selfish. The importance of autonomy can lie as much in how it connects us, by for example triggering compassion for suffering others, as it does in honouring individual choice. People who seek an assisted death may be prioritising their own wishes, but it is not inevitably true that this is an act of pure selfishness. For example, although the families of those who have travelled to Switzerland will inevitably regret the loss of their loved ones, for some (perhaps many) the ultimate act was carried out in recognition, not defiance, of the views of the extended family. As the children of Dr Ann Turner, who travelled to Switzerland for an assisted death, said in a press statement '[w]e could either support her in her hour of need, or we could turn our backs on our own mother and let her die a painful death alone'.[19] They also commented on the extent to which this was a family decision. Thus, perhaps what we really need is a recognition that choice and autonomy are not inherently disconnected from concern for others.

Jackson, for example, while accepting that autonomy should not exist in a 'sort of social and cultural vacuum, with needs and interests that emerge and can be satisfied without reference to the needs and interests of others . . .',[20] also concludes that

> acknowledging the significance of our social, economic and emotional context should not lead us to jettison the whole concept of autonomy. Rather we should perhaps think about how we might reconfigure autonomy in a way that is not predicated upon the isolation of the self-directed and self-sufficient subject.[21]

Moreover, Donchin points to the fact that '[a]ppeals to autonomy *rights* have an emancipatory aim that has often been one of the few defenses available

---

18 Valente, S M, (2004), at p 315.
19 Available at http://news.bbc.co.uk/1/hi/health/4761143.stm (accessed on 20/03/07).
20 Jackson, E, *Regulating Reproduction: Law, Technology and Autonomy*, 2001, Oxford: Hart Publishing, at p 3.
21 Ibid.

to women, particularly marginalised women, to resist pressures to override their own decision making authority'.[22] Thus, as Kalbian argues, feminists cannot afford to dump the concept of autonomy altogether and therefore they should support the position that 'autonomy is better understood when one views the person as a social being, whose identity relies on the context of her relationship with others . . .'.[23]

That the choice for death is not *only* a private decision with solely personal consequences can, therefore, be conceded, as can the vision of us all as being interrelated, without losing the value of the autonomy argument. In any case, the feminist arguments referred to above merely suggest that we should *consider* the impact of our decisions on others; they do not act as a block to making these choices. Most people would probably do this in any case, at least where there are others around to be considered. What we should resist, however, is some suggestion that we must always measure our decisions against some abstract notion of 'society'. Not only would this defy definition, it is an unreasonable imposition on our right to self-determine which is not required even if we agree with the feminist position on autonomy.

Nonetheless, Somerville continues to insist that the modern emphasis on respect for individual choice might 'result from a failure to balance a very strong (and necessary) emphasis on individual rights by any (or at least enough) consideration for communal claims'.[24] This is, as I have already suggested, to fail to take account of the possibility – perhaps even likelihood – that those who have reached such a serious decision have considered in considerable depth the impact of their death on others. The virtue of community cannot override the careful planning of others. If it did so, then every decision we make would need to be tested for its possible impact on others. Thus, my decision to enter into a simple contract would be validated only if I took account of its impact on society as a whole, or at least those closest to me. In any case, as Edwards says, '[o]ne is obliged to take into account consequences of one's actions which might harm others but it does not follow that these harms count for more than the suppression of one's free choice'.[25]

The exercise of self-determination can, therefore, be seen as both a social and a private action and can be supported on each basis. Without the autonomy to make social relationships, society would not exist. We may need to see autonomy as an aspect of our interconnectedness rather than as a characteristic of isolation, but this does not negate or even minimise the value of self-governance. As Parker says:

22 Ibid. at p 189.
23 Kalbian, A H, 'Narrative *ART*ifice and women's agency', *Bioethics*, Vol 19, No 2, 2005, 93–111, at p 94.
24 Somerville, M, at p 42.
25 Edwards, S D, 'Disability, identity and the "expressivist objection"', *Journal of Medical Ethics*, 2004: 30: 418–420, at p 419.

The communitarian claim that an emphasis on autonomy is *necessarily* individualistic and anti-communitarian is plainly false. To advocate an approach to ethical decision making based on the choices of individuals does not exclude the possibility that the values and choices of such individuals might have a social dimension.[26]

Ultimately, then, while it may be important to value autonomy within the context of the society of which we are a part, we should also accord it respect. Given that autonomy is the value which underpins liberal western democracies, interference with the free exercise of individual decision-making requires justification. As the feminist writer, Mary Ann Warren, says in another context, '[r]espect for personal autonomy requires that moral condemnations be directed only against actions which are demonstrably harmful, and/or which clearly violate the rights of other persons'.[27]

Most people would probably agree with this assertion, even if they disapproved of the choice I was making, and this leads to a second issue. Some people believe that it is – sometimes – necessary to protect people from the consequences of their own – autonomous – decisions, especially when these would result in death or other serious outcome. Particularly in relation to the vulnerable, as we will see later, this is an intelligible – even laudable – aim. However, as Harris points out, although '[c]oncern for welfare complements autonomy in that it provides the conditions in which autonomy can flourish and our lives be given their own unique meaning . . .',[28] nonetheless '[c]oncern for welfare ceases to be legitimate at the point at which, so far from being productive of autonomy, it operates to frustrate the individual's own attempts to create her own life for herself'.[29] This assumes, of course, that the decision to seek an assisted death is ever appropriately described as truly autonomous.

Is 'assisted' dying ever truly autonomous?

Even if we concede the value of self-determination or autonomy it is sometimes argued that, while suicide may (or, of course, may not) be an autonomous act, assisted death cannot be because it requires the involvement of third parties. On this argument, while the decision may be reached independently, the fact that it cannot be carried out by the person without help means that it is not a purely self-determining event.

Callahan, for example, maintains that there is a significant difference between suicide and assisted dying. The former can be seen as a private act,

---

26   Parker, M, 'Public deliberation and private choice in genetics and reproduction', *Journal of Medical Ethics*, 2000: 26: 160–165, at p 161.
27   Warren, M A, *Gendercide: The Implications of Sex Selection*, 1985, New Jersey: Rowman & Allanheld, at p 190.
28   Harris, J, (2003), at p 11.
29   Ibid.

whereas '. . . euthanasia should be understood as of its nature a social act. It requires the assistance of someone else and could not take place without it'.[30] Salem also says that '. . . there is a paradox underlying physician-assisted suicide. It is conceived of as an intimate, existential act and indeed a response to modern medicine, but at the same time it is a request for the *complicity* of physicians (and society)'.[31] Thus, for Salem, 'as long as physician-assisted suicide presupposes medical assistance it cannot be conceived as immersed in the realm of self-determination. Unless doctors are reduced strictly to being instruments to fulfill their patients' desires, physician-assisted suicide enacts what must be seen as a mutual decision'.[32] Keown also disputes the assertion that the important value of a chosen assisted death is in fact respect for an autonomous choice, claiming rather that 'the real, rather than the rhetorical, justification . . . is not the patient's autonomous request but *the doctor's judgment that the request is justified because death would benefit the patient*'[33] (original emphasis). This position also finds favour with other commentators, who argue that '[i]n all legislatures, the final decision for physician assisted suicide or therapeutic killing rests with the doctor. Patients' perception of total control over this type of death is illusory'.[34] As we will see later, however, neither of the assertions is, in fact, accurate.

Two further things need to be said about this characterisation of assisted dying. First, it presumes that autonomy can only be served when the individual him or herself carries out the act entirely independently of others. If so, then no decision to participate in, for example, any medical treatment can be described as autonomous since the patient relies on the doctor to carry out the act to which they have agreed. Second, the fact that someone else is involved is not necessarily sufficient to transform a private into a public act, with all of the consequences that flow from that. For example, the fact that we need a doctor to unblock fallopian tubes in order to facilitate a pregnancy does not require or permit individual decisions to establish a pregnancy to be second-guessed by the physician who assists by carrying out the surgery. Even where third party involvement is necessary to the achievement of an autonomous decision, therefore, we do not doubt that the key legitimising characteristic is the autonomous act, which does not become non-autonomous just because someone else's help is needed to give it effect.

30 Callahan, D, *The Troubled Dream of Life: In Search of a Peaceful Death*, 2000, Washington, DC: Georgetown University Press, at p 104.
31 Salem, T, 'Physician-assisted suicide: promoting autonomy – or medicalizing suicide?', *Hastings Center Report*, 29, No 3, (1999) 30–36, at p 31.
32 Ibid. at p 32.
33 Keown, J, *Euthanasia, Ethics and Public Policy*, 2002, Cambridge University Press, at p 77.
34 George, R J D, Finlay, I G and Jeffrey, D, 'Legalised euthanasia will violate the rights of vulnerable patients', *British Medical Journal*, 2005: 331: 684–685, at p 684.

Nonetheless, the importance of third party involvement was regarded as significant in one relatively elderly case heard by the European Commission on Human Rights. In the case of *R v UK* it was concluded that:

> The Commission does not consider that the activity for which the applicant was convicted, namely aiding and abetting suicide, can be described as falling into the sphere of his private life. . . . *While it might be thought to touch directly on the private lives of those who sought to commit suicide*, it does not follow that the applicant's rights to privacy are involved. On the contrary, the Commission is of the opinion that the acts [of] aiding, abetting, counselling or procuring suicide are excluded from the concept of privacy by virtue of their trespass on the public interest of protecting life, as reflected in the criminal provisions of the 1961 Act (emphasis added).[35]

Interestingly, however, on examination it is possible to derive a message from this decision which minimises rather than maximises the importance of the role played by third parties. In essence, the Commission is addressing the behaviour of the person who *assists* the dying – not the person who *seeks* the assistance. Were society, therefore, to decide that the provisions of the 1961 Act or the common law in Scotland no longer protected us against a 'trespass on the public interest of protecting life' then there would be no justification for continued criminalisation of the act of assisting. In other words, the Commission was not critiquing the autonomy of the decision for death, merely the fact that the actions of the third party were already against the law and culpable on that basis. The privacy right under consideration here was not that of the individual to choose an assisted death but rather the right of a third party to assist in facilitating it.

It is, however, also argued that autonomy or self-governance is *de facto* not possible in such circumstances. Burt, for example, suggests that the 'imminent approach of death' means that the concept of autonomy is 'radically unsettled'.[36] This argument, of course, is debatable. The presumption that people are inevitably profoundly disturbed or otherwise emotionally incapable of autonomous acts in the face of their death might be true in some cases. However, arguably it is less rather than more likely to be the case when the person has confronted the reality of their life and prefers non-existence to existence. It is surely those who wish to hold on to life who are more likely to be seriously troubled or depressed by the likelihood of death. Additionally, a consequence of accepting this is that it would need to be applicable in all circumstances where autonomy is taken to provide the basis for a lawful

35   *R v UK* (1983) 6 EHRR 140, at pp 166–167.
36   Burt, R A, 'The end of autonomy', *Improving End of Life Care: Why Has It Been So Difficult?*, *Hastings Center Report Special Report*, 35, No 6, (2005): S9–S13, at S10.

decision which results in death – for example, where a patient refuses life-sustaining treatment. However, as we will see later, the law's approach in these cases is entirely consistent with accepting the primacy of autonomy and the ethic of respect for persons demands that such decisions are vindicated.

Limits to decision-making authority?

As McCall Smith notes:

> As the shackles of a theocratic vision of human life were abandoned, the philosophy of liberal individualism … became universally more attractive. One effect of this was to promote the concept of autonomy to a dominating role in a substantial part of our public moral debate.[37]

This, he suggests, had the consequence that '… the body moved from being a public object, the focus of a broader vision of human dignity, to being an object of purely individual expression and concern'.[38] However, even if opponents of assisted dying were eventually prepared to accord primacy to the value of autonomy, there are nonetheless safeguards which many would probably agree should be in place to ensure that what seems *prima facie* to be a self-determining choice actually is a voluntary and free decision; that is, a decision that it is *in fact* autonomous. Some of these will be returned to later, but for the moment the most important is the question of capacity or competence; the ability to act autonomously.

Most particularly, it is feared that suicidal ideation or depression will lead people to make choices from which we should protect them; that they will choose death erroneously or inappropriately, motivated by factors which, in some cases, are able to be removed or at least ameliorated. As Woodman says, if we were to legalise assisted dying 'one of the safeguards that physicians want in place is the assurance that the patient who requests it is mentally competent to decide, and not propelled by a potentially treatable depression'.[39] The problem, as he points out, however, is that depression may or may not amount to a negation of competence. After all, '… doesn't anyone who is about to die feel some degree of depression? And who decides whether the sadness that they feel is clouding their judgement or heightening their understanding of their situation'?[40] If we negate every decision made by someone who is distressed at the prospect of their death (chosen or not) then we would have grounds to challenge any will made, for example, following a terminal

---

37 McCall Smith, A, 'Euthanasia: the strengths of the middle ground', *Medical Law Review* 7, Summer 1999, 194–207, at p 195.
38 Ibid.
39 Woodman, S, op. cit. at p 189.
40 Ibid.

diagnosis, every decision to spend as much money as we can before we die, and so on, and we would also need to bring the same concerns to refusal of life-sustaining treatment. True, these decisions – including the choice for an assisted death – may coexist with depression, but that does not in and of itself make them incompetent, even if they seem irrational to others. The right to make apparently irrational decisions – even those which may shorten life – is firmly entrenched in our law,[41] and this will be returned to later. Meantime, it is worth focusing on the impact of depression on end-of-life decisions. Smith and Pollack argue that '[t]he opponents of aid-in-dying argue that untreated depression is almost always the motivation behind a terminally ill persons' request to die'.[42] This, they argue, leads to two possible arguments. First, that 'a request for aid-in-dying confirms a diagnosis of depression which renders the person incompetent to make a life or death medical decision . . .', and second that 'if they were treated, the person would change his/her mind . . .'.[43]

In fact, as we will see later, depression does not seem to feature significantly in the reasons given by people for wanting to have an assisted death. That is not to say that it may not be a feature of the person's life, just as it may be when people reject life-sustaining treatment where the only consideration is competence, not emotional state of mind.

Where depression is present, it is of course to be hoped that an offer of treatment, where available and appropriate, would be made. However, even where treatment is available, it cannot be assumed that this would change people's minds about wanting an assisted death.

Perhaps more problematic is the idea that 'suicidal ideation' is a sign of mental illness; that precipitating or seeking death inevitably calls competence into question. Again, Smith and Pollack challenge this assumption. They note that

> [s]uicidal ideation and thoughts of death are key indicators of psychiatric illness in the medically well . . . but a survey of psychiatrists showed that only 3 per cent believed a request for aid-in-dying by a terminally ill person was *prima facie* evidence of a mental illness.[44]

Of course, it might be said, that psychiatrists may not be sufficiently skilled to make such judgements (although this is a somewhat strange claim) or that they may underestimate the existence of mental illness in those who want an assisted death. Again, however, this is no less true in the case of those who are

---

41   See, e.g. *Re C (Adult: Refusal of Medical Treatment)* [1994] 1 All ER 819; *Re B (Adult: Refusal of Treatment)* (2002) 65 BMLR 149.
42   Smith, D M and Pollack, D, 'A psychiatric defence of aid in dying', *Community Mental Health Journal*, Vol 34, No 6, 1998, 547–556.
43   Smith and Pollack (1998) at pp 551–2.
44   Ibid. at pp 548–9.

permitted to refuse life-saving treatments. Indeed, it has been pointed out that 'psychiatrists and other physicians have been successfully conducting such evaluations for years when persons request discontinuation of life sustaining interventions'.[45] Yet undoubtedly some psychiatrists (and others) continue to hold to the belief that requests for assistance in dying are inevitably based in depression or mental illness, either or both of which may be susceptible of treatment. The consequence of this would, of course, be that treatment might plausibly result in the person changing their mind. As Sullivan and Younger point out, '[e]valuating the role of depression in these refusals and determining the effect of depression on competence are difficult tasks . . .'[46] but they conclude that '[w]e must not overestimate or underestimate the value of treatment of depression for patients with severe medical illness . . .',[47] concluding that 'sometimes it is valuable to accept the patient's decision to die'.[48]

Can we limit the exercise of autonomy?

One further issue must be addressed under the heading of autonomy. In most jurisdictions where assisted dying is legalised, and in most where it is being discussed, limitations are placed on who may seek access to it. However, as Steinbock notes,

> . . . if autonomy is the basis for a right to PAS [physician assisted suicide], why should this right be limited to those who have a terminal illness? Cannot forcing someone to continue living under conditions he or she finds unbearable also be seen as a contradiction of his life, and an odious form of tyranny?[49]

In other words, on what basis can we challenge the rights of non-terminally ill people to make an autonomous choice to die? This issue is also addressed by Amarasekara and Bagaric, who say:

> If the doctrinal rationale for voluntary euthanasia rests on the principle of autonomy, then it logically follows that the pool of euthanasia candidates extends to all people who make an informed and free decision to die. Limiting euthanasia to people with a terminal illness or those in severe pain would be arbitrary. The charge of discrimination would be made by

---

45 Smith and Pollack (1998) at p 552.
46 Sullivan, M D and Younger, S J, 'Depression, competence, and the right to refuse lifesaving medical treatment', (1994) 151 *American Journal of Psychiatry*, 1994: 151: 971–8, at p 977.
47 Ibid.
48 Ibid.
49 Steinbock, B, (2005), at p 236.

those who wanted to die for any number of reasons including loneliness, unemployment, poverty, physical incapacity, or depression.[50]

These are valid points, but again do not defeat the appeal of autonomy-based arguments. If it is the case that everyone, and not just those more obviously 'in need', can lay claim to the same right to seek assisted dying, then so be it. That most of the permissive laws around the world place restrictions on accessibility is a commentary on the laws; not on the philosophical basis for the argument. What the limitations show is the reluctance of states to commit fully to an autonomy-based approach to assisted dying. In the Netherlands, for example, this may be explained by the fact that their law was not primarily based on concerns about patient autonomy; rather it finds its underpinning rationale in the conflict of duties confronting doctors when faced with a patient in unrelievable suffering.

Autonomy, therefore, while a strong argument in favour of allowing people to make their own life and death decisions, may not in and of itself be sufficient to convince opponents of the wisdom of legalisation. For example, Safranek argues that '[i]f both the virtuous and the vicious can act autonomously, then the mere possession of autonomy neither specifies an agent's moral character nor justifies his acts'.[51] On this account, '[t]he debate involving assisted suicide, like so many other social disputes, hinges on discrepant views of the good, rather than on autonomy or beneficence'.[52] These 'views of the good' have already been referred to in Chapter 1, where it was suggested that there is nothing inherently wrong in killing; an approach that even opponents of legalisation would accept, for example in the case of self-defence. If so, then it is not clear what these different views of the good amount to. In fact, virtually nobody believes that all killing in all circumstances is inevitably wrong. It is not, therefore, critical that both the 'virtuous' and the 'vicious' can act autonomously; what matters is whether or not the outcome of their acts is recognised as licit or illicit. Since killing is not always wrong, it cannot be the fact that killing is involved in assisted dying that would make it inherently wrong. To consider it as wrong, we would need to find additional supporting arguments about the *kind* of killing that assisted dying is in order to explain why it, and not for example, self defence, is wrong.

So, is assisted dying more 'wrong' than other forms of killing? It is difficult to find any grounds to explain why this would be a rational conclusion to reach. Why would a chosen death be less ethical than one brought about without our

---

50   Amarasekara, K and Bagaric, M, 'Moving from voluntary euthanasia to non-voluntary euthanasia: equality and compassion', *Ratio Juris*, Vol 17, No 3, September 2004, 398–423, at pp 409–410.

51   Safranek, J P, 'Autonomy and assisted suicide: the execution of freedom', 28 *Hastings Center Report* 28 No 4, (1998) 32–36, at p 32.

52   Ibid. at p 35.

consent, for example by way of withholding or withdrawing treatment? And if a chosen death is wrong, how can we explain the law's absolute prohibition on continuing life-sustaining treatment in the face of a competent refusal? Moreover, even if assisted dying is in some way 'wrong' why is it worse than (lawful) killing in a war which might merely be waged in pursuit of an unacceptable or disputed political agenda?

Compassion/relief of suffering

Nobody seriously disputes that modern medicine can keep people alive for longer than that life might be valuable to the person. In some situations, people may prefer a shorter life with quality to a longer life with suffering. Based both on their autonomous right to make such decisions for themselves, and on the compassion that may encourage others to help in the relief of suffering, why should they not be permitted to do so? Opponents of legalisation would say that there are ways around the problem of suffering which make assisted dying an unnecessary option.

Pain management

Palliative medicine – particularly in pain management – has developed apace. Many palliative care doctors insist that virtually all pain can be managed and that it is therefore completely inappropriate to contemplate assisted dying. Johnston, for example, claims that '[a]t present, the medicine, knowledge and technology is available such that adequate pain control measures can be implemented to control the pain of up to 99 per cent of patients'.[53] This may be so, but this is not an argument that can be universalised, nor is it of direct relevance. To be sure, the ability to relieve pain will be important; pain may well drive people towards believing that their life is intolerable, and certainly if that pain can be managed, many would choose continued life over death. However, Magnusson is one of the many commentators who point to the fact that '[e]uthanasia is not just about pain relief. Research indicates that indignity, dependency and lack of control are more important than pain in motivating the desire to die'.[54] Undoubtedly, pain could be better managed, and we know that '[t]he failure of physicians to relieve the pain of dying patients has been extensively documented'.[55] It is entirely sympathetic to the

---

53 Johnston, B P, *Death as a Salesman: What's Wrong with Assisted Suicide*, 1998, Sacramento: New Regency Publishing, at p 24.

54 Magnusson, R, *Angels of Death: Exploring the Euthanasia Underground*, 2002, Yale University Press, at p 90.

55 Tucker, K L, 'The death with dignity movement: protecting rights and expanding options after *Glucksberg* and *Quill*', *Minnesota Law Review*, Vol 82: 923–938, 1998, at p 935.

cause of legalisation to insist that pain management must be better, even if pain seems not to be the primary reason why people seek assisted dying.

However, although relief of pain seems to be a morally benign goal, in some cases, however few these are, pain can only be managed by what is referred to as terminal sedation. This means essentially putting someone into a coma and waiting for them to die. For those who value dignity (of which more later), this may relieve pain, but will not answer the issue of loss of control at the end of life.

Opponents of legalisation would counter that:

> As regrettable as terminal sedation is, there is no evidence that public opinion prefers the alternative of changing professional standards and the law to authorize euthanasia, thus running the risk of any further erosion of society's respect for life.[56]

This is, in fact, based on a fundamental error or overstatement. There is equally no evidence to the contrary. Indeed some evidence that the public supports legal reform does exist, even if some of it is derived from evidence which results from arguably flawed opinion polls.[57] In fact, as we have seen, societies throughout the world do not hold the position that life is always preferable when other values such as autonomy are taken into account. Moreover, the contention that the public supports terminal sedation rather than the alternative is refuted by at least one (albeit small) study. Starks et al '. . . recruited 60 individuals from 35 families: 28 family members reporting on 23 patients in the retrospective cohort and 12 patients and 20 of their family members in the prospective cohort'.[58] They discussed the issue of terminal sedation with seven patients and four retrospective family members. What they found does not support the contention that terminal sedation is seen as the lesser of two evils. As they report:

> Most felt that terminal sedation would only prolong the dying process and increase the burden on family members as they waited for the end to come. Three patients said they would consider this option only if the family thought it would be easier to live with, although they themselves would prefer a hastened death.[59]

---

56   Dowbiggin, I, *A Merciful End: The Euthanasia Movement in Modern America*, 2003, Oxford University Press, at p 175.
57   For discussion, see the House of Lords Select Committee on the Assisted Dying for the Terminally Ill Bill, *Report of the House of Lords Select Committee on the Assisted Dying for the Terminally Ill Bill*, HL Paper 86-1, especially Chapter 6.
58   Starks, H, Pearlman, R A, *et al*, 'Why now? Timing and circumstances of hastened death', *Pain Symptom Manage* 2005: 30: 215–226, at p 216.
59   Ibid. at p 218.

Moreover, there are philosophical reasons to doubt that terminal sedation is a better option than assisted dying. As Kamm points out, '... if aiming against the continued existence of rational agency for pain relief is what constitutes an impermissible use of persons as mere means, terminal sedation will be ruled out as well as PAS ...'.[60]

In any case, as I have already suggested, the indignity of the dying process, including loss of control, is one of the major reasons for seeking assisted dying; terminal sedation merely guarantees that loss, and for those who object to this it would surely not be a desired or desirable way to end one's life.[61] Further, terminal sedation is, arguably, indistinguishable from other assistance in dying; it requires an act by healthcare professionals and it is designed to bring about death. Proponents of terminal sedation as a last resort, however, try to make a distinction that would bring such sedation out of the realm of assisted dying and into the arena of simple medical treatment. Smith for example, says:

> Efforts must be undertaken to assure that terminal sedation does not fall into a quagmire of taxonomical confusion. If viewed as an action that validates personal autonomy or self-determination, this type of palliative care will no longer be seen incorrectly as either euthanasia or physician-assisted suicide. Rather with this reclassification or clarification in terminology will come an understanding of a medically proper way to assure a modicum of dignity at death.[62]

For the moment, leaving aside the question of whether this can possibly be described as a 'dignified' death, Smith rather seems to sell the pass by resting the justification for terminal sedation on the concept of autonomy, an argument usually used by those in favour of legalisation rather than those against. Indeed, it is unclear how on any argument the patient's request could turn terminal sedation from something that is different from assisted dying (which also hinges on patient request) into something that is just proper medical care. This may be a convenient argument, but it is of dubious merit. Certainly, some people may choose to die in this way, but that is insufficient to distinguish terminal sedation from other ways in which doctors could help patients to die. There is, then, no 'taxonomical confusion'; quite simply, terminal sedation is designed to facilitate or ensure the death of the patient. The fact that it does

60 Kamm, F M, 'Physician-assisted suicide, the doctrine of double effect, and the ground of value', *Ethics* 109 (April 1999), 586–605, at p 602.
61 For further discussion, see Ten Have, H and Clark, D, (eds), *The Ethics of Palliative Care: European Perspectives*, 2002, Buckingham, Open University Press, particularly Chapter 9.
62 Smith, G P, 'Terminal sedation as palliative care: revalidating a right to a good death', *Cambridge Quarterly of Healthcare Ethics*, (1998), 7, 382–387, at p 383.

so by removing the individual's awareness of his or her condition might make it a kind act where people do not wish to witness their own deterioration, but its aim is the same as other cases of assisted dying which patients are not currently permitted to choose.

On this subject, it is worthy of note that in the only case of which I am aware in which a patient *requested* terminal sedation – an act of autonomy according to Smith and therefore presumably licit – the patient's request was initially denied. Kelly Taylor has two genetic conditions which cause her unrelievable pain. She has also been given less that one year to live. She requested that she be given sufficient morphine so that she would lapse into unconsciousness and, having previously indicated by way of an advance directive that she would at that stage accept neither assisted nutrition or hydration, she would die. Mrs Taylor's argument is, first, that this is merely an example of the use of the double effect principle (of which more later) and second, that her Article 3 right not to be subject to inhumane and degrading treatment protects her choice.[63] Despite what Smith has argued, her doctors, the hospital and the British Medical Association are all in agreement that to agree to her wishes would be unlawful. Her consent, and autonomous choice, do not therefore seem in fact to turn what would otherwise be unlawful into something that is part of 'proper' medical treatment.

Palliative care specialists are among the strongest opponents of legalised assisted dying; perhaps unsurprisingly so. But their claims that pain can be relieved in virtually all cases must be subject to a more rigorous interrogation than is common. We should not permit the legitimate esteem in which they are held to blind us to the paternalism inherent in their approach. Palliation can remove much pain, as we have seen, but as Cassel says:

> All too often we focus only on pain as if it were the only symptom that accompanies death, when in fact there are many other symptoms affecting dying patients that are much more difficult to treat than pain. These sometimes are protean, and can be difficult to diagnose and to understand, but often as unremitting and terrible for the patient experiencing them: symptoms such as nausea, vomiting, shortness of breath, inability to handle secretions, and nightmares and episodic, terrifying delirium, sometimes caused by the very medications doctors give to treat the pain. . . . These symptoms as a source of suffering cannot always be abolished.[64]

---

63 Dyer, C, 'Dying woman seeks backing to hasten death', *British Medical Journal*, 334, 329, (17 February 2007).

64 Cassel, C K, 'Physician-assisted suicide: progress or peril?', in Thomasma, D C and Kushner, T, (eds), *Birth to Death: Science and Bioethics*, 1996, Cambridge University Press, 218–230, at p 221.

In addition, Davies challenges the view that the hospice movement's undoubted expertise in dealing with the dying has removed the need for consideration of assisted dying or rendered it redundant. Death can be accompanied by degrading and disturbing symptoms some of which cannot be relieved (without terminal sedation). As Davies says:

> even if it were possible to alleviate all of these – and the hospice doctors do not claim that it is – there are still many people who do not want to go on to the bitter end and do not see why that should be required of them.[65]

Since '. . . even with the very best palliative case some patients still suffer unbearably at the end of life and want help to die . . . ',[66] we are left with only paternalistic reasons to bolster the argument against allowing patients to choose an assisted death. Suffering, after all, is a subjective and not an objective phenomenon and may well endure irrespective of the therapies that modern medicine can offer.[67]

While Somerville fusses with the *speculation* that legalising assisted dying might in fact cause suffering rather than relieving it, because '[p]eople might fear that it would be practised in ways that would reduce personal control . . .',[68] she conveniently ignores the *evidence* that people's fear about loss of control is intimately related to their condition; only if assisted dying were non-voluntary or involuntary would Somerville's fears be realistic. Rather, she – like many opponents – prefers speculation to solid evidence.[69] As Quill says:

> The myth that excellent palliative care is incompatible with the provision of legal access to physician-assisted death as a last resort has been largely debunked by five years of data from Oregon. Physician-assisted suicide has accounted for relatively few deaths (less than 0.1 percent per year), and more than three-quarters of the patients who have died under the provisions of the act have been simultaneously enrolled in hospice programs. Patients who have chosen the option of physician-assisted suicide have been motivated primarily by loss of autonomy, loss of control of their bodily functions, decreased ability to enjoy life, and

---

65 Davies, J, 'The case for legalising voluntary euthanasia', in Thomasma and Kushner, op. cit., 83–95 at p 88.

66 *Dignity in Dying: The Report*, London: Dignity in Dying, February 2006, at p 12.

67 Shand, J, 'A reply to some standard objections to euthanasia', *Journal of Applied Philosophy*, Vol 14, No 1, 1997, 43–47.

68 Somerville, M, p 37.

69 Angell, (1990), op. cit.

tiredness of dying. Unrelieved pain has never been the main reason, and clinical depression has not seemed to confound the decision.[70]

We are left therefore with the conclusion that palliation should be both available and offered, but not that its availability – even successes – presents a strong case against legalisation of assisted dying. While the wider availability of, and developments in, palliative care might 'reduce the demand for assisted suicide . . . it will not eliminate the demand'.[71] Moreover, '. . . contrary to claims by some opponents of euthanasia and PAS, use of palliative care is not necessarily an effective response to patients' request for euthanasia and PAS'.[72]

One additional point emerges from this discussion. Although reports consistently suggest that the prime reason for requesting assisted dying relates to loss of dignity, etc, it is sometimes forgotten that the suffering associated with loss of control is intimately linked to the value of autonomy and self-determination. Thus, while some suffering can be alleviated, at the heart of the relief of suffering argument is, in fact, autonomy. Were the argument to be viewed from this perspective, it would bolster autonomy-based claims and place palliation firmly in the appropriate place – as an important, but by no means definitive, contributor to the debate. While the House of Lords Select Committee on Medical Ethics,[73] and the House of Lords Select Committee on the Assisted Dying for the Terminally Ill Bill,[74] were quite obviously impressed by the medical evidence they received, conceptualising the question of suffering as an aspect of an autonomy-based rather than palliation-based argument would suggest that their emphasis on medical perspectives is seriously misplaced.

The argument, however, does not end there. Even if we can agree that the desire to live in a certain way, and to experience death as we choose, can defeat the arguments of those who insist that we should always prefer life to death, opponents have further cards up their sleeves.

70   Quill, T E, 'Dying and decision making – evolution of end-of-life options', *New England Journal of Medicine*, 350: 20: 2029–2032, at p 2030.
71   Orentlicher, D, *Matters of Life and Death: Making Moral Theory Work in Medical Ethics and the Law*, 2001, Princeton and Oxford, Princeton University Press, at p 40.
72   Emanuel, E J, Daniels, R, Fairclough, D L, Clarridge, B R, 'The practice of euthanasia and physician-assisted suicide in the United States: adherence to proposed safeguards and effects on physicians', *Journal of the American Medical Association*, Vol 280(6), 12 August 1998, 507–13, available at http://gateway.uk.ovid.com/gwl/ovidweb.cgi (accessed on 11/08/06), at p 10.
73   *Report of the House of Lords Select Committee on Medical Ethics*, op. cit.
74   *Report of the House of Lords Select Committee on the Assisted Dying for the Terminally Ill Bill*, op. cit.

The slippery slope

One of the most commonly used arguments against legalisation of assisted dying is that this would perch us at the top of a slippery slope. This argument was rather simplistically given credibility by the Report of the Select Committee on Medical Ethics, which claimed that '. . . to create an exception to the general prohibition of intentional killing would inevitably open the way to its further erosion whether by design, by inadvertence, or by the human tendency to test the limits of any regulation'.[75] The slippery slope argument is said to take two distinct forms, the logical and the empirical, and broadly presupposes that if we once permit A (which might be acceptable), we inevitably will have to permit B (less acceptable), and even C (completely unacceptable).

The logical form of the argument suggests that '(for example) the acceptance of PAS at a patient's request leads to acceptance of the practice where the initiative has not come from the patient but is at the doctor's prompting'.[76] An example of the logical slippery slope is encapsulated in the following quotation:

Once euthanasia is legalised for competent patients, it is likely that there will be pressure to legalise it for the incompetent, the compassion that is universally felt for those with a terminal illness which is accompanied by undignified symptoms or unbearable pain is experienced no less for minors and intellectually impaired patients who are in the same condition. Their helplessness in fact probably *adds* to their vulnerability and emotional appeal.[77]

Or, as Burgess puts it:

. . . the real worry . . . must be the fear of a slide through habituation into wholesale killing of a kind the reformers never contemplated legalising. The idea seems to be that medical professionals who engage in euthanasia – and the general public – will come to regard (beneficent) killing as routine. When this occurs, there will be pressure for further liberalisation until we reach a stage where courses of action now regarded as atrocious will then be regarded as permissible. (We will then be, in effect, at the bottom of the slope.)[78]

75 *Report of the House of Lords Select Committee on Medical Ethics* op. cit. at p 49, para 238.
76 Freeman, M, 'Death, dying, and the Human Rights Act', *Current Legal Problems*, Vol 52, 218–238 (1999) at p 233.
77 Amarasekara and Bagaric, (2004), at p 405.
78 Burgess, J A, 'The great slippery-slope argument', *Journal of Medical Ethics* 1993: 19: 69–174, at p 171.

Further examples of the logical slippery slope are provided by Hendin and Klerman, who argue:

> If those advocating legalization of assisted suicide prevail, it will be a reflection that as a culture we are turning away from efforts to improve our care of the mentally ill, the infirm, and the elderly. Instead, we would be licensing the right to abuse and exploit the fears of the ill and depressed. We would be accepting the view of those who are depressed and suicidal that death is the preferred solution to the problems of illness, age, and depression.[79]

The logic of this position, however, can be challenged, not least because it assumes that A and C are the same or similar creatures. As Frey says, 'no one really believes that because we allow that there can be justified killings in law, our society has reached anarchy or a state of nature'.[80] Nor is it inevitable (logically) that allowing people to make their own end-of-life decisions means that those who do not wish to make such a choice will be forced to. Moreover, respect for autonomy implies no disrespect for groups such as the disabled who may feel themselves to be particularly vulnerable to this argument, see below. Nonetheless, many see the logical slippery slope as a real reason for concern. Smith goes further, saying, '[s]ince our values often follow our pocketbooks a right to die could quickly morph into a duty to end your life for the benefit of society and/or your family'.[81] Again, however, these commentators – however compelling their rhetoric – are making untestable presumptions about how autonomous people will react to the permissibility of choosing death and what effect that would have on those who have no wish for an assisted death. If the choice that is legally endorsed is a voluntary one, it clearly does not follow that coerced choices will be regarded as valid; at least not on the same grounds – an entirely different justification would be needed once autonomy is stripped from the equation. What these commentators argue for in fact denies the value of autonomy and seems to presume that we cannot recognise the difference between decisions based on individual choice and those which are coercive or paternalistic. That coerced or pressurised decisions might occur (as they probably currently do) is an argument for caution and good regulation; not an argument for prohibition. Moreover, they presume that allowing people to make their own end-of-life decisions is in some way to erode the moral compass

79 Hendin, H and Klerman, G, 'Physician-assisted suicide: the dangers of legalization', *American Journal of Psychiatry* 1993: 1650: 43–145, at p 145.
80 Frey, R G, 'The fear of a slippery slope', in Dworkin, G, Frey, R G and Bok, S, *Euthanasia and Physician-Assisted Suicide: For and Against*, 1998, Cambridge University Press, pp 43–63, at p 52.
81 Smith, W J, 'Why secular humanism about assisted suicide is wrong', 31–32, Spring 2003, available at http://www.secularhumanism.org, at p 31.

which people can legitimately lay claim to. The fact that, for example, some relatives may be greedy, or uncaring, cannot be extrapolated to the position that *all* are, nor to the conclusion that we are incapable of resisting pressure and will be rendered non-autonomous simply because of their greed. If this were all it took to negate autonomy it would be a pretty worthless concept.

The empirical form of the slippery slope argument 'does not allege that the consequences are inevitable but that they will happen in practice because safeguards to prevent it either cannot be designed or will not work'.[82] Finnis, for example, asks

> ... what conceivable legislative pronouncement, elegant preamble, government pamphlets, elaboration of hospital paperwork, physician reporting, official enquiries and all that, could remove or even appreciably diminish the patient's subjection to the pressure of the thought that my being killed is what my relatives expect of me and is in any case the decent thing to do, even though I utterly fear it and perhaps perceive it as the uttermost and ultimate indignity, an odious, devastating subjection to the needs and will of others?[83]

However, speaking in the House of Lords Debate on the Assisted Dying for the Terminally Ill Bill, the distinguished philosopher Mary Warnock said, '[t]here can be no evidence that this Bill poises us on the top of a slippery slope, let alone one that leads to the widespread euthanasia of the vulnerable — an argument that we hear over and over again'.[84] In any case, disaster is neither imminent nor likely. Gorowitz explains this rather colourfully: '[i]t is not enough to show that disaster awaits if the process is not controlled. A man walking east in Omaha will drown in the Atlantic – if he does not stop. . . . Collectively we have significant capacity to exercise judgment and control . . .'.[85]

In any case, we have no evidence that a slope will actually emerge, although some commentators would suggest that just such a slope has already emerged in the Netherlands. They cite as evidence an apparent weakening in controls, resulting in endorsement of assisted dying for vulnerable young children, or a purported increase in unrequested deaths, as clear proof that the empirical slippery slope is a reality. This, they conclude, will either lead to, or reflects, a reduction in our respect for the lives of others. Shand, however, argues that

---

82 Freeman, (1999), at pp 233–4.
83 Finnis, J, 'Euthanasia, morality, and law', *Loyola of Los Angeles Law Review*, Vol 31: 1123–46, 1998, at p 1136.
84 *Hansard*, Vol 681, Col 1221, (12 May 2006), Baroness Warnock.
85 Gorowitz, S, *Doctors' Dilemmas: Moral Conflicts and Medical Care*, 1982, New York: Oxford University Press, at p 168.

it might be said that the introduction of euthanasia, rather than weakening the value we place on life, actually strengthens it by ensuring that the *life* of the individual is not despoiled by its finishing in a degrading manner and by respecting the opinions of the individual.[86]

Finnis, a noted opponent of legalisation, produces what he clearly believes to be the death-blow to those who suggest that the empirical slippery slope is a fantasy:

> When we sum up . . . official Dutch statistics for the fifth year of their euthanasia regime, we find that in 26,350 cases, death was accelerated by medical intervention intended wholly or partly to terminate life. That is *over 20% of all Dutch deaths*. In the United States that would be over 400,000 deaths. Of these, well over half – 59% (15,528) – were without any explicit request. In the United States that would be over 235,000 unrequested medically accelerated deaths per annum.[87]

What Finnis has done, however, is to elide *medically* assisted dying (which happens all the time as we will see in the next chapter) with *chosen* assisted dying. The argument in this discussion relates to a chosen death; not to the (arguably more worrying) fact that doctors already regularly choose death for their patients, albeit that they disguise it, using arguments such as futility or the doctrine of double effect.[88]

Beauchamp and Childress agree – as I suspect we all might – that if there were empirical evidence to support the slippery slope, then 'the argument is cogent, and such practices are justifiably prohibited'.[89] However, they also ask '[d]oes the evidence indicate that we cannot maintain firm distinctions in public policies between patient-requested death and involuntary euthanasia?'[90] The answer must be that '[d]etailed empirical evidence is required and detailed empirical evidence is conspicuously lacking'.[91]

Although we cannot simply dismiss the idea that, however unpalatable, people may feel some pressure in a permissive, albeit regulated, environment to choose death because they feel themselves to be a burden on their loved ones, as Amarasekara and Bagaric say the slippery slope argument leads to 'a large amount of conjecture. While guesses and hunches provide fertile discussion

86 Shand, (1997), at p 45.
87 Finnis, (1998), at p 1128.
88 For further discussion, see Chapter 3.
89 Beauchamp, T L and Childress, J S, *Principles of Biomedical Ethics*, 4th edn, 1994, Oxford University Press, at p 231.
90 Ibid.
91 Burgess, (1993), at p 171.

points for both sides of the euthanasia debate, such armchair speculation is not likely to advance the debate beyond the level of the rhetoric'.[92] Although, therefore, we should be alert to the possibility that such slopes might conceivably emerge, we cannot base our position on more than compassion and caution. We do not have the evidence necessary to suggest that this is a real fear, nor is it likely we will ever have it unless those countries which have legalised assisted dying suddenly descend into the medical equivalent of Pol Pot's killing fields.

Being a burden

Johnston says that '[i]mplicit in the push to legalize assisted suicide is that, at its heart, it is not meant for those whom we care for, but for those whom we no longer care for'.[93] That is, that such people have become a burden or a nuisance and are therefore dispensable. In essence, this too is a form of the slippery slope argument, which I have already argued is rather weak. In any case, it can be turned on its head. As Shand says, '[b]ecause euthanasia is *not now* a practical option for most people, is illegal, carries with it a social stigma, and may have traumatic psychological consequences for relatives, many people feel forced to go on living when they would rather die'.[94]

However, for some the idea that people may (misguidedly or not) believe their lives to have become worthless, or a burden, is a strong – even definitive – argument against allowing them to make choices about death. One such commentator is Keown, a prolific and committed opponent of legalisation, who presents the worst-case scenario in this way:

> The fact that, through depression or pain or loneliness, some patients may lose sight of their worth is no argument for endorsing their misguided judgement that their life is no longer worth living. Were the law to allow patients to be intentionally killed by their doctors the law would be accepting that there are two categories of patients: those whose lives are worth living and those who are better off dead. What signal, moreover, would that send out to the sick, the elderly, the disabled and the dying?[95]

---

92   Amarasekara, K and Bagaric, M, *Euthanasia, Morality and the Law*, 2002, New York, Peter Lang Publishing Inc., at p 64.
93   Johnston, op. cit. at p 132.
94   Shand, (1997), at p 43.
95   Keown, J, 'Defending the Council of Europe's opposition to euthanasia', in McLean, S A M (ed), *First Do No Harm: Law, Ethics and Healthcare*, 2006, Aldershot: Ashgate, 479–494, at p 488.

Additionally, Gunderson says that '[f]or the chronically or terminally ill, knowing that one is a permanent and difficult burden can be excruciating'.[96] There is no doubting the sincerity of these commentators, but their comments beg one fundamental question, which is picked up by Shand, who argues that

> ... there may be nothing wrong with the decision to end one's life based on the opinion that one will be a burden – one may indeed be a burden, and there may be only so much the people who care for us can do to dissuade us of this view – it may be perfectly reasonable not to want to be a burden.[97]

Indeed, being a burden – rather than simply perceiving oneself to be one – is arguably a morally acceptable and perfectly reasonable factor to take into account when planning for the future. For Davies, in fact, '[t]his is the altruistic impulse, admired throughout history when expressed as self-sacrifice. ... Why should any suggestion by the failing person that they are becoming a burden be, as it commonly is, so vehemently denied'?[98] Indeed, he points to the link between autonomy and altruism, describing them as rights which 'are undisputed during competent adult life'.[99] There is, he claims, nothing praiseworthy 'about enduring unrelievable suffering until a "natural" death occurs' nor in seeking to force this 'upon someone who sees no point in such a course of action'.[100]

Like it or not, many people approaching the end of their lives believe themselves to be a burden on others – they may indeed be one. While this is sometimes proposed as a strong argument against legalisation, we need to unpick the meaning of being a burden rather than simply conceding this argument. Assume that I am capable of making my own (competent) decisions as to whether or not I am a burden, and of deciding whether this is tolerable or not. This might well affect my decisions about my life (and death). For example, I may wish to ensure that the legacy I have been building for years is not totally destroyed by the costs of caring for me, or perhaps more appropriately, that the family who so kindly offer to take me in do not have their lives ruined by their efforts to meet my needs. A carer's life is often a bleak one, and I may reasonably wish to avoid that for my loved ones. The fact that one is a personal or even financial burden on family or friends should not necessarily be discounted as irrelevant to one's life choices. Although death is final, and is

---

96 Gunderson, M, 'Being a burden: reflections on refusing medical care', (2004) *Hastings Center Report* 34, No 5, 37–43, at p 37.

97 Shand, (1997), at p 44.

98 Davies, J, 'Altruism towards the end of life', *Journal of Medical Ethics* 1993: 19: 111–3, at p 112.

99 Ibid., at p 113.

100 Ibid.

not equivalent to other, remediable lifestyle decisions that we might make in the face of perceiving ourselves as a burden, and although there may be ways around this particular perception, in the long run where no alleviation can be found, it is not illegitimate to prefer death to life, nor is this a non-autonomous decision. It is for me to weigh benefits and burdens in the balance and decide which are important; not for others to do so on my behalf.

The doctor/patient relationship

It is generally assumed that the doctor/patient relationship would be implicated were assisted dying to be made legal. This is true in most, but as we will see not all, jurisdictions where legalisation has taken place. Although, therefore, arguments for the legalisation of assisted dying do not inevitably rest on the involvement of doctors, it is commonly assumed that doctors will necessarily be involved and this provides the basis of one further common argument against assisted dying. 'Doctors', says Johnston, 'should be kept from killing because of all professions, they are the most able and the most likely'.[101] Certainly, they are best placed to carry out assisted dying, if the hoped for outcome is death rather than failure with the possibility of ensuing disability, and of course they have direct access to the means to provide an assisted death successfully. It seems, however, a rather strange argument that doctors should not be permitted to participate because they are likely to succeed! However, the possible effect on the relationship between them and their patients must be considered.

It is often said that the doctor/patient relationship is one of the most important in our lives – perhaps particularly at the end of our lives. Anything that threatens that relationship, therefore, is to be avoided. Arguably, this claim is overstated on two counts. First, although we depend on doctors for medical advice and the provision of therapy, the importance given to that relationship can overstate the authority of the doctor and the dependence of the patient. Second, it assumes that allowing willing doctors to assist in facilitating a competent request for assisted dying necessarily has negative rather than beneficial consequences for the relationship.

It is true that in the clinical setting, patients are essentially dependent, at least in a technical sense, on their doctors. What has been called the 'sick role' may well infantilise patients and this is certainly a matter of concern. However, it is not inevitably the case that the nature of the relationship prohibits freedom of choice; if so, there would be no purpose served by the ethical and legal requirement that patients are provided with information about the risks, benefits and alternatives to treatment recommendations before making their

101 Johnston, op. cit. at p 111.

decisions. If people are incapable of making independent decisions because they are patients then there would surely be no purpose served by the disclosure requirement, nor value in the requirement to obtain consent.[102]

Second, the assertion that the doctor/patient relationship is threatened by doctors acceding to the convinced, competent and knowledgeable decisions of their patients seems somewhat strange. Is it not just as likely that the relationship suffers when patients' choices are ignored? However, in order to explain their position doctors who oppose legalisation draw heavily on their own professional ethic, which stands in direct contrast to the wishes of those patients seeking assistance in dying. The Hippocratic prohibition on assisting patients to die, and the exhortation to 'do no harm', on this argument take priority over the desires of the patient. Thus,

> [i]t is argued that the norms of medicine prohibit a physician from ever acting with the intent to kill a patient or to aid him in killing himself. For this reason it is essential . . . to maintain a sharp distinction between allowing patients to die . . . and acts of assisted suicide.[103]

Two responses can be made here. First, it is not clear why the ethic derived from an ancient Oath, which is honoured more in the breach than in the observance, should be uncritically accepted as ethically definitive. Second, as we will see later, the distinction between killing and letting die is by no means clear-cut or ethically sound.

In yet another version of the slippery slope argument, the House of Lords Select Committee on the Assisted Dying for the Terminally Ill Bill was, however, concerned that involving doctors in assisted dying would have negative effects.

> The essence of the concern here is that, if assisted suicide and voluntary euthanasia should be legalised and if implementation of the law were to be carried out within the health care system, these procedures will of necessity become a therapeutic option; that over time there will be drift from regarding the death of a patient as an unavoidable necessity to regarding it as a morally acceptable form of therapy; and that pressure will grow as a result for euthanasia to be applied more widely – for example, to incompetent people or to minors – as a morally acceptable

---

102 The literature on the importance of consent based on information sharing is huge. See, e.g., McLean, S A M, *A Patient's Right to Know*, Aldershot: Dartmouth, 1989; Mason, J K and Laurie, L T, *Mason and McCall Smith's Law and Medical Ethics*, 7th edn, 2006, Oxford University Press.

103 Dworkin, G, 'The nature of medicine' in *Euthanasia and Physician-Assisted Suicide: For and Against*, op. cit. at p 6.

form of medical therapy which is considered to be in the patient's best interests.[104]

The second strand to this argument has already been dealt with, but it is worth considering the first in more depth. If it is the case that assisted dying would become a therapeutic option if legalised, it is difficult to see why this is problematic; is this not precisely what proponents are arguing for? Why this should be a matter of concern is less than obvious. In addition, '. . . physicians are providers of comfort as fundamentally as they are healers of illness. When these two roles conflict, it is not clear why the healing role should take priority over the comforting role'.[105] If, therefore, the option of assistance in dying provides comfort to the patient, its availability as a treatment option is surely a benefit. As Shand says, such an option may enhance rather than reduce the trust between doctor and patient because '[t]he trust between patient and doctor is that the doctor will *do his best* for the patient; it begs the question to assume that this will consist in not carrying out acts of euthanasia'.[106]

Moreover, there may be additional benefits to legalisation, given what patients may want from assisted dying:

> . . . even accepting the premise that healing is the fundamental physician role, permitting assisted suicide can facilitate that role. Although assisted suicide will shorten some patients' lives, it will prolong other patients' lives. What patients want from the right to assisted suicide is not so much the ability to die as the knowledge that they will have control over the timing of their death. With such control, they may be more willing to undergo aggressive medical treatments that are painful and risky. If the treatments did not succeed but only worsened the patients' conditions, the patient would be assured that they could end their suffering with assisted suicide. Without such assurance, they might well forgo the treatments entirely.[107]

To return to consideration of the doctor rather than the patient, it is arguable that prohibiting willing doctors from participating in fact is a breach, rather than a protection, of their ethical commitments to care. Quill, *et al*, for example say:

> Given current professional and legal prohibitions, physicians find themselves in a difficult position when they receive requests for assisted

104 *Report of the House of Lords Select Committee on the Assisted Dying for the Terminally Ill Bill* op. cit. at p 40, para 102.
105 Orentlicher, op. cit. at p 41.
106 Shand, (1997), at p 46.
107 Orentlicher, op. cit. at p 40.

suicide from suffering patients who have exhausted the usefulness of measures for comfort care. To adhere to the letter of the law, they must turn down their patients' request even if they find them reasonable and personally acceptable. It they acceded to their patients' requests, they must risk violating legal and professional standards, and therefore they act in isolation and in secret collaboration with their patients. . . . There is more risk for vulnerable patients and for the integrity of the profession in such hidden practices, however well intended, than there would be in a more open process restricted to competent patients who met carefully defined criteria.[108]

This is a point that needs to be taken seriously, as evidence suggests that – irrespective of the state of the law – some doctors are currently engaged in assisting their patients to die, suggesting that for some at least this is seen as the 'right' or 'ethical' professional thing to do. The question of the opacity of decision-making and its effects will be returned to in the conclusion to this book, but there is reason to believe that the deception involved harms not only the ethics of the doctors involved but also potentially their relationship with their suffering patients.

Despite this, the call has gone out to doctors to resist firmly any move towards legalisation. 'Now', say Gaylin, Kass, Pellegrino and Siegler, 'is not the time for promoting neutral discussion. Rather it is the time for the medical profession to rally in defence of its fundamental moral principles, to repudiate any and all acts of direct and intentional killing by physicians and their agents'.[109] Kass agrees with this, saying that 'should doctors become technical dispensers of death, they will not only be abandoning their posts, their patients, and their duty to care; they will set the worst sort of example for the community at large . . .'.[110] In a rallying cry worthy of the most eloquent evangelical, he continues that

> should physicians hold fast, should doctors learn that finitude is no disgrace and that human wholeness can be cared for to the very end, medicine may serve not only to the good of its patients, but also, by example, the failing moral health of modern times.[111]

108 Quill, T E, Cassel, C K and Meier, D E, 'Proposed clinical criteria for physician-assisted suicide', *New England Journal of Medicine*, 327: 1380–1384 (1992) at p 1383.
109 Gaylin, W, Kass, L R, Pellegrino, E D and Siegler, M, 'Doctors must not kill', *JAMA*, 8 April 1988, Vol 259, No 14, 2139–2140.
110 Kass, L R, '"I will give no deadly drug": why doctors must not kill', in Charlesworth, M, (ed) *Bioethics in a Liberal Society*, 1993, Cambridge University Press, 231–246, at p 246.
111 Ibid.

Pretty words indeed, but the problem is that, in the finest paternalistic tradition, they completely ignore the wishes and interests of (some) patients, as well as arguably rather overstating the importance of doctors in setting community values.

Finnis adds to this, speculating on the future of the medical ethic itself. He says that an inevitable outcome of legalisation of assisted dying would be that the ethics of healthcare professionals in the future would change rapidly – presumably towards an ethical position which is worse than that held to today. Change in the law would, on his argument, mean that tomorrow's practitioners would be, presumably, less 'ethical' than their contemporaries.[112]

Any such change is, in Finnis's view, to be resisted, presumably because he believes the current ethic to be the right one (assuming of course that we can identify just what it is). Of course, as an opponent of legalisation, he would. However, his view is not the complete answer, even if he might hope that it is. Not only do other commentators disagree with him, but so do some healthcare professionals; the ethic to which he claims they subscribe does not, in fact, represent their actual position. The assumption of the high moral ground simply disguises the paternalism inherent in opposition to legalisation; that someone else knows better than the patient what is the right path for them. This can be disguised as slippery slopes or the ethic of care but, however presented, it is essentially disingenuous. Additionally, the unfounded claim that the change would be 'very rapid' seems to be no more than an attempt to scare; how can Finnis know this? And if the outcome is the satisfaction of patients' strongly held wishes, and a vindication of their rights, why would the possible speed of the change be anything other than welcome?

Finnis's position on assisted dying is, however, apparently shared by the medical establishment – although as we will see later, not unanimously. The British Medical Association's objections to legalisation seem to be based both on the perceived inherent wrongness of killing and on the nature of the doctor/patient relationship. To that extent, it can be argued that it is insufficiently subtle. Not only do we not hold all killing to be wrong, it is also arguable that the doctor/patient relationship might be improved by doctors being enabled lawfully to accede to the interest of some of their patients in choosing an assisted death. In any case, the issue is surely about what Hall *et al* refer to as 'trust worthiness', rather than trust. For them, 'whether one deserves trust – is an ethical or value-laden construct. Trust itself, however, is a psychological state that is subject to objective measurement'.[113] It cannot be assumed that patients' trust in their doctors will inevitably suffer if they are allowed to assist in their death. Respecting patient's rights might enhance rather than reduce this trust.

112 Finnis (1998), at p 1133.
113 Hall, M, Trachtenberg, F, Dugan, E, 'The impact on patient trust of legalising physician aid in dying', *Journal of Medical Ethics* 2005: 31: 693–697, at p 693.

Accepting that patients' rights rather than doctors' (perceived) reluctance should drive the agenda does raise one final question, which was briefly touched on above; namely, that there is no theoretical reason why doctors – or indeed others – should be the judge of who can have access and who cannot. This, Keown believes, gives the lie to the dominance of patients' rights. He says '[n]o responsible doctor would kill a patient merely because the patient requested it, however autonomously, any more than a responsible doctor would amputate a healthy leg just because the patient requested it'.[114] Of course, that depends on one's definition of 'responsible'. His anti-legalisation colleague, Finnis, takes this thought even further, arguing that '. . . unless doctors are to be permitted to kill anyone and everyone who makes a "stable and competent" request for death, they are going to have to proceed on a classification of lives as "worth living" or "not worth living"'.[115] Arguably, of course, to be consistent it will be necessary that proponents of legalisation accept the proposition that assisted dying should be available to anyone who competently requests it and this will be considered later. However, even if that is so Finnis is mistaken to conclude that this involves *doctors* in deciding on whether or not a life is worthwhile: the entire point is that it is the *patients* who would decide this.

Although I have chosen, for reasons given earlier, to take the doctor/ patient relationship as the paradigm for this discussion, as I also indicated, this is not necessary. While arguments cannot be viewed entirely in a vacuum, the appropriate construct is not the narrow one of the patient and physician but rather the wider one of which rights society is willing to recognise and protect. While there may need to be a second order consideration of the question of precisely who is involved in assisted dying, I suggest that this is by no means a central issue, and indeed it can be used to obfuscate the values at the root of the question. We could, for example, take doctors entirely out of the equation, however impractical that might seem, and still have a body of argumentation pointing towards legalisation. Nonetheless, the House of Lords Select Committee on Medical Ethics was deeply swayed by the opinions of healthcare professionals in reaching its conclusions. As its report says:

> Some people may consider that our conclusions overall give too much weight to the role of accepted medical practice, and that we advocate leaving too much responsibility in the hands of doctors and other members of the health-care team. They may argue that doctors and their colleagues are no better qualified than any other group of people to take ethical decisions about life and death which ultimately have a bearing not only on individual patients but on society as a whole. But no other group of people is better qualified to do so. . . . By virtue of

114 Keown, J, 'Mr Marty's muddle: a superficial and selective case for euthanasia in Europe', *Journal of Medical Ethics*, 2006: 32: 29–33, at p 32.
115 Finnis (1998), at p 1144.

their vocation, training and professional integrity they may be expected to act with rectitude and compassion.[116]

They may indeed be expected to do this, but it is difficult to see what relevance this has to the fundamental question of whether or not to respect the competent decisions of their patients to seek assistance in dying. In any case, the expertise of doctors – while not doubted – is not unlimited. As Mr Justice Munby has said,

> ... doctors can properly claim expertise on medical matters; but they can claim no special expertise on the many non-medical matters which, as we have seen, go to form the basis of any decision as to what is in a patient's best interests.[117]

Devaluing disability

A more serious concern relates to the possibility that, given that many people who seek assisted dying might qualify as disabled, there would be a disproportionate impact on this group, many of whom may already feel themselves to be vulnerable. Since the Disability Discrimination Act 2005 has expanded the categories of disability to include – some – people who have cancer, HIV infection or multiple sclerosis,[118] the potential membership of this group has been considerably expanded. While current arguments in the disability community have focused on whether disability is the consequence of a medical condition or a social environment, expansion of the definition of disability might be thought to render that debate moot. Thus, the contemporary dominance of the so-called social model of disability may be challenged by the inclusion of others who have not traditionally been conceived of as disabled. Yet, there remains, in the United Kingdom at least, considerable support for the social model. Saxton, for example, says that 'if suffering does indeed attend life with disability, then the place to begin ameliorating that suffering is with the eradication of social discrimination – not with the eradication of people with disabilities'.[119] Further, as the National Council on Disability (US), has said:

116 *Report of the Select Committee on Medical Ethics*, HL Paper 21-1, 1994, at p 56, para 272.
117 *R (on the application of Burke) v General Medical Council* (2004) 79 BMLR 126, at p 162.
118 Disability Discrimination Act 2005, s 18.
119 Saxton, M, 'Why members of the disability community oppose prenatal diagnosis and selective abortion', in Parens, E and Asch, A, (eds), *Prenatal Testing and Disability Rights*, 2000, Washington, DC: Georgetown University Press, 147–164, at pp 147–148.

For many people with disabilities, it is more often the discrimination, prejudice, and barriers that they encounter, and the restrictions and lack of options that this society has imposed, rather than their disabilities or their physical pain, that cause people with disabilities' lives to be unsatisfactory and painful. . . . Society should not be ready to give up on the lives of its citizens with disabilities until it has made real and persistent efforts to give these citizens a fair and equal chance to achieve a meaningful life.[120]

It is undoubtedly the case the people with disabilities have been discriminated against socially, politically and even clinically over many years and to that extent the social model has real relevance. We live in a society which accommodates disability rather poorly and where people who are impaired or disabled perceive themselves to be less valued than their non-disabled counterparts. This position is not simply based, as are some of the arguments against legalisation, on unproven or unproveable anxieties and aspirations: it is based in experienced reality and rightly generates a call for equality of treatment. It is not difficult, therefore, to imagine that people who already feel themselves to have been sidelined in a society which does not afford them equal value or respect might also fear that they would be the victims of any liberalisation of the law in this area.

Unsurprisingly, therefore, much is made by opponents of legalisation of the possibility that people with disabilities will suffer even further discriminatory treatment in a more legally relaxed environment. Steinbock, for example, holds out the possibility that '. . . there are groups of patients who may be especially vulnerable: the disabled, those with mental illness, poor people, and minority group members'.[121] Gill too points to the reality of life with disability in a world which is already prejudiced against such lives, pointing to their disempowerment and vulnerability:

Throughout most of their lives, the choices persons with disabilities make to live and work as they wish are socially nullified. . . . Many persons with disabilities live a coerced existence every day. Some may be closer to the edge than anyone realizes until some event pushes them over the threshold into suicidal despair.[122]

Even if we concede that risks might arise for people with disability were assisted dying to be legalised, we must however resist the more extreme

---

120 'Assisted suicide: a disability perspective', available at http://www.ncd.gov/newsroom/ publications/1997/suicide.htm (accessed on 16/06/05), at p 2.
121 Steinbock, B, (2005), at p 237.
122 Gill, C J, 'Depression in the context of disability and the "right to die"', *Theoretical Medicine* 25: 171–198, 2004, at p 183.

versions of this argument. As we have seen, it is not uncommon in this debate to see analogies being drawn between the legalisation of assisted dying and the experiences of those who suffered under the Nazi regime's systematic annihilation of those who it deemed to be 'unfit' or 'undesirable'. Thomasma, for example, points to that black period in history, maintaining that '[s]ome of the factors shaping today's debate are very close to those that shaped the discussions in Nazi Germany that led to social programs to eliminate the vulnerable and weak'.[123]

With respect, this claim seems erroneous and needs to be debunked. The current debate on the legalisation of consensual and voluntary assisted dying rests on the assumption of the value of autonomy; not on a state generated eugenics policy. The Nazis had no interest in supporting or endorsing the autonomy of individuals – far from it. Their entire ideology was based in state control and the elimination of individuality by classifying people on the basis of their membership of groups. It may be true that laws currently in place in jurisdictions where assisted dying has been legalised are poorly drafted and this may be a cause for concern, particularly for people with disabilities, but this condemns the laws themselves; not the intention behind the policy. This will be returned to later, but it is an important concern. Fear for the safety and well being of people with disabilities is also expressed by Yuill, who claims that:

> Right-to-die campaigners condemn the lives of the disabled as bereft of dignity, apparently associating dignity solely with control over bodily functions. According to this definition, if someone loses their bodily 'autonomy', they no longer have human dignity. In my mind, dignity comes from bearing up under suffering we meet throughout our lives rather than letting it destroy us, and from facing fears rather than caving in to them.[124]

This is also a mischaracterisation. People who want to facilitate autonomous choices at the end of life do not thereby disvalue disability. Rather, they accept that for some people, disability is a relevant consideration in making their own life-defining decisions. Advocates of choice at the end of life are just as likely as anyone else to rail against the injustice often meted out to people with disability – even to canvass vociferously for a more just and equitable society. What they do not do, however, is to reject the possibility that disability may be a relevant constituent in the autonomous choice of people, even were a non-discriminatory society in existence.

123 Thomasma, D C, (1998), at p 399.
124 Yuill, K, 'Ten myths about assisted suicide: the flaws in the arguments for ending lives', available at http://www.spiked-online.com/Printable.0000000CA82B.htm (accessed on 29/06/06).

This is not simplistically to adopt the so-called medical model of disability which arguably easily leads to disvaluing disabled life. Rather it accepts that, while impairments may be disabling as much because of society's failure to accommodate them as for any other reason, nonetheless the fact of disability in itself may be relevant to how people see their future. For example, the suffering associated with cancer is disabling, but it is also clearly relevant to the way in which people manage their healthcare decisions and their end-of-life choices. As Shakespeare, himself a noted disability scholar, says:

> The disability rights movement has developed a social model under-standing of disability, in which people are disabled by society, not by their bodies. This has made it harder for the disability rights community to engage with debates about illness, impairment and end of life. It could be argued that a social model philosophy enables some to disengage from troubling questions about bodies and mortality.[125]

He also argues that it 'seems inconsistent that disabled people should not be able to take control over the manner of their death'.[126] Moreover, there is something inherently unsatisfactory about the idea that people with disabilities are uniquely threatened by relaxing the law on assisted dying. It presumes a number of things, perhaps most importantly that people with disabilities are in some sense infantilised; that they are not able to make their own decisions. Surely, however, this is an assumption which degrades those with disability. Batavia powerfully rejects this position, saying:

> Most disabled persons do not consider themselves vulnerable or oppressed and want to make the decisions that fundamentally affect their lives. We do not believe that the right to assisted suicide is premised on our society's widespread misperception that people with disabilities have a diminished quality of life. It is based on respect for the autonomy of terminally ill persons in determining the quality of their lives during their final days.[127]

Any robust defence of the equality of people with disabilities, and respect for their autonomy, inevitably leads to the conclusion that to deny them choice because they are disabled is every bit as discriminatory as other societal

---

125 Shakespeare, T, 'Submission to the House of Lords Select Committee on the Assisted Dying for the Terminally Ill Bill', at para 2.7, (personal communication); available at Vol II of the Report, 254 (with Ms Alison Davies).

126 Shakespeare, T, *Disability Rights and Wrongs*, 2006, Abingdon: Routledge, at p 132.

127 Batavia, A I, 'Disability and Physician-Assisted Suicide', *New England Journal of Medicine*, Vol 336: 1671–73, June 5, 1997 (available at http://www.content.nejm.org (accessed on 19/01/06) (transcript), at p 3.

attitudes may be. It also challenges the idea that allowing people who are not classified as disabled the right to choose will inevitably result in irresistible pressure being imposed on people with disabilities such that they are unable to make their own decisions. As has been said:

> Perhaps the most disturbing aspect of this debate is the revelation that many people with disabilities believe that their physician would be too quick to help them die as a 'solution' to their health problems. *But many other people with disabilities, including me, do not have this belief.*[128] (emphasis added)

To some – hopefully significant – extent, the anxiety expressed within the disability rights community can also be countered by reminding ourselves that the sole intention of proponents of legalisation is to render it permissible that people who have made a competent, voluntary decision to end their lives in a particular way are empowered to do so. In our imperfect world, of course, it may be that people with disabilities are more likely to feel themselves to be a burden on others, and may therefore be seduced into unnecessarily terminating their lives. To be sure, we must do something about this if that is the case and we must strive to minimise – or better yet eradicate – any social, medical, political or personal agenda which results in them feeling this way. However, we must also, even if we can identify individual and collective acts of discrimination against people with disabilities, bear in mind that those with disabilities should not be denied a right if it is legally extended to others.

In other words, the danger in much of the disability activists' rhetoric is that *in itself* it may serve to diminish people with disabilities and ignore, or potentially ignore, the presumption of equality of rights which would avoid discriminatory practices. In part it does this by categorising people with disability as inherently vulnerable. In some cases, of course this may be true, but by no means every disabled person feels this way about themselves. In addition, as Hoffmaster points out, vulnerability is not a fixed notion. We may, as he suggests, 'bandy [it] about confidently but carelessly', but we do not 'know what it means and that it means the same thing for everybody'.[129] Even the Disability Rights Commission, while not currently supporting assisted dying, nonetheless recognises that if this is a right which is accorded to non-disabled people it should also be accorded equally to those with disabilities. We may agree with the Disability Rights Commission that '[i]f a disabled person expresses the wish to die the first task must be to try to enable them

---

128 Ibid. p 4.
129 Hoffmaster, B, 'What does vulnerability mean?', *Hastings Center Report*, March–April 2006, 38–45, at p 38.

to make the choice to live . . .',[130] but this is surely no less true of those not described as disabled.

In any case, the aim of the disability rights lobby is not to place people with disability in a worse position than the one they are currently in by further alienating them from the 'mainstream'. As Silvers says:

> Characterising people with disabilities as incompetent, easily coerced, and inclined to end their lives places them in the roles to which they have been confined by disability discrimination. Doing so emphasises their supposed fragility, which becomes a reason to deny that they are capable, and therefore deserving, of full social participation.[131]

Shakespeare further notes that the assumption that everyone with disability would oppose legalisation of assisted dying is not borne out in fact, with 63 per cent of those polled in 2003 supporting legalisation of assisted dying.[132] Of course, this should not be surprising. The attempt by opponents to categorise people with disabilities as one homogeneous, vulnerable group deserves to – and does – fail. Yet Gill continues to cleave to the notion that the threat is real, arguing:

> Until the lives of people with disabilities and chronic illnesses are valued equally to the lives of non-disabled people, and until health professionals learn more about disability to temper their biases, legalised assisted dying will continue to endanger this segment of the population. Dim assessments of life with disability influence judgements about offering life-sustaining interventions. Currently, there is no way to insure that observers who assess the rationality of a disabled individual's desire to die are sufficiently knowledgeable about disability and sufficiently unimpaired by conditioned prejudice regarding disability, to act in support of that individual's genuine self-determination rather than in response to their own unconscious bias against life with a disability.[133]

Inequality of rights, of status and of opportunity undoubtedly attends some people with disabilities. Whether or not this inevitably means that their end-of-life choices are any different from those of others is, however, more

---

130 Disability Rights Commission, 'Health and independent living', available at http://www. drc-gb.org/publicationsandreports/campaigndetails.asp?section=he&id=307 (accessed on 16/06/05), at p 1.

131 Silvers, A, 'Protecting the innocents from physician-assisted suicide: disability discrimination and the duty to protect otherwise vulnerable groups', in Battin, M, *et al* (eds), *Physician Assisted Suicide: Expanding the Debate*, 1998, New York: Routledge, at p 132.

132 Referred to in Shakespeare, T, op. cit. at p 127.

133 Gill, (2004), at p 189.

speculative. In a somewhat odd position, the Disability Rights Commission on the one hand claims to value individual autonomy while at the same time seems to suggest that it is not something that people with disabilities actually have because of the pressures on them.

One further account of the discrimination likely to be experienced by people with disabilities comes from Amarasekara and Bagaric, who protest that those whose disability renders them incompetent will suffer further by being excluded from any legalisation of assisted dying. Noting that the incompetent would not be allowed to have assistance in dying, they say that 'arguably it is unreasonable that they should be expected to suffer the pain and distress from which competent patients have been freed by legally choosing to be euthanised'.[134] They further complain that '[t]he preconditions of sanity and rationality give rise to indirect discrimination because they disproportionately affect members of a disadvantaged group by excluding many who are terminally ill from access to voluntary euthanasia'.[135] This too is a somewhat strange argument. Are they arguing that people who are not competent to choose should nonetheless be allowed to do so? Are they saying that an argument based on voluntariness or autonomy is discriminatory against those who cannot make a choice?

It is entirely consistent with existing law – and ethics – that those who lack competence are protected from the outcome of their – incompetent – choice; indeed that they are not permitted lawfully to make some decisions for themselves. Nonetheless, Keown asks '. . . if death would benefit the patient why should it be denied the patient merely because of incompetence'?[136] Again, this misunderstands the autonomy-based argument for legalisation, which is not derived from the abstract notion that death is necessarily a benefit to be meted out to people; rather it is the right to choose death which is valued. One might as well say that we should ignore the question of competence altogether. This would indeed be a threat to people with disability and would turn the entire debate on its head. We would then be making judgements about the quality of other people's lives rather than facilitating their own evaluation of that quality.

However, it must be accepted that a better understanding of life with disability would be valuable. Gill suggests that '[l]earned rejection of the disabled self . . . may provide an *internal* pressure impelling some individuals toward self-annihilation while social oppression provides a relentless *external* pressure to give up on life'.[137] If so, then we must argue for care to be taken in evaluating what might otherwise seem to be a genuine choice. However, as Mayo and Gunderson conclude:

134 Amarasekara and Bagaric, (2004), at p 405.
135 Ibid., at p 407.
136 Keown, (2006), at p 32.
137 Gill, (2004), at p 181.

> [t]he arguments advanced by disability critics of PAD [physician assisted death] make a compelling case for strengthening . . . safeguards, particularly for patients with disabilities. They have failed to show any *additional* risks to patients who may already opt to cut short a fate they view as worse than death.[138]

Nonetheless, the perception remains for commentators such as Coleman and Gill that 'disabled people are beginning to feel that we are riding on the Titanic'.[139] Further, they argue that '[a]ssisted suicide is not a free choice as long as people with disabilities are denied adequate healthcare, affordable personal assistance in our own homes, assistive technology, equal education, nondiscriminatory employment, and free access to our communities' structure and transportation systems'.[140] Finally, they suggest that the perception that assisted dying offers a real choice is misguided, since

> the majority who are offered this option are people that society is all too ready to abandon as too costly and unproductive – people who can only depend on the protection of the law. The depth and breadth of this abandonment is only understood by those who live it every day.[141]

A few points can be made in response to these arguments. First, proponents of legalisation will readily concede that any apparent choice should in fact be real. This means not only that it is informed, but also that genuine alternatives are available. However, this does not differentiate those with disabilities from others; both are in precisely the same boat. Moreover, the argument for legalisation does not rest on the 'offer' of assisted dying; it rests on the *request* for it.

In support of opposition to legalisation, the National Council on Disability (US) claims that:

> Current evidence indicates clearly that the interests of the few people who would benefit from legalizing physician-assisted suicide are heavily outweighed by the probability that any law, procedures, and standards that can be imposed to regulate physician-assisted suicide will be misapplied to unnecessarily end the lives of people with disabilities and entail

---

138 Mayo, D and Gunderson, M, 'Vitalism revitalized: vulnerable populations, prejudice, and physician-assisted death', *Hastings Center Report,* July–August 2002, 14–21, at p 18.

139 Coleman, D and Gill, C, 'Testimony to congress on behalf of Not Dead Yet', available at http://www.notdeadyet.org/docs/house1.html (accessed on 18/06/03). Transcript, p 1.

140 Ibid., at p 2.

141 Ibid., at p 5.

an intolerable degree of intervention by legal and medical officials in such decisions.[142]

Burgdorf, while accepting that '[t]he benefits of permitting physician-assisted suicide are substantial and should not be discounted ...',[143] nonetheless also believes that '[t]he dangers ... are immense ...'.[144] These powerful voices against legalisation, however, do not end the debate. For example, when Oregon legalised physician-assisted suicide, the doomsayers were equally loud and equally anxious. The fear was that the disadvantaged would be the group most likely to have their lives ended in this way, yet, as Dahl and Levy point out, 'the overwhelming majority of patients seeking physician-assisted suicide are financially well off, highly educated, and have health insurance'.[145] In other words, the argument that those who are more vulnerable would be prime targets for legalised assisted dying has proved – in Oregon at least – to be ill-founded, if not downright misleading.

Moreover, there is arguably something a little old-fashioned about some of the disability rights activists' concerns. Previously, much of their focus was on a specific group, for example those with certain kinds of disability as it was previously defined. One concern about legalising assisted dying, therefore, was that '[i]f we attempt to change the natural ecosystem by eliminating disability, we will no doubt upset the balance of nature just as we are doing through the degradation of the environment and the pollution of our natural habitats'.[146] Clearly, this argument is less obviously applicable to people with cancer (some of whom are now legally defined as disabled) than it is, say, to those who suffer from a developmental difficulty. The ecosystem is not obviously challenged by allowing people with cancer to choose whether or not life with suffering is something that they want to continue to experience.

This is not to say that people with disabilities – however defined – should not have a clear voice in this debate, even although it is unlikely that they will harmonise with each other. This supports the concern expressed earlier that the attitude of society to those with disabilities is based in part on the tendency not to hear the voices of people with disability or to make negative assumptions about the quality of their lives, rather than addressing the positives. It does not,

---

142 'Assisted suicide: a disability perspective', available at http://www.ncd.gov/newsroom/publications/1997/suicide.htm (accessed on 16/06/05), at p 3.

143 Burgdorf, R L, 'Assisted suicide: a disability perspective', available at http://www.ncd.gov/newsroom/publications/1997/suicide.htm (accessed on 16/06/05) (National Council on Disability), Transcript, at p 2.

144 Ibid.

145 Dahl, E and Levy, N, 'The case for physician-assisted suicide: how can it possibly be proven?', (2006) 32 *Journal of Medical Ethics*, 335–338, at p 335.

146 McPherson, G W and Sobsey, D, 'Rehabilitation: disability ethics versus Peter Singer', *Archives of Physical Medicine and Rehabilitation*, Vol 84, Issue 8, August 2003, 1246–1248, at p 1247.

however, generate a principled basis to oppose legalisation; rather it demands serious and mature consideration of the consequences of so doing.

Respect for persons' dignity

Moving away from this argument, a further position is proposed – primarily by those who support assisted dying; namely, that what is being argued for is a right to die with 'dignity'. While some argue that dignity is far too slippery a concept to have meaning, its use is common in the assisted dying debate (and elsewhere), and for some it is central to the argument. Cassel, for example, says:

> Dignity is an important need and not something we can diminish by categorising it as just a popular political slogan. People are asking for something concrete when they are asking for death with dignity. . . . Addressing this need for dignity might be more profoundly significantly human than all the other caring that physicians do.[147]

Steinbock, on the other hand, questions just what is meant by dignity in this context. She says that this is problematic, 'partly because it is very vague (what is it to die with dignity?) and partly because it may seem to embody objectionable and even discriminatory attitudes toward the disabled . . .'.[148]

Somerville adds that

> [w]e need to consider also the wider effects of recognizing a right to die with dignity and holding that it includes a right to euthanasia; that right could be converted into a duty to die with dignity. And that, in turn, could become a right of society to insist that the people die 'with dignity' . . . or even an obligation to die (the corollary of which is a right to kill through euthanasia).[149]

However, this elision of right to choose and duty to die can be resisted both theoretically and practically, as it is yet another version of the slippery slope argument which has already been discounted. Allmark also suggests that, having lost dignity, 'it is far from obvious that suicide or euthanasia will rescue it. Furthermore, opting for euthanasia without good reason could presumably itself constitute an affront to human dignity'.[150]

147 Cassel, C K, 'Physician-assisted suicide: progress or peril?', in Thomasma, D C and Kushner, T, op. cit. at p 222.
148 Steinbock, B, (2005), at p 237.
149 Somerville, M, op. cit. at p 43.
150 Allmark, P, 'Death with dignity', (2002) 28 *Journal of Medical Ethics*, 255–257, at p 257.

The problem, however, remains that dignity is not a clear-cut concept. For that reason, it seems to me to be an unhelpful concept in this debate. When people talk about dying with 'dignity' they are in fact talking about death being a better option than the life they have and not being forced to live in conditions which they regard as demeaning or unduly burdensome. Thus, the debate is really about respect for persons, rather than dignity. Singer proposes therefore that the real issue is that

> . . . if the goods that life holds are, in general, reasons against killing, those reasons lose all their force when it is clear that those killed will not have such goods, or that the goods they have will be outweighed by bad things that will happen to them. When we apply this reasoning to the case of someone who is capable of judging the matter, and we add Mill's view that individuals are the best judges of their own interests, we can conclude that this reason against killing does not apply to a person who, with unimpaired capacities for judgement, comes to the conclusion that his or her future is so clouded that it would be better to die than to continue to live. Indeed, the reason against killing is turned into its opposite, a reason for acceding to that person's request.[151]

Of course, as with other autonomy types of argument, we must also evaluate respect for persons against the idea that each individual stands as part of a community; not as an isolated, selfish person. Thus, Brooks, for example, suggests that the consequences of this approach – which might broadly be described as utilitarian or communitarian – are that:

> When dealing with questions of 'euthanasia' the utilitarian ethic necessarily involves considerations of harm and benefit accruing to individuals other than the patient. . . . These are all considerations of *harm* 'done' to others by permitting the patient to live. That is to say, they are factors militating in favour of the patient's *death* (emphasis in original).[152]

Harris, however, responds that:

> Even if we accept Brooks's version of utilitarianism as requiring that we promote the greatest happiness of the greatest number, it is far from clear that we would be forced to the conclusions Brooks fears. For one thing, most people would be made very unhappy by the idea that someone could or would be killed to appease the distress or ameliorate

151 Singer, P, 'Voluntary euthanasia: a utilitarian perspective', *Bioethics*, Vol 17, Nos 5–6, 2003, 526–541, at p 530.
152 Brooks, S A, 'Dignity and cost-effectiveness: a rejection of the utilitarian approach to death', *Journal of Medical Ethics*, 1984, 10, 148–151, at p 150.

the finances of their relatives; and the distress of all of us at the very idea of this, would easily counterbalance the happiness of the relatives. The greatest happiness of the greatest number would thus require that we saved the life of the unlucky geriatric.[153]

While taking seriously the notion of interconnectedness, I have already suggested that every death in and of itself affects all of us; that it is chosen does not change that. Indeed, it might be plausible that a chosen death, which follows discussion with those who care for us, minimises rather than maximises the effect on others. There is some evidence that relatives and friends of people who die following an assisted death 'had less traumatic grief symptoms, less current feelings of grief and less post-traumatic stress reactions than friends and family of patients who died of natural causes'.[154] Irrespective, any harm caused is most immediately and crucially harm to the person him or herself. Clearly, death is most intimately experienced by the person choosing it, just as the refusal to respect a choice for death most closely affects the person whose choice it is. Thus, as Harris says:

> If the harm of ending a life is principally a harm to the individual whose life it is and if this harm in turn must be understood principally as the harm of depriving that individual of something that they value and want, then voluntary euthanasia will not be wrong on this account. Such a view prioritising the individual's autonomy and her liberty to pursue it in her own way may be termed the liberal view of euthanasia.[155]

One question, however, remains outstanding. Words such as 'autonomy' and 'dignity' are not set in interpretational stone; the exercise of one person's autonomy may not sit comfortably with the autonomy of others. Equally, even assuming we know what dignity is, or can offer some definition, it is unlikely that everyone would agree on it. Safranek and Safranek, for example, argue that '[t]he crucial constitutional question at stake is whose view of dignity and autonomy should be legislated: that of the minority, for whom assisted dying comports with dignity and autonomy, or the majority, for whom it does not'?[156] Of course, the use of words such as 'minority' and 'majority' in this quotation is contentious, but leaving that aside for the moment, the point is that

---

153 Harris, J, 'Arresting but misleading phrases', *Journal of Medical Ethics*, 10, 155–157, (1984) at p 156.
154 Swarte, N B, Marije, L, *et al*, 'Effects of euthanasia on the bereaved family and friends: a cross sectional study', *British Medical Journal*, Vol 327, 26 July 2003, p 189.
155 Harris, J, 'Euthanasia and the value of life', in Keown, J, (ed), *Euthanasia Examined: Ethical, Clinical and Legal Perspectives*, 1995 (reprinted 1999), Cambridge University Press, 6–22, at p 10.
156 Safranek, J P and Safranek, S J, 'Assisted suicide: the state versus the people', *Seattle University Law Review*, Vol 21: 261–279 (1997) at p 273.

there will be different views about what amounts to a dignified, autonomously chosen death. Callahan further challenges the notion of dignity as the basis for permitting the choice for assisted dying, arguing that 'it is a strange kind of community that would require consensual homicide to realize its members' individual dignity'.[157] Rather, he argues, that the consequence would be to harm the individual 'by predicating his dignity and final self-determination on the right to be killed by another'.[158]

Yet again, however, this misunderstands the point. Proponents of legalisation do not 'require' consensual killing to protect dignity; rather they argue that for some people – although not everyone – the right to make this choice would achieve, or help to achieve, that aim. They have no intent to suggest that consensual killing should be required – indeed, it makes no sense to use words such as 'require' and 'consensual' in the same sentence.

Before concluding, one other – and in my view weak – argument sometimes used by those in favour of legalisation is that it would simply bring the law into line with what is already going on.

It's happening anyway

It is widely accepted that, like other laws, the law that precludes assisted dying is sometimes breached. Price suggests that '[p]erceiving and appreciating that physicians are already involved in assisted suicide might help facilitate constructive discussion of potential reforms by focusing attention on the central issues'.[159] Indeed, even in the Council of Europe, the difference between legal rhetoric and social reality was deemed – by some speakers at least – to be relevant, with one Council of Europe representative saying that:

> In most countries, there is a big gap between criminal law, which defines euthanasia as a criminal offence in all circumstances, and a social reality in which a painless death with dignity is regarded by the patient as the sole solution to unbearable suffering. For liberals, this social reality is much more important than conservative legislation that shows no compassion for fellow citizens who wish to have the right to decide their own fate when they are terminally ill and suffering unbearable pain and humiliation with no prospect of improvement, those who have a lasting wish to die, and see no alternative, need compassion, from not only doctors but politicians.[160]

157 Callahan, op. cit. at p 115.
158 Ibid.
159 Price, D P T, 'Assisted suicide and refusing medical treatment: linguistics, morals and legal contortions', 1996 *Medical Law Review*, 4, Autumn, 270–299, at p 299.
160 Council of Europe Assembly Debate, 27 April 2005, available at http://assembly.coe. int/documents/records/2005-2/e/0504271000e.htm (accessed on 24/06/05), Mr Dees (Netherlands), Transcript, p 4.

However, commenting on a report (the Marty report[161]) emanating from the Council of Europe, in which the difference between what happens and what is supposed to happen, was taken to be significant, Keown asks, in my view entirely sensibly, '. . . why does the Report seem to assume that the problem with the alleged gap between law and practice lies with the former rather than the latter, that the law is bad and the practice good'?[162] Laws are broken and ignored regularly; as I have argued earlier, this is no reason in itself to repeal them. However, where there *is* some value in observing the difference between what is supposed to happen and what actually does happen is in the attempt to identify whether changing the law would result in a *worse* situation emerging. Dahl and Levy, for example, suggest that '. . . assessing PAS is a comparative matter: we need to know what potential there is for abuses under a particular legislative regime, as compared, not only to other legislative regimes that permit PAS, but also to others that ban it'.[163]

This can be a helpful way of using information about current experiences; much more useful than the proposition that just because something already occurs it should be tolerated or legalised. This is especially the case if one believes that transparency and accountability in decision-making offer a better chance of protecting the vulnerable, and validating the rights of people to make their own life choices than does a hidden and unaccountable practice. On this basis evidence about what already happens is not irrelevant, and some evidence is available:

> A recent study comparing end of life decision making in six European countries – Belgium, Italy, Sweden, Denmark, Switzerland, and the Netherlands – indicates that permitting PAS or voluntary euthanasia . . . may actually decrease the number of cases in which doctors withhold or withdraw life sustaining medical treatment without the patient's explicit request.[164]

The possibility that permitting chosen deaths will transfer authority from doctors to patients is surely to be welcomed. As we will see later, there are many reasons to be concerned that decisions which end in death are sometimes not made by patients themselves – rather they result from value judgements made by others. One major reason for prioritising choice is that it may reduce the incidence of such cases; a positive result in probably everyone's terms.

---

161 Available at http://assembly.coe.int/Documents/WorkingDocs/Doc03/EDOC9898.htm (accessed on 29/08/06).
162 Keown, (2006), at p 30.
163 Dahl, E and Levy, N, 'The case for physician assisted suicide: how can it possibly be proven?', *Journal of Medical Ethics* 2006: 32: 335–338, at p 337.
164 Ibid.

Thus, the question then becomes focused differently. As Tucker suggests, the important question to be answered is not whether legalisation should take place but rather 'whether the practice should proceed underground and unregulated, or openly and regulated to protect patients, regularize access, and accommodate legitimate state interests'.[165]

Finally, and this has been touched on briefly already, Steinbock reminds us that just because there are some situations in which we might approve assisted dying, this does not fully address the regulatory question. Just as the Disability Rights Commission doubts whether existing law actually protects people from inappropriate or coerced decisions, Steinbock also suggests that the really important question 'is rather whether it is possible to draft a statute that will cover all and only the justifiable cases'.[166] This point will be returned to in more depth later.

Conclusion

Where, then, does this leave us? I said at the beginning of this section that both proponents and opponents have powerful arrows in their quiver and that resolution of their differences would be likely to be very difficult, if not impossible. However, inaction is arguably not an option. Sticking with the status quo awards victory to opponents; accepting the arguments of proponents of legalisation would surely offend those who sincerely believe that legalisation would be a moral and social disaster. Meantime, some people – sometimes illegally – have their choices respected, while others are denied that opportunity. Permission to choose death may arguably also put some others at risk, as has already been canvassed. So, we must effectively choose which values are more important than others. One way of doing this is a relatively crude form of number crunching. Singer, for example, admits that if we legalise assisted dying, then some people may die unnecessarily, but counters that 'this has to be balanced against the presumably much larger number of people who, had voluntary euthanasia not been permitted, would have remained alive, in pain or distress and wishing that they had been able to die earlier'.[167]

However, while the distress element of this is important, arguably the numbers are not. I have already suggested that this would not be a satisfactory basis on which to judge the debate. First, for some people *any* unnecessary death is unacceptable, but perhaps more tellingly, his argument that more people would suffer is based purely on speculation. We do not know, and

---

165 Tucker, (1998), at p 924.
166 Steinbock, B, (2005), at p 237.
167 Singer, P, 'Voluntary euthanasia: a utilitarian perspective', *Bioethics*, Vol 17, Nos 5–6, 2003, 526–541, at p 532.

frankly have no way of calculating, this. We do know that the fear of being maintained against our wishes is real, and as Woodman says:

> This particular fear seems to have grown in direct proportion to our physicians' abilities to perform these life-prolonging feats. . . . Many who once considered death too unpalatable to contemplate are beginning to realize that living can be worse than dying. As a result, more and more suffering people are asking their physicians to help them die, not keep them alive.[168]

On the other hand, others would argue that permitting assisted dying is an affront to the compassion which we should expect of society; that we should focus rather on 'improving care and suicide prevention to help the suicidal and disabled overcome the desire to end their lives'.[169] Neither of these, however, is mutually exclusive. Not even the most ardent supporters of legalising assisted dying are cavalier about the value of life. Most of us prefer life to death and are afraid of dying and death. Improving facilities in order to offer a real choice to those who are suffering is surely non-controversial. However, even in Utopia, there may be people who would still wish to make a self-determining choice for death. Even if their numbers are few, the question must be on what basis – empirical or theoretical – we should deny that wish.

As has already been suggested, the dominant ethic in contemporary law and society is respect for autonomy. Even if autonomy is seen in a more communal light than it sometimes is, it remains central to the lawfulness of any intervention, and would serve the same purpose were the intervention to be an assisted death. In the liberal tradition, people's freedoms are legitimately interfered with only when so doing prevents harm to others. The likelihood of harm being caused to third parties by legalising assisted dying is speculative; the harm to – some – individuals from not permitting it is real. Indeed, although assisted dying is characterised by opponents as a negative, it also encapsulates positive characteristics,[170] unless we believe that all life of any quality should be hung on to. Moreover, it has been argued that '. . . the concept of liberty must protect important personal decisions, such as the right to assisted suicide, from the tyranny of pluralism, i.e., the majority vote of elected representatives of the people themselves'.[171]

Before concluding it is necessary to consider one further concern; that is, that in handing over the right to practice assisted dying to doctors we merely medicalise the issue. That is that far from handing authority to individuals

168 Woodman, S, op. cit. at p 19.
169 Smith, W J, 'Why secular humanism about assisted suicide is wrong', 31–2, Spring 2003, available at http://www.secularhumanism.org, at p 32.
170 Shand, (1997), pp 43–47.
171 Safranek and Safranek, (1997), at p 265.

by legalising assisted dying in fact we radically empower doctors. Somerville suggests that we medicalise such issues 'in order to deal with those that make us feel uncomfortable or that are prohibited outside a medical situation'.[172] Finnis also suggests that legalisation 'will obviously be a huge accession of power to physicians and healthcare personnel'.[173] Keown adds that legalisation would,

> for the first time, allow certain private citizens to kill other private citizens on the basis of the arbitrary judgment, historically denied in Western law and medical ethics, that they would be better off dead. In short, the rule of law, to which the arbitrary exercise of power is repugnant, not least the power of life and death, surely tells not for but against legalisation.[174]

What each of these commentaries omits, however, is that unless doctors abuse their powers and authority there is no reason to fear the fact that they have it. They also presume that the possession of the authority to help patients will lead to an 'arbitrary exercise of power', but how can this be so if its exercise is grounded in the autonomy of the patient? If assisted dying is based on personal rather than medical choice, then it is not vulnerable to Keown's attack. Competent decisions to choose death are not arbitrary – rather they are personal and considered. The fact of medical involvement allows professionals to facilitate the realisation of autonomous choice and enables them to respect the competent wishes of their patients; it does not give them the right to take over.

Of course, the liberal tradition is counterbalanced by the concept of harm, because 'members of society cannot tolerate every act of liberty, and therefore they invoke the harm principle to eschew acts that conflict with their view of the human good'.[175] Our problem, however, is that either avenue seems to predict harm. Legalisation might cause harm to those who fear they will be vulnerable to abuse of the law; failing to do so leaves those with a genuine and competent desire for an assisted death to suffer. It is necessary, therefore, to identify a principled rather than a pragmatic way to resolve this seemingly intransigent problem. Finnis, although an opponent of legalisation, agrees:

> The hard cases, the real sufferings of real people, are not to be shuffled away in our deliberations about euthanasia. We need to ponder them, not least to ask ourselves what we should be doing about pain and

172 Somerville, M, op. cit. at p 47.

173 Finnis, (1998), at p 1139.

174 Keown, J, 'Defending the Council of Europe's opposition to euthanasia', in McLean, S A M, op. cit. at p 482.

175 Safranek and Safranek (1997), at p 267.

depression and other relievable sources of misery. But we should also look for the line, any line seriously proposed, and ask the line-drawers what sense they can make of distinguishing between the cases on each side of it – in matters so important as autonomy, oppression, and existence itself.[176]

In the long run, we are left to draw that line. This, I have suggested, can most appropriately be done in accordance with the principles of libertarianism, justified in the service of respect for persons, their autonomy and their reasoned decisions in the face of suffering. None of the arguments against legalisation is capable of outweighing the values inherent in respect for these considerations. In the absence of plausible evidence of harm, the libertarian view must triumph. It will not do to suggest that, '[t]he push for legalized euthanasia/PAS is, to a great extent, the result of a failure of medical training and practice . . .'.[177] It is far more than that; it is the assertion of the right to live life – and experience death – as we choose and in a way that is compatible with our own values. Smith and Pollack conclude that:

> Competent, terminally ill persons suffering in the final months of life deserve to have a right to aid-in-dying. This right should be viewed as a last resort, but is a necessary component of palliative care for those suffering from terminal illness. Aid-in-dying makes sense because it is a compassionate response to the realities of modern dying and because it respects individual autonomy. This right not only provides a means of ending extreme physical suffering near the end of life. Aid-in-dying also provides psychological reassurance throughout a terminal illness because it relieves the common fear of a painful, undignified death.[178]

However deeply felt, many of the objections to legalised assisted dying start from a position which reflects a religious or quasi-religious view of the meaning of life and the meaning of suffering, draw illogical conclusions as to the purported likelihood of the slide between voluntary and involuntary decisions, and reinforce the paternalism which historically characterised the relationship between doctor and patient. Of course, not all of them begin from a position informed by faith. Magnusson, for example, notes that 'many opponents of legalised euthanasia are simply more "communitarian" in outlook, believing that individual freedoms and interests should be tempered

176 Safranek and Safranek (1997), at p 1142.
177 Falkenheimer, S A, 'Euthanasia: who needs it?', The Center for Bioethics and Human Dignity available at http://www.cbhd.org/resources/endoflife/falkenheimer_2005-01-31_print.htm (accessed on 08/11/05).
178 Smith and Pollack (1998), at p 547.

by communal values, social goals, and traditional constraints'.[179] However, even for those who adopt this 'communitarian' approach, it is equally logical to support legalising assisted dying, since – in the absence of harm to society – their communitarian beliefs would support maximizing liberty or 'happiness'. In the long run, the arguments against legalisation may not *in fact* rest in principle. As Hull says, it may be that the real problem in this area is that legalisation 'puts power where opponents don't want it: in the hands of patients and their loved ones'.[180]

179 Magnusson, op. cit. at p 37.
180 Hull, R T, 'The case for physician-assisted suicide', available at http://www.secularhumanism. org (Spring 2003), 35–36, at p 35.

Chapter 3

Choosing death

We have seen in the last chapter that a distinction is often drawn, generally by those who oppose legalisation of assisted dying, between some deaths in which there is third party involvement but are deemed to be appropriate or acceptable and deaths brought about with active third party assistance at the request of the patient, which are deemed to be inappropriate. I have already suggested that these distinctions are untenable and in this chapter I will explain precisely why this is the case. To adopt the position that opponents of assisted dying want to take, there must necessarily be some meaningful distinction that can be drawn between the various types of life-ending behaviour. This is usually done by postulating that there is a distinction between actively killing someone and letting someone die. The former it is said is, and should remain, an illegal action; the latter is essentially part of medical care and treatment. In the latter case, it is argued, the death does not come about because of the actions of the healthcare professional but rather occurs because of the underlying condition affecting the patient. In this chapter, I will show why this distinction carries no moral or ethical weight and will argue that it should be directly rejected by the law.

In any case, it is clear that the law not only respects, but in some cases actively supports, the choices that people make to bring about the end of their lives. Paradoxically, however, it tries to draw distinctions between certain kinds of decisions for death by applying different principles, even although the same ones could in fact be applied. Thus, autonomy is the driving principle in cases where life-sustaining medical treatment is lawfully refused, and could equally be applied to the choice for a directly assisted death. However, the law has to date declined to be consistent in its use of this principle, resorting to sophistry and scaremongering to permit the former and reject the latter. Concerns which are apparently discounted in the case of treatment refusal – such as the impact on others – become important in situations where the person wants the same outcome but needs direct assistance. Before reconsidering the acts/omissions distinction it is worth addressing each of the situations where people may seek to end their lives and evaluating the legal response.

Refusal of life-sustaining treatment

Consent is the legal and ethical device that validates medical interventions and that renders them both lawful and morally acceptable. The converse of this is also held to be true; that no medical treatment can be given – legally or ethically – in the face of a competent refusal. Treatment without consent can amount to an assault or a battery. Central to the value of consent is the concept of autonomy; consent makes treatment lawful because it is an expression of the person's will. As was said in the US case of *Schloendorff v Society of New York Hospital*: 'Every human being of adult years and sound mind has a right to determine what shall be done with his own body; and a surgeon who performs an operation without the patient's consent commits an assault.'[1]

In other words, the important principle in all medical interventions – or their rejection – is that of autonomy or self-determination. The individual is sovereign over his/her own body, to paraphrase Mill. Courts have traditionally sought to balance the sanctity of life doctrine with the importance of autonomy, difficult though that may be, but ultimately have been impelled to concede that autonomy trumps the sanctity of life. Based on this conclusion, the individual is entitled to make choices, even those which will result foreseeably and intentionally in their death. The most recent paradigmatic case to highlight this is the case of *Ms B*.[2]

In this case, a woman who had become tetraplegic and required ventilation for her continued survival repeatedly requested doctors to remove the ventilator in order that she might die. At first there was speculation as to her mental health, but this was resolved in the course of the dispute. Ms B was deemed to be competent to make decisions about her own medical treatment and it is quite clear from both the law and professional guidelines that individuals who are competent have a right to refuse even life-sustaining treatment. Her doctors, who believed that there was an alternative regime which might permit her to survive – albeit in a condition which she found unacceptable – repeatedly refused to comply with her wishes and Ms B was forced to take the case to court in order to have her wishes respected. Ms B rejected the weaning regime proposed by her doctors, saying in a written response that 'weaning is essentially a long-term treatment for those patients who want to live without ventilation. This is not what I want as it has no positive benefits for me given my level of disability'.[3] Let there be no doubt what Ms B was asking for. While conceding that she would want to live were her circumstances otherwise, she also made it quite clear that she regarded the weaning process as likely to result in 'a slow and painful death', which would also in her view rob her of dignity.[4] She clearly and unequivocally wanted to die.

---

1   105 NE 92 (NY, 1914).
2   *Re B (Adult: Refusal of Treatment)* (2002) 65 BMLR 149, at p 172.
3   Ibid., at p 160.
4   Ibid.

In an unusual move, the judge in this case – Dame Elizabeth Butler-Sloss – interviewed Ms B in the hospital setting. She was quite clearly impressed with Ms B and very sad that her decision to end her life remained consistent. On the other hand, she was also clear that Ms B could not be forced to undertake any alternative regime, nor could she be forced to continue to be ventilator dependent. Indeed, even more unusually, the judge imposed a small fine on the doctors involved in her care for their failure to respect her wishes. Ms B was, therefore, supported by law in her decision. Some time later the ventilator was removed and Ms B subsequently died.

Ms B's request for assistance in bringing about her death was, therefore, endorsed by law. However tragic this situation, and however much the judge, the doctors and other health professionals regretted Ms B's decision, it was her right to make it and hers alone. As Dame Elizabeth Butler-Sloss said:

> One must allow for those as severely disabled as Ms B, for some of whom life in that condition may be worse than death. It is a question of values and ... we have to try inadequately to put ourselves into the position of the gravely disabled person and respect the subjective character of experience.[5]

Ms B was not asking simply for the ventilator to be withdrawn – that could have been done had she accepted the alternative weaning regime and she would have continued to live. Rather, she rejected life in her condition and deliberately chose to die. In accepting that for some people the state of their life could be worse than the prospect of their death, Dame Elizabeth seems to concede that it may sometimes be, for that individual, preferable to die. Moreover, she was critical of the doctors caring for Ms B who refused to consider either accepting her request or referring her to other doctors who might have been prepared to act on it. She described the position into which Ms B had been placed by the doctors as 'impossible', concluding that the 'one-way weaning process appears to have been designed to help the treating clinicians and the other carers and not in any way designed to help Ms B'.[6] Ms B was held to be competent, based on the 'presumption that a patient has mental capacity to make decisions whether to consent to or refuse medical or surgical treatment offered to him/her'.[7]

The healthcare professionals who ultimately disconnected the ventilator and delivered the drugs to ease her passing, with the full blessing of the law, participated intimately in her death; indeed, it was arguably precisely because they recognised that their involvement was also direct that the first set of healthcare professionals refused to participate. The British Medical Association

5   Ibid. at p 172.
6   Ibid. at p 173.
7   Ibid. at p 174.

notes that this can be a very difficult situation for healthcare professionals, but cautions that 'they must not put pressure on . . . [patients] . . . to accept treatment'.[8] On all logic, Ms B's death was assisted. It is therefore clear that refusal of treatment that is life-preserving is permitted in UK law; that patients can orchestrate their own deaths even when they need assistance in so doing. However, not everyone is in a situation where they can choose to have an assisted death of this sort; not because their intention is any different, not because of questions about causation and not because the outcome – death – is different, but because of the pragmatic fact that they do not have life-sustaining treatment that they can refuse, and this will be discussed in more depth later in this chapter. There are, however, other examples where a positive choice for death is respected in law even where that decision binds future treatment rather than evidencing a contemporaneous choice.

Advance directives

Where an individual has made what is known as an advance directive (sometimes known as an advance statement or living will) refusing treatment in the future should certain circumstances arise, that individual is making a decision that life in certain conditions is not preferable to death. Now enshrined in law in England and Wales by the terms of the Mental Capacity Act 2005, such directives have legal validity so long as they are competently made and applicable to the circumstances. In Scotland, although no statute exists, it has long been assumed that a valid and applicable advance directive would be binding on doctors and other healthcare professionals.

It is worth noting in passing that it is legally clear that patients cannot by an advance directive insist on *receiving* treatment in the future.[9] It might, therefore, be argued that autonomy is not in fact the principle at the root of how doctors relate to their patients in these cases. If autonomy was the most important consideration then surely people should be allowed to exercise that right of self-determination to insist on, as well as to refuse, treatment? These two scenarios are, however, different. There are additional reasons why a demand for useless treatment should be resisted, even if we accept the importance of the autonomy model. First, is the impact any such demand would have on the general welfare of society. Just as opponents of legalisation point to the possible effects on the rest of the community if people were allowed to make the choice for an assisted death, so too we can reasonably look to the effect of the waste of resources that could be involved in the endless provision of futile

---

8   British Medical Association, *Withholding and Withdrawing Life-Prolonging Medical Treatment: Guidance for Decision Making*, 3rd edn, 2007, Oxford: Blackwell Publishing, at p 45.

9   *R (on the application of Burke) v General Medical Council* (2004) 79 BMLR 126; *Burke v General Medical Council* [2005] EWCA Civ 1003 (CA).

treatment. No doctor could be placed under a duty to provide such treatment, in the interests both of the patient and the wider community. Second, unlike the argument about the effect on third parties of legalising assisted dying which is based on speculation, the effects of acquiescing in the provision of futile treatment are far from speculative. Thus, the harm element of the liberal tradition would be met were valuable and scarce social goods to be distributed in a way that is nothing more than wasteful. The autonomy argument, therefore, falls in the face of the harm that would result to others in this case.

In the case of treatment refusal, however, people who become incompetent can, by dint of having made the earlier statement, ensure that doctors do not continue with unwanted treatment. Should such a directive be triggered by circumstances, doctors are obliged to stand by and allow a patient to die, even if there is treatment that could save them. The doctor's duty to save life becomes, yet again, secondary to the respect given to individual autonomy. If, as I have argued, there is no moral difference between killing and letting die, then in this case the medical personnel who do not institute potentially life-sustaining treatment are in precisely the same position as those who actively end a patient's life; they are complicit in the death of their patient.

Even before the passing of the 2005 Act, it was widely accepted that advance directives, properly made and applicable to the circumstances, would be legally binding on healthcare professionals. There is some case law that supports this conclusion. In *Re C*[10] a man who had been diagnosed as suffering from paranoid schizophrenia was allowed by the court to refuse medical treatment which his clinicians believed to be life-saving. In addition, the court also agreed that, should he lapse into incompetence, his advance declaration refusing treatment should be taken as binding on his doctors. In the case of *Re AK*[11] a 19-year-old man who was suffering from motor neurone disease and was able to communicate only by moving his eyelids sought and obtained court authorisation to have treatment withdrawn two weeks after he was unable to communicate. In this case, the judge said:

> It is . . . clearly the law that the doctors are not entitled so to act if it is known that the patient, provided he was of sound mind and full capacity, has let it be known that he does not consent and that such treatment is against his wishes. To this extent an advance indication of the wishes of a patient of full capacity and sound mind are effective.[12]

Each of these patients made a choice for death; each choice was respected, even though it involved the participation of healthcare staff. The importance of this is to demonstrate yet again that the law does not always reject as illicit a

10 *Re C (Mental Patient: Medical Treatment)* (1993) 15 BMLR 77.
11 (2001) 58 BMLR 151.
12 *Re AK* (2001) 58 BMLR 151, per Hughes, J, at p 156.

choice for death, nor are doctors always unwilling to participate in such deaths. That this is accepted does not, however, mean that it is uncontroversial.

In light of the fact that people may change, it might be thought rather strange that such decisions, which will result in death, should be respected – particularly, but not exclusively, if the sanctity of life is the dominant value – and indeed a significant literature has grown up around this question. For example, if I currently believe that living with Alzheimer's would be intolerable, I can now direct that, should I become unable to care for myself and/or recognise my family, I would not wish any life-sustaining treatment to be provided. However, once I am in that condition I may appear happy – should doctors treat an infection which threatens my life? Battin, for example, argues that, if autonomy is the guiding principle then at least prima facie the choice made should be respected at the time when it is triggered by circumstances.[13] However, she also notes that there is an argument that the person who made the decision is no longer the same person; why, therefore, should the person she *was* be able to bind the person she *is*? On the other hand, clearly the person she *was* fully intended, with her own unique understanding of what she would or would not want, to bind the person she might *become*. van Delden says that advance directives 'protect autonomy interests of the now incompetent person. They do so by promoting a previous wish into an actual one . . .'.[14] However, he also argues that they also 'ignore the time interval between the two'.[15] This raises, amongst other questions, what he calls the issue of 'the continuity of the person'.[16] It is this question that concerns many commentators, but it is of concern not because the choice to die is problematic. Rather it is potentially a problem because of doubts about whether or not previous autonomy-based decisions should be given effect to when the person is no longer autonomous.

Equally, of course, it could be argued that where it can cure or palliate symptoms, treatment should be given irrespective of the previously expressed wishes of the individual. In these circumstances, for example, Ryan argues that the directive should not be given effect to as it assumes that the patient when competent was in fact able to determine what s/he would have wanted in the future. This, he argues, is a flawed assumption.[17] Moreover, Dresser has argued that:

13 Battin, M P, *The Least Worst Death: Essays in Bioethics on the End of Life*, 1994, Oxford University Press, at pp 147–148.

14 van Delden, J J M, 'The unfeasibility of requests for euthanasia in advance directives', *Journal of Medical Ethics*, 2004: 30: 447–452.

15 Ibid. at p 449.

16 Ibid.

17 Ryan, C J, 'Betting your life: an argument against certain advance directives', *Journal of Medical Ethics*, Vol 22, Issue 2, 95–99.

If a patient can no longer appreciate the values that motivated the pre-commitment choice, treatment decisions should take into account what now matters to the patient. . . . Competent persons are free to elevate their critical interests above experiential interests. But after they lose decisional capacity, they have a different set of concerns. Experiential interests become central to their lives. Experiential interests should also be central to decisions about their life-sustaining treatment.[18]

Despite this debate, however, the law is clear; I can now bind future healthcare decisions, so long as they are to reject treatment. What can be drawn from this discussion is that, even though there are some profound philosophical questions which need to be answered, the law has chosen to adopt a route to facilitate non-treatment choices – and therefore an assisted death – based on previous choices made possibly without understanding how the person might feel once they are in a particular situation. It is interesting, therefore, that where there is a real ethical debate to be had – as opposed to the dubious ones entertained in the debate about assisted dying – the law has come down firmly in favour of allowing people to choose to die and has seemingly ignored this ethical question.

So far we have considered two situations in which a choice for death is legally accepted. In each case, the exercise of autonomy prevents the imposition of unwanted, albeit perhaps life-saving, treatment and facilitates death. If autonomy is of such importance, it might reasonably be expected that it would carry the same weight in all situations where people choose death. Whereas the decisions described above might be said to leave some questions unanswered – at least in the case of advance directives – they are legally acceptable. However, the request for assistance by an individual who has no life-sustaining treatment to refuse is, oddly, the one case where the patient's contemporary, competent decision is rejected.

Requests for assisted dying

Ms B's case can be contrasted with the case of Diane Pretty. In this case, Mrs Pretty sought the assurance of the Director of Public Prosecutions that, in the event that her husband assisted her to die, he would not be prosecuted. Mrs Pretty suffered from advanced motor neurone disease and her death was imminent, albeit that it would not occur before her condition deteriorated to the point at which she would be unable to perform most bodily functions for herself. For her, the prospect of continued life in those circumstances was

---

18 Dresser, R, 'Precommitment: a misguided strategy for securing death with dignity', *Texas Law Review* 81 (2002–03) 1823–1847 at p 1840.

anathema. She, like Ms B, did not wish life in that condition to be extended. In an attempt to achieve what she regarded as a dignified death, she pursued her case through the courts in England and all the way to the European Court of Human Rights.[19] At every stage, her request for assistance in dying was denied. If we leave aside for the moment the question of her husband's involvement, given that arguably this generated its own unique questions, the right that she was claiming is worthy of consideration as her arguments were cast in the broader terms of a 'right to die', or, perhaps more accurately, a right to receive assistance in dying, albeit that her claims were specifically targeted at a particular piece of legislation.

In the European Court of Human Rights, Mrs Pretty argued that a number of her Convention rights were being infringed by the failure of the UK Government to legalise assistance in dying. From the point of view of outcome and intention, what Mrs Pretty was seeking was access to the same right that was accorded to Ms B: the right to choose to die when she wanted to. However, the difference between the two cases rested – as it commonly does – on the purported distinction between killing and letting die. In Ms B's case, it was possible – albeit by some strange reasoning – to conceptualise her death as resulting from an omission, even though from a common sense perspective removing the ventilator which kept her alive is an act. In Mrs Pretty's case, active assistance would also have been required to bring about the same result, yet the physical form of the behaviour needed to do so was used to distinguish between the two cases. In each case, nonetheless, the patient had a considered and durable intent to die; the only real question was how that death was brought about. However, while Ms B's case rested on the common law, Mrs Pretty's required her to challenge a statutory provision – s 2(1) of the Suicide Act 1961 which makes assisted suicide a crime in England and Wales.

Mrs Pretty sought to argue her case on a number of Convention rights which she argued were breached by the terms of the Suicide Act 1961 (which, it should be remembered, does not apply in Scotland). She started her submissions with the most fundamental of all Convention rights – the right to life, which is contained in Article 2. This Article reads as follows:

> 1. Everyone's right to life shall be protected by law. No one shall be deprived of his life intentionally save in the execution of a sentence of a court following his conviction of a crime for which this penalty is provided by law.

19 *Pretty v United Kingdom* (2002) 66 BMLR 147.

Mrs Pretty argued that this Article was designed to protect individuals from the unwarranted behaviour of third parties – for example, that it reinforced laws prohibiting the non-consensual taking of life. She claimed that it should, however, be interpreted as also encapsulating freedom of choice. In her claim,

> [w]hile most people want to live, some want to die, and the article protects both rights. The right to die is not the antithesis of the right to life but the corollary of it, and the state has a positive obligation to protect both.[20]

Further, she argued that what she was seeking was different from voluntary euthanasia, to which the Court of Human rights responded, in agreement with Lord Bingham,[21]

> ... there is in logic no justification for drawing a line at this point. If article 2 does confer a right to self-determination in relation to life and death, and if a person were so gravely disabled as to be unable to perform any act whatever to cause his or her own death, it would necessarily follow in logic that such a person would have a right to be killed at the hands of a third party without giving any help to the third party and the state would be in breach of the Convention if it were to interfere with the exercise of that right.[22]

However, the Court was unwilling to concede this right, not only because of concern about the consequences that might follow were it recognised, but also because for the Court of Human Rights to hold that English law breached her human rights, she would need to have proved not just that the Convention could accommodate regimes which legalise assisted dying, but more importantly that it was a breach of the Convention not to do so. This was surely an impossible hurdle unless the right to life could reasonably be interpreted as encapsulating a 'right' to die.[23]

A second article raised in aid of Mrs Pretty's claim was Article 3, which reads:

> No one shall be subjected to torture or to inhuman or degrading treatment or punishment.

---

20 Ibid. at p 155.
21 *R (on the application of Pretty) v Director of Public Prosecutions and Secretary of State for the Home Department* [2001] UKHL 61.
22 (2002) 66 BMLR 147 at p 156.
23 Ibid. at p 159.

Mrs Pretty argued as follows:

(1) Member states have an absolute and unqualified obligation not to inflict the proscribed treatment and also to take positive action to prevent the subjection of individuals to such treatment. . . . (2) Suffering attributable to the progression of a disease may amount to such treatment if the State can prevent or ameliorate such suffering and does not do so. . . . (3) In denying Mrs Pretty the opportunity to bring her suffering to an end the United Kingdom . . . will subject her to the proscribed treatment. . . . (4) Since . . . it is open to the United Kingdom under the Convention to refrain from prohibiting assisted suicide, the Director [of Public Prosecutions] can give the undertaking sought without breaking the United Kingdom's obligations under the Convention. (5) If the Director may not give the undertaking, s 2 of the 1961 Act is incompatible with the Convention.[24]

Yet again, however, the Convention could not be taken as imposing an obligation on the United Kingdom to legalise assisted dying, nor on the Director of Public Prosecutions to pre-empt a decision on possible prosecution. Mrs Pretty also sought to rely on Article 8 of the Convention which reads:

1. Everyone has the right to respect for his private and family life, his home and his correspondence.

2. There shall be no interference by a public authority with the exercise of this right except such as is in accordance with the law and is necessary in a democratic society in the interests of national security, public safety or the economic well-being of the country, for the prevention of disorder or crime, for the protection of health or morals, or for the protection of the rights and freedoms of others.

However, for the Court, '[a]rticle 8 protects the physical, moral and psychological integrity of the individual, including rights over the individual's own body, but there is nothing to suggest that is confers a right to decide when or how to die'.[25] Interestingly, in a different context, another judge, Mr Justice Munby, had declared that the right to die with dignity was protected by Articles 3 and 8, albeit that in this case the patient was seeking to have ANH continued, rather than seeking an assisted death.[26] In addition, he said that these Articles also protect the individual 'from treatment, or from lack of treatment, which will result in one dying in avoidably distressing circumstances'.[27] He further

24 Ibid. at pp 159–160.
25 Ibid. at p 163.
26 R (on the application of Burke) v General Medical Council (2004) 79 BMLR 126.
27 Munby, J, at p 157, para 80.

declared that '. . . the personal autonomy which is protected by art 8 *embraces such matters as how one chooses to pass the closing days and moments of one's life and how one manages one's death*'.[28] (emphasis added) Although this judgement was overturned on appeal, these specific contentions were not directly attacked by the Appeal Court. Although the judges in the appeal were at pains to warn not to cherry-pick from the earlier judgment, neither did they specifically reject his analysis on this point. Mr Justice Munby's views are, therefore, of considerable interest for this argument.

One further article on which Diane Pretty relied was Article 9, which states:

1. Everyone has the right to freedom of thought, conscience and religion; this right includes freedom to change his religion or belief and freedom, either alone or in community with others and in public or private, to manifest his religion or belief, in worship, teaching, practice and observance.

2. Freedom to manifest one's religion or beliefs shall be subject only to such limitations as are prescribed by law and are necessary in a democratic society in the interests of public safety, for the protection of public order, health or morals, or for the protection of the rights and freedoms of others.

The European Court of Human Rights was clear that respect was indeed owed to freedom of thought and religion, but nonetheless held that '. . . her belief cannot found a requirement that her husband should be absolved from the consequences of conduct which, although it would be consistent with her belief, is proscribed by the criminal law'.[29]

Finally, Mrs Pretty sought to rely on Article 14; the non-discrimination right. However, as this right can only be used where one or more of the other Convention rights has been engaged, it had no relevance to her case.

Although generally referred to as a 'right to die' case, Mrs Pretty's argument did not in fact only address the question of whether or not there is or should be a general right to have assistance in dying, although the Court did express some concerns about the possible consequences of permitting this. Rather, it directly tested the specific terms of a statute against the margin of appreciation that all States are allowed to exercise. In other words, even though some Member States of the Council of Europe have legalised assisted dying, this does not mean that other States have a corresponding obligation to do the same. Each State has the right to legislate according to the prevailing morality

28 Ibid. at p 150, para 62.
29 Ibid. at p 169.

in its own community. The terms of the Convention, then, cannot provide individuals in Member States with the right to assisted dying, even though the provision of such a right will equally not amount to an infringement of the Convention.

As we have seen, Mrs Pretty's case was not the first time that the 1961 Act had been challenged. In the case of *R v United Kingdom*[30] the European Commission of Human Rights considered whether or not the Suicide Act 1961 s 2 violated either Article 8 or 10 (freedom of expression) of the Convention on Human Rights. The applicant had been convicted for putting people who wanted assistance in dying in touch with someone else, who then assisted them in committing suicide. The Commission held that these acts were excluded from the concept of privacy (Article 8) because they breached the public interest in protecting life. As to Article 10, the Commission described

> ... the State's legitimate interest in this area in taking measures to protect, against criminal behaviour, the life of its citizens particularly those who belong to especially vulnerable categories by reason of their age or infirmity. It recognises the right of the State under the Convention to guard against the inevitable abuses that would occur, in the absence of legislation, against the aiding and abetting of suicide.[31]

It is interesting that the Commission used the speculation about 'inevitable abuses' as part justification for its decision; as ever, without any evidence of the likelihood, far less the inevitability, of such abuses occurring. For the moment, however, the 1961 Act – in those parts of the United Kingdom in which it applies – would seem to be an unmoveable objection to legalisation of assisted dying. If assisted dying were to be legalised, therefore, it would require repeal of the 1961 Act and some justificatory provision in Scots law, by way of a specific exclusion from criminal charges for bringing about death in specific circumstances. Simply trying to achieve an assisted death by appealing to Convention rights seems doomed to failure.

The clinical perspective

Although patients – and some commentators – may not perceive there to be much, if any, difference between acts and omissions, it is probably the case that many healthcare professionals do, as we have already seen. It is almost certainly the case that healthcare professionals find the death of any patient a tragedy. Their training and motivation focus on restoring health rather than on witnessing or contributing to the end of a life. Death is a failure, not a blessing. However, realistically they must also accept that they cannot offer

30   (1983) 33 DR 270.
31   Ibid. at p 272.

a cure in every case and that their patients will in some circumstances die. Not surprisingly, for healthcare professionals it is probably morally and professionally preferable that a patient dies of causes other than those directly brought about by themselves and their fellow professionals. The act of killing will presumably seem to them to be less morally acceptable than allowing a patient to die. This difference is explained by Gillon:

> Medicine, law and everyday morality distinguish clearly between a strong universal though *prima facie* prohibition on killing and a very much more equivocal attitude to letting die. The assumption underlying this general approach seems to be that all of us owe a strong *prima facie* duty to all others not to kill each other but that we may or may not, depending on the circumstances and the relationships involved, owe a duty to each other to preserve each other's lives.[32]

This distinction, however, could be taken to bear on the issue of murder rather than a chosen death, and in any case, as Gillon says, it rests on a prima facie, and not therefore immutable, proposition. In other words, any ethical difference between killing and letting die – real or perceived – could equally hinge on whether or not the death was chosen or imposed. Gillon's analysis, then, might be of even more relevance in cases where the person does not make the choice to die (such as patients in permanent vegetative state (PVS)) rather than people in the position of Ms B or Diane Pretty. In any case, as Singer asks:

> Can doctors who remove the feeding tubes from patients in a persistent vegetative state really believe that there is a huge gulf between this, and giving the same patients an injection that will stop their hearts beating? Doctors may be trained in such a way that it is psychologically easier for them to do the one and not the other, but both are equally certain ways of bringing about the death of the patient.[33]

It seems clear, however, that some doctors do draw such a distinction, whether because they genuinely believe it to be real or because they prefer to categorise their behaviour in that way. In either case, that healthcare professionals may be uncomfortable with bringing about death in one way rather than another, while interesting, is scarcely definitive of the issue. While I do not dispute the integrity and professionalism of doctors, it is unclear why this gives them

---

32 Gillon, R, 'Euthanasia, withholding life-prolonging treatment and moral differences between killing and letting die', *Journal of Medical Ethics* 1998: 14: 115–117 at p 115.
33 Singer, P, *Rethinking Life and Death: The Collapse of our Traditional Ethics*, 1994, New York: St Martin's Griffin, at p 221.

any special insight into what patients actually want, or why their views are particularly important, either for these individuals or for society as a whole.

The Select Committee on the Assisted Dying for the Terminally Ill Bill also noted that the views of the medical profession may on occasion be at odds with those of patients. As its Report says:

> We were told that, while it might be argued that there was little differ-ence from the patient's standpoint between on the one hand allowing a refusal of futile or burdensome treatment and on the other refusing assistance with suicide or voluntary euthanasia, from the standpoint of the physician the two situations were quite different – in that he is acceding in one case to a patient's request to let his or her illness take its natural course, while in the other he would be required to bring the patient's life to an end prematurely.[34]

That may be so, but it does not explain why the medical view should prevail over that of those who wish their suffering to be relieved with assistance. Jackson argues that when the debate is driven by what medical professionals regard as a moral distinction this leads to a situation which, from the patient's perspective, 'makes very little sense'.[35] Indeed, she claims that '[l]awful and unlawful life-shortening practices can be distinguished . . . only by adopting the medical practitioner's perspective'.[36] In addition, this perspective on the purported difference between acts and omissions is, of course, not shared by every healthcare professional, as recent debate in the British Medical Association has shown, and at the time of the Select Committee's review the Royal College of Physicians and the Royal College of General Practitioners had declared themselves neutral on assisted dying. In 2005, conference voted to amend the BMA's traditional stance in opposition to legalisation to one of neutrality. This was overturned, after extensive campaigning, in 2006. The fact that the medical professions are themselves divided on this issue reflects the fact that doctors cannot be presumed all to share the views of those who were given such weight by the Select Committee.

In any case, the views of healthcare professionals are of limited importance in a debate which hinges on principle. Bowing to the sensitivities of the medical professions is a pragmatic and not a moral or ethical step. While we must accept the refusal of a healthcare professional to participate in actively ending life, we cannot and should not make their views the cornerstone of what is

---

34 The House of Lords Select Committee on the Assisted Dying for the Terminally Ill Bill, *Report of the House of Lords Select Committee on the Assisted Dying for the Terminally Ill Bill*, 4 April 2005, p 22, para 49.

35 Jackson, E, *Regulating Reproduction: Law, Technology and Autonomy*, 2001, Oxford: Hart Publishing at p 433.

36 Ibid.

good, permissible, ethical or lawful. Moreover, there is a certain amount of reputable evidence that doctors and other healthcare professionals are already participating in acts of assisted dying in ways which go beyond what might be called 'passive' involvement. Although the House of Lords Select Committee on the Assisted Dying for the Terminally Ill Bill cast doubt on the value of some of the opinion research that has been done in this area, a pattern emerges from around the world which shows that some doctors *are* involved in assisting their patients to die, irrespective of what the law says. It cannot therefore be assumed that the authority given to the opinion of opponents of legalisation within the medical professions is not in fact misplaced. What of those who would argue *for* legalisation, as some healthcare professionals do?

The recent House of Lords Select Committee also noted the argument that 'if society wishes to legalise acts which run counter to accepted medical ethics, it would be wise to consider whether such acts might not be carried out by other means'.[37] However, what doctors actually believe to be 'ethical' may have been simplistically assumed by many commentators, including the Select Committee itself. In a study which mimicked the landmark study undertaken by van der Maas *et al*[38] in the Netherlands (where assisted dying was at that time tolerated and is now legal), Kuhse *et al* concluded that, while 19.5 per cent of deaths in the Netherlands 'involved a medical decision whether partly or explicitly intended to hasten death or not prolong life'[39] the comparable percentage in Australia – where assisted dying is illegal – was 36.5 per cent. It would seem, therefore, that whatever the law says, and whatever medical ethics purports to say, doctors are no more homogeneous in their views as to what is 'ethical' than is the general public. If so, this reinforces concern about using 'medical ethics' as a touchstone for the distinction between what is lawful and what is not.

Opinions gathered by medical professionals' own professional associations vary. It is wrong, therefore, to extrapolate from the views of some healthcare professionals – such as those involved in palliative medicine, who unsurprisingly seem to be by and large firmly opposed to legalisation of assisted dying – to the conclusion that all healthcare professionals hold to that view. Furthermore, it is arguably disingenuous of the Select Committee on the one hand to discount the conclusions drawn from opinion polls of the public (which are widely in support of legalisation) while at the same time being

37 *Report of the House of Lords Select Committee on the Assisted Dying for the Terminally Ill Bill*, op. cit. at p 83, para 242.

38 van der Maas, P J, *et al*, 'Euthanasia and other medical practices involving the end of life in the Netherlands, 1990–1995', (1996) 335 *New England Journal of Medicine*, 1699–1705.

39 Kuhse, H, Singer, P, Baume, M, Clark, M, Rickard, M, 'End-of-life decisions in Australian medical practice', 166 *Medical Journal of Australia* 191–196 (1997) available at http://www.mja.com.au/public/issues/feb17/kuhse/kuhse.html (accessed on 22/02/07), Transcript, p 6.

prepared to give considerable weight to representations from the medical profession which are every bit as likely to be unrepresentative or biased. In any case, it must be restated that the arguments canvassed here do not depend on public or any other opinion polls.

Acts and omissions revisited

Leaving aside, therefore, any speculation as to the feelings of healthcare professionals, and even the public, what is in fact important is to identify how best we can evaluate the interconnectedness of intention, causation and outcome. It seems clear that both Mrs Pretty and Ms B had precisely the same intention and sought precisely the same outcome, yet in one case this was permissible and in the other it was denied. If we agree that the acts/omissions distinction is artificial and irrelevant, then the element of causation is the same in each case. Therefore, we can conclude that:

> Physician-assisted suicide is not fundamentally different from the with-holding or withdrawing of medical treatment. In each case, the patient's interest in self-determination gives the patient a right to die, whether by refusing treatment, having treatment withdrawn, or accepting the assistance of a physician.[40]

That the law strives to convince that there remains an important distinction between killing and letting die speaks more to policy than principle – or even logic. In effect, it tries to maintain this purported difference by using a number of devices to distinguish between cases which are essentially similar. In this way, the courts aim to uphold their declared commitment to the sanctity of human life. This will be returned to later. However, it is not just the law that holds this alleged distinction to be critical to, if not definitive of, this debate. For example, Somerville says:

> Euthanasia should be seen as different in kind, not merely degree, from other medical acts or omissions that could or would shorten life. One crosses a great divide in undertaking intentional killing. Although pain and other symptoms of serious physical distress should be relieved, it must always be the pain or other symptoms that one seeks to eliminate, and not the person with the pain or symptoms.[41]

---

40 Notes 'Physician Assisted Suicide and the Right to Die with Assistance', 105 *Harvard Law Review* (1991–1992) 2001–2040, at p 2040.

41 Somerville, M, *Death Talk: The Case Against Euthanasia and Physician-Assisted Suicide*, 2001, Montreal and Kingston: McGill-Queen's University Press, at p 84.

Still other commentators, however, would argue that the reality is more subtle. Beauchamp and Childress, for example, argue that '[b]oth killing and letting die are *prima facie* wrong, but can be justified under some circumstances'.[42] Thus, we may hold to the position that neither letting die nor actively killing is a self-evidently right or moral action, but that – with sufficient justification – each of them could become one. Importantly, though, in logic the same arguments would be needed to justify either of them. Yet, we do not require any such justifications in respect of those seeking passive assistance to die, for example in situations such as those faced by Ms B. In these cases, all that is required is that the decision is made autonomously by a competent patient. The reasons for the choice are not inquired into, the patient's state of physical health is not scrutinised. What is important, then, is respect for an autonomous choice competently made by the patient. However, when the dying is accompanied by an active intervention from a third party, issues about competence, rationality and – usually – physical condition are engaged with, scrutinised and analysed. This anomaly is, interestingly, reflected even in those countries or states where assisted dying has been legalised. No legislation exists anywhere that does not try to limit the categories of those who are entitled to gain access to assisted dying, although as we will see the legal regime in the Netherlands – to the horror of its critics – has allowed for the categories of those who can be assisted to die to be expanded.

A further paradox lies in the fact that the only question asked in the case of Ms B was whether or not she was legally competent. Her reason for making the decision to die, whether or not it was rational and whether or not she was terminally ill – she was not – were matters of complete irrelevance. Yet Diane Pretty, who nobody ever suggested was anything other than competent and who *was* terminally ill, had her reasons for wanting to die closely scrutinised and suffered the indignity of the very death she had feared, predominantly because the law persists in declaring the priority of the sanctity of life (even when manifestly it does not always accord it that status) and insists on the distinction without a difference which is the acts/omissions doctrine in this context. As Williams says:

> The distinction ... enables the 'right' resolution, but the method by which that result is achieved is defective when it is based on an untenable fabrication which relies, to a great extent, on judicial intuition and preconceived categorisations of what is acceptable and what is not.[43]

42 Beauchamp, T L and Childress, J S, *Principles of Biomedical Ethics*, 4th edn, 1994, Oxford University Press at p 225.
43 Williams, G, *Intention and Causation in Medical Non-Killing: The Impact of Criminal Law Concepts on Euthanasia and Assisted Suicide*, 2007, London: Routledge-Cavendish, at p 56.

Despite this, she maintains that there are 'considerations of public policy' which mean that the distinction should be retained.[44] She argues that one such consideration rests on the fact that, if we did not make such a distinction, then doctors throughout the country would be regularly 'killing' their patients because, for example, non-treatment decisions are made routinely. Of course, this is merely a semantic problem which could be easily resolved, simply by accepting that killing can in specified circumstances be acceptable. A second reason, she suggests, is that 'the distinction avoids placing an "intolerable" burden on people who would otherwise be liable without limit'.[45] Williams concludes that the distinction 'even if it is a fabrication – is important because it illustrates the relevance of moral factors which distinguish between people who are seen as either good or bad'.[46] While the practical reasons proffered by Williams may have some merit, it must be doubted whether or not they should be defended at the expense of principle. It is surely not the words we use to label behaviour that are important; it is what that behaviour derives from and results in. Equally, it is not obvious that the distinction does *in fact* point to good and bad people. A doctor who withholds treatment may not be a 'good' person. Indeed, s/he may do so with the intention that the patient dies and, as we will see in the next chapter, s/he may do so without reference to the wishes of the patient and even when treatment could prolong life. So too, a doctor who actively assists a patient to die need not be a 'bad' person. S/he may be acting out of genuine compassion, on the considered request of his/her patient and with respect for that patient's dignity and autonomy.

My conclusion from what has gone before, therefore, is that there are major inconsistencies in the way in which the law approaches end-of-life decision-making, and that the ethical or moral bases for the distinctions drawn, and the outcomes which result from them, are unclear, if not downright disingenuous. Perhaps in an effort to promote the view that the sanctity of life is the most important of all social, ethical and legal principles, the law has found a number of – essentially unsatisfactory – ways in which to permit some deaths to happen and refuse to allow others, even while simultaneously admitting that the sanctity of life principle is defeasible to the importance of autonomy. Perhaps the ultimate paradox is that the deaths that the law seeks to condemn are those which involve a considered request from competent, suffering people. It is a strange ethical and legal position that permits this situation to arise, particularly when it is based on arguments which are inherently flawed. As Jackson has said, '. . . the moral principle that doctors must not kill their patients makes no practical sense in the light of our willingness to accept the medical profession's extensive and routine involvement in the shortening of

---

44 Ibid.
45 Ibid. at p 61.
46 Ibid. at p 69.

patients' lives', although she concludes that it nevertheless 'continues to have extraordinary symbolic resonance'.[47]

Superimposing distinctions such as acts and omissions onto the otherwise unambiguous commitment to respect for autonomy, and sticking rigidly to the idea that there is something inherently different about active and passive end-of-life decisions, distorts the ethical and legal landscape and leaves some needy people in a position where the help that they desperately want is denied to them. As we will see, it also means that healthcare professionals who do wish to assist their patients to have a chosen death either risk criminalisation for so doing or are prevented by flawed reasoning from being able to respond to genuine requests from competent adult patients. The reluctance of the law to concede that patient autonomy in these circumstances is every bit as important as it is in other cases where it is prioritised over sanctity of life may be understandable. However, it is arguably long past the time that this situation was revisited in order to evaluate it for clarity of thought and consistency of argument.

That some jurisdictions have been able to do this is a testament to their maturity. That the United Kingdom still struggles with it is a testimony to the power of unelected, and probably unrepresentative, groups in the community. In Scotland, for example, when a Member of the Scottish Parliament attempted to raise enough signatures to have a Bill legalising assisted dying considered by the Parliament, he was unable to muster even the small number of votes that were needed to begin the parliamentary debate. This democratic deficit is one that should not be tolerated, particularly as it seems to bow to arguments which, I have argued, are not unchallengeable or self-evidently strong. This is not to say that people who hold views opposed to legalisation of assisted dying are in any sense holding to these decisions in bad faith – quite the opposite. However, there are reasons to question whether or not their particular perspectives should dominate. Leaving the law in its current state simply permits the views of one group to dominate over another, irrespective of the extent to which their views inflict pain and suffering on others.

Further, Orentlicher notes that:

> Some commentators have drawn a moral distinction between a patient's rejecting the burdensomeness of medical treatment and a patient's rejecting the burdensomeness of life. . . . There are two problems with this distinction. First, many permitted withdrawals of treatment represent a rejection of burdensome life rather than burdensome treatment. . . . Second, it is not meaningful to distinguish between the burdensomeness of treatment and the burdensomeness of life in the context of decisions about life-sustaining treatment. When a person's life is dependent on

47 Jackson, op. cit. at p 436.

medical treatment, the only life the person has is a life with the treatment; the life and the treatment are inseparable.[48]

This is an important point which is too often overlooked. While it may be appealing to imagine that we can in some way separate the suffering from the sufferer, the reality of course is that they are essentially indistinguishable. It makes no sense to attempt this separation, or at least no sense beyond a rather weak effort to salve our consciences by playing with words. It also allows us to pretend that people do not in fact want to shed their burdensome life, when of course some will want to do exactly that. That some of us would never contemplate such a choice is no reason to deny that others will.

The fact that the arguments opposed to legalisation can be so effectively countered must raise doubts about their place in underpinning our legal system. To be sure, it is always possible to find argument and counter-argument in situations which are this complex and sensitive, but analysis of the arguments for and against legalisation lends weight to the view that in contemporary bioethics and law autonomy is indeed the overarching, perhaps even overriding, principle to which the law purports to pay considerably more than lip service. The reluctance of the law to confront the consequences of this head on, combined with the disingenuous tools that it uses to maintain the current position, is surely unworthy of a great legal tradition.

What matters in the end is that sometimes death is seen as the better, or the preferred, option. That some people can have their death brought about – whether or not they have asked for it – yet others who have expressed a sustained and competent request for it cannot is surely an unfortunate and cruel legacy of a legal system struggling to find the appropriate weight to be given to competing moral values by unnecessarily and unreasonably drawing lines in the sand; lines which are ultimately based not on principle, but on untested and speculative fears about consequences. In fact, even consequences which might be conceived of as positive have been used to argue against legalisation. For example, it has been reported that in the Council of Europe, a proposal to permit legalisation of euthanasia was rejected in part because 'it would call on European countries to define procedures for ending treatment of such patients or for discontinuing lifesaving medical treatment when doctors believe there is little hope for survival'.[49] Why this would be a bad outcome is far from clear. Respect for persons surely requires that such a clarification is appropriate, and indeed medical associations in many countries have tried to do just that whether or not they are contemplating legalisation of assisted dying.

48   Orentlicher, D, *Matters of Life and Death: Making Moral Theory Work in Medical Ethics and the Law*, Princeton and Oxford: Princeton University Press, 2001, at p 33.
49   Ertelt, S, 'European human rights group condemns euthanasia of disabled', Lifenews. com, 27 April 2005, available at http://66.195.16.55/bio940.html (accessed 16/06/05).

At this stage one further concern is generally wheeled out; namely that respecting the views of some people will inevitably lead to pressure on other, more vulnerable people to 'choose' death. If so, this is every bit as true in the case of treatment refusal – which must be respected – and advance directives – which are given the force of law. In the long run:

> Even though we might imagine some justifiable cases of assisted suicide, it is argued, there is too great a risk that vulnerable patients will end their lives non-voluntarily or will succumb to pressures from others to end their lives. . . . These risks are real, but they are just as real for patients who ask that their life-sustaining treatment be withdrawn.[50]

Refusing life-sustaining treatment and asking for assistance in dying are essentially indistinguishable – unless we resort to sophistry. Consistency and principle would therefore require that they be treated in the same way. If we are not to force unwanted treatment on the competent but unwilling person, then we must also accept that we should assist those who competently seek assistance to die. Leaving the law as it currently stands means, where a patient refuses treatment, 'that the doctor's actions (encouragement as well as assistance) are in all instances outside the control of the criminal law'.[51] Only his or her active involvement brings the criminal law into play, yet the reasons for this are unclear. If we are concerned that patients may choose death because of pressure or 'encouragement' from doctors or others, this is no less true in cases where the patient's choice is not intensely scrutinised. In cases of treatment refusal, just as in requests for assisted dying, the patient intends to die. Indeed, it could be argued that those most at risk of any abuse from the system are those who are incompetent – where death can often be chosen by third parties – not those who have balanced their choices and reached a conclusion that is best for *them*. While statutory and common law rules closely regulate the latter situation, 'comparatively few safeguards exist when doctors take decisions, such as the withdrawal of artificial ventilation, which will end the lives of their incompetent patients'.[52]

The presumption seems to be that no harm flows from allowing doctors to decide that someone can die – so long as they bring this about 'passively' – but that it does or would follow were people allowed to make their own decisions and obtain help – actively. However, this is an assumption rather than a fact. Some people would rather argue that '[l]egalizing and thereby regulating physician-assisted death does not put terminally ill patients at greater risk than

50 Orentlicher, op. cit. at p 45.
51 Price, D T, 'Assisted suicide and refusing medical treatment: linguistics, morals and legal contortions', *Medical Law Review* 4 Autumn 1996, 270–299, at p 292.
52 Jackson, op. cit. at p 440.

do other, already accepted practices in the treatment of the terminally ill'.[53] Moreover, in the case of physician-assisted suicide, the doctor's involvement is generally confined to the handing over of a prescription; generally a morally neutral act. What turns this otherwise value-free action into a crime? It cannot surely be the foresight that the patient will use this to bring about their death, unless we concede that foresight and intention are equivalent; a position vehemently disputed by those who oppose legalisation. In fact, of course, the two both can and should be equated, leading to the conclusion that each should either be tolerated or not; drawing distinctions between the two – as opponents would want to do – merely sustains a distinction without a difference. Nor can it be the fact that the act of handing over the prescription may result in death; doctors are not infrequently involved in bringing about the death of their patients.

Failing to recognise that withholding/withdrawing treatment, respecting competent refusals of treatment, and active assistance in dying are essentially facets of the same ethical plane drives a wedge between logic and principle. Those who are unwilling to recognise this doubtless do so in good faith but, while free to hold their own position, need to consider what justification, if any, there may be for imposing it on others. Orentlicher also adds that this distinction ignores the fact that 'many treatment withdrawals reflect an intent to die. . . . When physicians discontinue life-sustaining treatment for these patients, they are doing so to facilitate an intent to die'.[54]

Moreover, we must also be concerned that the law is inconsistent in how it approaches these extremely important decisions. Forcing someone to survive against their own considered preferences is an insult to the respect owed to that person, particularly when based on reasoning which is at best arguable and at worst inherently flawed and seems designed to reinforce an ideologically biased policy rather than to vindicate rights. As Rachels says:

> There are times when the protection of human life has no point, and the western tradition has had difficulty acknowledging this. The noble ideal of 'protecting human life' is invoked even when the life involved does the subject no good and even when it is not wanted.[55]

It is surely time that we recognised this. The number of people who would want to have assisted dying may be small, but their suffering is real and when their competence is not in question, their choice for death should be respected, even if it involves direct assistance.

---

53 Gunderson, M and Mayo, D J, 'Restricting Physician-Assisted Death to the Terminally Ill', (2000) 30 *Hastings Center Report* No 6, 17–23, at p 22.
54 Orentlicher, op. cit. at p 35.
55 Rachels, J, *At the End of Life: Euthanasia and Morality*, 1986, Oxford University Press, at p 24.

It is easy to see why there might be some *personal* difference perceived between killing and letting die; that is, those involved, or likely to be involved, might prefer to withhold or withdraw treatment rather than helping someone to die more directly, for example by delivering a lethal injection. Indeed, in research conducted by myself and a colleague some ten years ago, when asked, if one or other was legalised which would they prefer, our respondents (about 1,000 doctors and pharmacists) would prefer legalisation of assisted suicide by a 2:1 margin over voluntary euthanasia.[56] This seems to suggest that even those who would be prepared to assist in the death of a patient would prefer to be involved only indirectly. Interestingly, as an aside, the public's position was exactly the opposite – by the same margin, they would prefer voluntary euthanasia to assisted suicide.

However, personal preferences – while interesting – are not definitive of the morality of the issue. As Battin argues:

> ... we must recognise that the distinction between killing and letting die does not succeed in carrying the moral weight often placed on it. Even if it were always possible to draw clear conceptual lines between the two, the conceptual distinction almost always brings along with it an unjustified moral distinction in the bargain. For example, to describe a procedure as 'mercy killing' invites the inference that because it involves killing it is wrong; this is to take the moral baggage along with the conceptual distinction, though the inference does not follow. To claim that it is permissible to let new born infants die, if their defects are so severe that they cannot survive, but not to kill them, is also to beg the question; one cannot assume that in such cases killing is worse than letting die. Rather, each such issue needs to be argued on its own merits, and the conceptual distinction between killing and letting die cannot do all the work instead.[57]

On this view, the *outcome* is what should be considered rather than the *means* by which it is brought about. Thus, for example, whether a patient refuses life-sustaining treatment or asks for assistance in dying, the morality of the event should be judged not by the fact that death is the consequence but rather on how we categorise the behaviour itself. This view can be contrasted with the views of the House of Lords Select Committee on Medical Ethics, which, reporting in 1994, claimed that 'the right to refuse medical treatment is far removed from the right to request assistance in dying'.[58]

56 For discussion see McLean, S A M and Britton, A, *Sometimes a Small Victory*, 1996, Glasgow: Institute of Law and Ethics in Medicine.
57 Battin, op. cit. at p 19.
58 House of Lords Select Committee on Medical Ethics, *Report of the House of Lords Select Committee on Medical Ethics*, HL Paper 21-1, 1994, para 236.

Battin, on the other hand, makes a philosophical attempt to equiparate killing and letting die – or at least to argue that one is not necessarily always morally different from the other – as opposed to the more formal, legalistic attempt by the House of Lords Select Committee to maintain some kind of distinction between them. Although few, if any, of us look upon death as a friend, there are some for whom it may appear that way. The criminal law at least has accepted that it is either futile or inappropriate to prosecute people who commit or attempt suicide. However, for some individuals, either circumstances or psychology may prevent them from exercising the choice to commit suicide. This will be of particular significance for those whose decisions are contextualised within a clinical setting because they already suffer from a particular condition. One of the groups most protected against self-harm is those who are in hospital which, incidentally, is the most likely place for people to die in many parts of the modern world. Thus, those who would be technically free to commit suicide were they in a non-clinical setting will be actively prevented from so doing once they come under the care of healthcare professionals. This situation is described by Illich in this way:

> Traditionally the person best protected from death was the one whom society had condemned to die. Society felt threatened that the man on Death Row might use his tie to hang himself. Authority might be challenged if he took his life before the appointed hour. Today, the man best protected against setting the stage for his own dying is the sick person in critical condition. Society, acting through the medical system, decides when and after what indignities and mutilations he shall die. The medicalization of society has brought the epoch of natural death to an end. Western man has lost the right to preside at his act of dying. Health, or the autonomous power to cope, has been expropriated down to the last breath. Technical death has won its victory over dying. Mechanical death has conquered and destroyed all other deaths.[59]

It can, of course, be argued that healthcare professionals merely carry out their duty of care in preventing suicide; that is, their obligation to prevent harm from coming to their patients requires careful attention to life preservation, not to facilitating their suicidal intentions. Thus, arguably, healthcare professionals could be said to have an obligation to prevent people from exercising a choice for death. Therefore, for those who are psychologically, physically or situationally incapable of committing suicide, this argument runs that it should be unlawful for doctors or other healthcare professionals to be complicit should they choose to end their lives. Interestingly, not even those

---

59   Illich, I, *Limits to Medicine. Medical Nemesis: The Expropriation of Health*, 1975, London and New York: Marion Boyars, at pp 207–208.

most opposed to the legalisation of assisted suicide would necessarily regard this as being the most appropriate or the best outcome. Finnis, for example, who is a committed opponent of legalisation, suggests that:

> When one does not know that the requests are suicidal in intent, one can rightly, as a health care professional or as someone responsible for the care of people give full effect to request to withhold specified treatment or indeed any and all treatment, even when one considers the request misguided and regrettable. For one is entitled and indeed ought to honour these peoples' autonomy and can reasonable accept their death as a side effect of doing so.[60]

However, he then proceeds to make a distinction between 'suicide' and 'requests for assistance in dying':

> ... suicide and requests which one understands to be requests for assistance in suicide are a very different matter. It is mere self-deception to regard the choice to kill oneself as a 'self-regarding' decision with no impact on the well-being of people to whom one has duties in justice. ...
> If one is really exercising autonomy in choosing to kill oneself, or in inviting or demanding that others assist one to do so or themselves take steps to terminate one's life, one will be proceeding on one or both of two philosophically and morally erroneous judgments: (i) that human life in certain conditions or circumstances retains no intrinsic value and dignity; and/or (ii) that the world would be a better place if one's life were intentionally terminated.[61]

With respect, his argument here seems to hinge on somewhat obtuse reasoning. For example, it suggests that patients can legitimately choose a course of action that will knowingly and deliberately bring about their death, only so long as they do not actively intend to die – but are passively permitted to do so! Quite apart from the inherent problems with this contention, it is not explained just how doctors are to make this decision or on what grounds – nor indeed what is their qualification for doing so.

Moreover, Finnis proposes that the apparent autonomy of the decision to request assistance in suicide rests on what he calls 'philosophically and morally erroneous judgements'.[62] This arguable proposition points to one of the weaknesses of the attempt to distinguish between the situations

---

60 Finnis, J, 'A philosophical case against euthanasia', in Keown, J (ed), *Euthanasia Examined: Ethical, Clinical and Legal Perspectives*, 1995, Cambridge University Press, (reprinted 1999) pp 23–35, at p 33.

61 Ibid. pp 33–34.

62 Ibid.

under discussion here. It is perfectly possible to seek an autonomous right to end one's life, with or without assistance, without believing either of the propositions Finnis uses to explain why such decisions are 'philosophically and morally erroneous'. Equally, there is nothing inherently bizarre, wrong or objectionable in believing either or both of them. In other words, even if one does believe them, these are still perfectly reasonable positions to adopt given a particular set of circumstances and to suggest, as Finnis seems to, that somehow this makes them philosophically erroneous is to take the underpinning philosophy to which he holds and seek to impose it on others who do not share that perspective. Believing that one's own life is no longer of value, or that the world would be a better place if one were dead, can be perfectly legitimate, intelligent and rational; failure to accept this is inimical to respect for the persons themselves.

Moreover, although Finnis and others who agree with him would want to argue that suicide in and of itself is wrong, they do not deny that sometimes a choice that results in death is intelligible; even acceptable. However, they rest their case on the view that there is some morally significant distinction between killing and letting die that justifies rejection of one and tolerance of the other. This seems to be based on the idea that people should be prevented from preferring and/or choosing death, perhaps because of the claim that all suffering can be relieved – which has already been discounted – or, more likely, on the basis that life is a gift from God which man should not be allowed to reject. What is morally superior about dying from a pre-existing illness, or the refusal of life-sustaining treatment, rather than choosing the time of one's own death is obscure at best. The distinction between the cases is vanishingly small, if indeed it exists at all.

However, despite what has gone before, the distinction between acts and omissions seems to have been given credibility in law as well as by some commentators. This, however, fails to take account of the fact that:

> Patients request physician-assisted suicide for the same reasons that they refuse life-saving treatment: they want control over when they die, where they die, and their physical and mental state at the time of their death. The principle of self-determination demands that the State respect the individual's judgment about how much pain he wishes to tolerate before death, unless there are overriding public policy interests. Recognising a right to die with assistance also furthers the policy of giving patients control over the course of their medical treatment: this right not only gives terminally-ill patients another option, but it also removes a substantial disincentive for refusing life-saving care, that is, the fear of lengthy uncontrolled suffering prior to death.[63]

63 Notes (1991–1992), at p 2026.

We have already seen that some commentators hold that there is a significant moral difference between acting to bring about a death and passively
allowing someone to die, with the moral preference falling on the side of
'letting die'. As we have also seen, others would argue that such differences
are imaginary; indeed, that it is less moral to bring about death in a protracted,
potentially painful and distressing way than it would be to bring about death
'cleanly' and speedily. Yet, nonetheless, many still wish to maintain this
distinction. Tom Sackville, then Parliamentary Under-Secretary of State for
Health, said that:

> It is essential to draw a clear distinction between euthanasia, which is
> a positive intervention to end life, and the withholding or withdrawal
> of treatment that has no curative or beneficial effect. The question of
> whether to withhold treatment from someone who is not benefiting
> from it is different from euthanasia, although it raises similar moral
> and ethical questions.[64]

Like others who hold to this position, while conceding that there are
'similar moral and ethical questions' in the two cases, he does not explain why
these similarities should not form the basis for our approach to end-of-life
decisions. In other words, like a number of other commentators, he focuses
on the – contrived – differences rather than on the similarities between the
two situations. Quite why this is a legitimate position to adopt is unclear,
particularly when one analyses just what these differences might be. It might
be accepted by everyone that the outcome, death, is the same, and if we do
not follow the dubious argument that disconnecting a ventilator or failing to
provide ANH, for example, can be categorised as an omission when – in many
cases – it clearly involves an act in common-sense terms, then we are left with
intention as being the moral touchstone of the permissibility of the behaviour.
Thus, it might be argued, the doctor who withholds or withdraws treatment
does so not with the intention that the patient dies, but rather only with the
knowledge or foresight that this will be the outcome. This leads to one further
argument in this area: the extent to which intention and foresight can or should
be separated.

Double effect

This distinction is central to the doctrine of double effect, which broadly
speaking allows that a 'bad' outcome can be tolerated when it is brought about
unintentionally by an act which is otherwise good. Thus, it is permissible to
provide massive doses of analgesia, which might result in a patient's death,

so long as the intention is to alleviate pain and not to bring about death, even though that death is foreseen. The difference between intention and foresight is therefore central to the applicability of this doctrine, which is supported by some religions and by the law in the United Kingdom.[65] However, on a moral basis it seems difficult to argue that there is any meaningful difference. If death is the 'bad' consequence which is to be avoided except when it is inevitable, then knowing – or foreseeing – that one's behaviour will result in a death brings about an equally 'bad' result. Furthermore, this assumes that death, however it occurs, is always a bad thing and fails to take account both of its inevitability and, in the case of a chosen death, its perceived desirability. The decision as to whether or not death is to be preferred surely rests with the individual. Therefore, the outcome – for the person – is not a 'bad' outcome, nor is it always 'bad' that death occurs. If so, then the principle of double effect adds little if anything to the debate; rather it serves to obfuscate, not enlighten.

From a legal perspective, the difference between intention and foreseeability rests on highly dubious grounds, even although it has been used in the past by UK courts and is insisted upon by some moral philosophers. In the case of *R v Woollin*,[66] on the other hand, the court held that where an outcome is virtually certain – foreseeable – then it legally qualifies as being intentional. This judgement seems to shake the foundations of the acceptability of the doctrine of double effect, which has traditionally been used to excuse certain life-ending behaviour while at the same time criminalising that which has death as an intended rather than a foreseen outcome.[67] This doctrine is also open to philosophical dispute. As Dickenson says, '[s]ome bioethicists and most supporters of euthanasia, regard the doctrine of double effect as a hypocritical remnant of Catholic moral theology', although noting that 'it is accepted by many practitioners'.[68]

Doctors who remove assisted nutrition and hydration, or who fail to provide life-saving treatment, must surely be 'virtually certain' that the outcome of so doing will be the death of the patient. Are we to criminalise their behaviour too? Frankly, were we to do so, modern medicine would be in crisis, especially in the case of those caring for the acutely or terminally ill and on intensive care wards. As we have seen, Williams seeks to use this conclusion as a reason for maintaining the difference between act and omission, and it has already been argued that this is not necessary; we can simply re-categorise or re-label the behaviour in question, especially if it is accepted that they are morally equivalent and that neither is inherently 'bad'.

65   *R v Adams* [1957] Crim LR 365.
66   [1999] 1 AC 82.
67   *R v Adams* [1957] Crim LR 365.
68   Dickenson, D L, 'Are medical ethicists out of touch? Practitioner attitudes in the US and the UK towards decisions at the end of life', *Journal of Medical Ethics*, 2000: 26: 254–60, at p 257.

Her approach is equally unsatisfactory in relation to double effect. We only adopt this sophistic approach because we are reluctant to agree that killing and letting die can be morally equivalent and therefore each can be acceptable in some circumstances. This merely liberates doctors knowingly to assist patients to die – whether or not they want to – without exposing them to the critical searchlight of the law; it does nothing to clarify the morality of the behaviour in question nor does it manifest respect for the person. In addition, it must not be forgotten that doctors, who are as we have seen required to accede to a competent refusal of life-sustaining treatment, are also aware that in so doing they are assisting their patient to die. Doctors who accept treatment refusal and who withhold or withdraw life-sustaining treatment, like it or not, are complicit in a death, and in some cases that death will have been chosen. There would appear, therefore, to be a very fine line – if there is one at all – between a variety of medical practices which result in death; not in terms of causation and not in terms of intention.

This is an important point, which seems to have been accepted by the House of Lords. In the leading case of *Airedale NHS Trust v Bland* [69] (see p 116) the court did not shirk from the reality that the actual intention behind the declaration being sought was to bring about death. In a commentary on this case, Price notes that '[t]he House of Lords considered that the physicians involved *did* possess the requisite intention to kill'.[70] He concludes, then, that '[d]eath and not just the withholding of food or other treatment is intended in these treatment refusal cases . . .'.[71] Otlowski also contends that '[t]the distinction between active and passive euthanasia and the underlying acts and omissions doctrine is most problematic and unsatisfactory . . . the distinction is of debatable moral and philosophical significance'.[72] Orentlicher further points out that '. . . we cannot assume for any *particular* act or omission that there is or is not moral culpability. In some cases, an omission is as reprehensible as an act'.[73] Finally, Jackson suggests that '[t]he doctrine of double effect, with its emphasis upon the doctor's intention, offers a particularly stark illustration of the law's tendency to adopt the perspective of the medical practitioner'.[74] It also, of course, makes presumptions about the proper role of medicine. Hilliard, notes that:

Applying the principle of double effect seems to assume that physicians should never intend death. But asserting that physicians should never

69 (1993) 12 BMLR 64.
70 Price, (1996), pp 282–283.
71 Ibid.
72 Otlowski, M F A, *Voluntary Euthanasia and the Common Law*, 1997, Oxford: Clarendon Press, at p 12.
73 Orentlicher, op. cit. at p 30.
74 Jackson, op. cit. at p 435.

intend death involves presuppositions regarding the proper goals of medicine that may not be warranted given the circumstances in which terminally ill, suffering patients often find themselves.[75]

On this argument, double effect is, or should be, contextual in nature. That is, bringing about some deaths is not a 'bad' outcome that requires us to utilise the somewhat convoluted reasoning of this principle. In effect, the use of double effect is inappropriate in these circumstances. While it might assuage the consciences of doctors, it has no morally relevant role in certain – perhaps the majority of – cases. In any case, the practical applicability of the doctrine must surely be brought into contention, following the claim of a leading palliative care specialist that '[s]ymptom control is a science. Morphine and other drugs given appropriately at the end of life do not shorten life. . . . Morphine may even prolong life by ensuring that patients are comfortable and not exhausted through intractable symptoms'.[76] This contention, which was made by Baroness Finlay as she introduced the Palliative Care Bill into the House of Lords on 16 November 2006, arguably makes it impossible to defend the doctrine of double effect on any pragmatic – as well as theoretical – basis. If patients die as a result of the provision of morphine or other analgesia then, according to Baroness Finlay, it cannot have been administered 'appropriately'. That being so, presumably this 'inappropriate' provision would be culpable, and double effect would not be available as a justification.

Causation

A final area for consideration relates to the question of causation: the necessary link between the act, or omission, and the outcome. Callahan, for example, suggests that '[t]hough the result of killing and allowing to die may be the same in one way – a patient is dead in either case – that hardly means that the causal difference between the two incidents is morally irrelevant'.[77] However, as we have already seen, this argument rests on relatively weak foundations. If there is no difference in outcome, and if foreseeability and intention can be equated, then there is no basis from which to assert that there is a moral difference between the two. Presumably, however, Callahan means to suggest that when 'allowing to die' is proposed, the death does not result from a direct link between the doctor's behaviour and the outcome. However, while it may be that in some cases the person does die because of a pre-existing condition,

---

75 Hilliard, B, *The US Supreme Court and Medical Ethics*, 2004, St Paul, MN: Paragon, at p 333.

76 *Hansard*, Col 1275, (23 Feb 2007), available at http://www.publications.parliament.uk/pa/ld200607/ldhansrd/text/70223-0001.htm (accessed on 03/04/07).

77 Callahan, D, *The Troubled Dream of Life: In Search of a Peaceful Death*, 2000, Washington, DC: Georgetown University Press, at p 77.

in many cases the death brought about by omission is not directly caused by the underlying condition; it is quite clearly associated with the omission itself, just as it would be in a death brought about by an act. Patients such as Anthony Bland do not die of PVS; they die because nutrition and hydration have been removed. PVS is not in itself a terminal condition – patients who are nourished and hydrated can live for many years in that condition. We seek to disguise this by saying, for example, that an omission merely permits 'nature to take its course'. Moreover, in legal terms causation is not a matter of philosophical debate. Rather, it is 'a question of policy, not mechanical connection'.[78] On this approach, assisted deaths are not fundamentally different from those resulting from withholding or withdrawing medical treatment:

> Distinguishing physician-assisted suicide from the withdrawal of treatment on the basis of causation fails, because causation, in the right-to-die context, depends on whether the physician owes a duty to the patient, which is itself a policy question. To say that the patient's illness, rather than the withdrawal of life-sustaining treatment 'causes' the patient's death simply means that a court will not hold the physician liable for the death.[79]

Moreover, in the case of withholding/withdrawing and requests for assisted dying, '[i]n each case, the patient's interest in self-determination gives the patient a right to die, whether by refusing treatment, having treatment withdrawn, or accepting the assistance of a physician'.[80] Grayling asserts that 'withholding treatment is an act based on a decision, just as giving treatment is an act, based on a decision'.[81]

Conclusion

It can be seen, therefore, that none of the efforts to draw fine distinctions in order to separate different forms of ending of life from each other succeeds in doing so satisfactorily. Indeed, despite this alleged difference being routinely used by courts, at least two judges in the House of Lords in the *Bland* case[82] (see p 116) expressed their concern about using the alleged difference between acts and omissions as a yardstick for their decision. Lord Browne-Wilkinson, for example conceded that

> . . . the conclusion that I have reached will appear to some to be almost irrational. How can it be lawful to allow a patient to die slowly, though

---

78 Notes (1991–1992) pp 2001–2029.
79 Ibid.
80 Ibid. p 2040.
81 Grayling, A C, 'Right to die', (2005) 330 *British Medical Journal*, 799, at p 799.
82 *Airedale NHS Trust v Bland* (1993) 12 BMLR 64.

painlessly, over a period of weeks from lack of food but unlawful to produce his immediate death by a lethal injection, thereby saving his family from yet another ordeal to add to the tragedy that has already struck them? I find it difficult to find a moral answer to that question. But it is undoubtedly the law. . . .[83]

It is scarcely surprising that he should have had such a difficulty. Indeed, in the same case, Lord Mustill described himself as experiencing 'acute unease' about using the acts and omissions distinction to reach the conclusion that Anthony Bland could die. He explained his unease by saying that it was 'due in an important part to the sensation that however much the terminologies may differ, the ethical status of the two courses of action is for all relevant purposes indistinguishable'.[84] In reaching his judgment, he further expressed his concern that the decision 'may only emphasise the distortions of the legal structure which is already both morally and intellectually misshapen'.[85]

It would seem, therefore, that even some of our most distinguished judges are unhappy about using the purported acts and omissions distinction as an ethical and/or a legal device to find a way to resolve issues at the end of life. If this distinction is suspect in cases where patients have no input, it seems to be if anything more suspect when patients themselves are requesting the right to die at a time of their own choosing. In other words, although we seem to be prepared to make death-inducing decisions on behalf of those who cannot express their own views, we are prepared to use the acts/omissions distinction to avoid legitimising the choices of people who have made their own decisions. Given this, quite why it should be that it is permissible to facilitate death in a patient who is not able to ask for it and yet impermissible in the case of a patient who does competently ask for it is one of the mysteries of this entire debate. Moreover, double effect is open to serious challenge and, while it might comfort some people involved in the death of another, it is scarcely more than a smokescreen. Finally, the argument based in causation also fails, leaving opponents with little credibility – in as much as their position depends on any of these arguments.

Some personal choices for death, therefore, are vindicated in law – and in ethics – even where it is absolutely clear precisely what is being chosen. The primary rationale for acceptance where it occurs is the value ascribed to autonomy, which assumes competence. Whereas, however, the autonomy of Mrs Pretty was thwarted, that of Ms B was given legal effect. Yet, apart from the fact that Ms B required what might be termed only passive assistance to end her life, each woman apparently made the same, competent choice to have her life ended. Of course it is true that in some cases an apparent choice for

83 Ibid. at p 131.
84 Ibid. at p 132.
85 Ibid.

death might be driven by external or internal pressure, but this is true whether the decision is to reject treatment or to seek help in dying. Indeed, Jackson suggests that

> ... in so far as there is a risk that patients might opt for a course of action that will result in their death out of a sense of obligation, or as a result of more direct pressure, this must be equally or perhaps even more true when death is achieved by treatment withdrawal.[86]

Most particularly, as Dworkin points out, if the fear is that doctors, or others, can manipulate an individual into 'choosing' death this is no less true when the cause of the death is treatment withdrawal or rejection, rather than an act to bring it about. Even if we believe that pressure may come from the wider society, for example people perceiving themselves as a burden or prolonging life is seen as too expensive, '[i]f the patient's death is cheaper for the system, then it is cheaper whether the patient commits suicide or is withdrawn from a life-support system'.[87]

In conclusion, it can be said that assisted dying is effectively equivalent to withholding and withdrawing treatment. The patient in each case is asserting an autonomy-based claim to have their choices at the end of life respected – at least where they are involved in the decision. Equally, refusing life-sustaining treatment is one further way in which end-of-life decisions can be manifested, even although in each case the intended and foreseen outcome is the patient's death. Despite attempts to distinguish between these examples in order to disguise their similarities, it remains true, in logic if not in policy, that each of them is an act or an event with the same outcome.[88] Therefore, while '[a] mentally competent patient has an absolute right to refuse to consent to medical treatment for any reason, rational or irrational, or for no reason at all, even where that decision, may lead to his or her own death . . .',[89] an equally competent patient cannot achieve the same outcome simply because s/he needs active help. This is despite the fact that it has been held in the UK's highest civil court that in the event of conflict, 'the principle of the sanctity of human life must yield to the principle of self-determination . . .'.[90]

There are other groups whose death may be brought about knowingly and deliberately without – in many cases – their opinion having been sought. Consideration of these groups will be undertaken in the next chapter. Although

86 Jackson, op. cit. at p 429.
87 Dworkin, G, 'Public policy and physician-assisted suicide', in Dworkin, G, Frey, R G and Bok, S, *Euthanasia and Physician-Assisted Suicide: For and Against*, 1998, Cambridge University Press, pp 64–80, at p 67.
88 Grayling, (2000), at p 799.
89 *Re MB* (1997) 38 BMLR 175, at p 182.
90 *Airedale NHS Trust v Bland* (1993) 12 BMLR 64, at p 112 (per Lord Goff).

I indicated at the beginning of this book that my argument concerned the competent adult person, it would be remiss not to consider others whose death is brought about without reference to their wishes, because these cases point even more clearly to the problems which have been illustrated in this and the previous chapters. In any case, when we concede that there is a difference between acts and omissions and when we accept the principle of double effect, we do not enhance protection for those who are vulnerable. In fact, this makes them more rather than less open to the potential for abuse. Those who are, or might be thought of as, vulnerable are not assisted by drawing a veil over the reality of what is happening. Indeed, we might be more cautious in our treatment of them if we accept that what is being done is *in fact* designed to bring about their death.

Chapter 4

Choosing death for others

We have seen in the previous chapter that in some cases people are allowed to choose to die – in part by characterising the act bringing about that death as an omission. However, the requests of other competent people to have their choice for an assisted death will not be respected as long as assisted dying is unlawful. I have proposed that there is in reality no difference between requests for the termination of life-sustaining treatment and those for an actively assisted death: neither in terms of intention nor in causation. Therefore, the rationale for the legal distinction between these cases must be highly dubious and the justification for differential treatment is absent. Of course, it might be said, the real difference rests on respect for the sanctity of all life; that by removing treatment we are simply 'letting nature take its course'. However, this argument, as I have suggested, fails to convince. In any case, a mere glance at the reality of end-of-life decisions is sufficient to demonstrate that we do not in fact always respect the sanctity of all life, and this is true not only in situations where the person refuses treatment but also where the person cannot express an opinion about life and death either because of their clinical condition or because of their age.

Given what may seem to be an anomalous rather than a principled position, this chapter will reflect on the fact that in some cases death can be brought about not on the request of the person him or herself but rather based on the opinions and choices of others, whether doctors, families or courts. If there are sustainable objections to legalising assisted dying I have already suggested that they disappear in the face of a competent decision by the individual, yet in the cases to be discussed in this chapter that justification is absent. How then can it be that we deny people a chosen death yet are – legally and ethically – apparently content, or at worst reconciled, to terminate the lives of the incompetent?

Permanent vegetative state

The paradigmatic example of this question relates to patients who are in what is now called a permanent (rather than persistent) vegetative state

(PVS). These patients have irrevocably lost the capacity to communicate, to feed themselves or to experience pleasure or pain. First described over 30 years ago by Jennet and Plum,[1] PVS entails the loss of higher brain function. The brain stem, however, remains intact, meaning that patients can survive with appropriate care for as long as they do not succumb to another life-threatening condition – for example, an untreated or untreatable infection. Survival, of course, depends most critically on the provision of nutrition and hydration by mechanical means, since the patient will be unable to swallow or otherwise ingest food and liquid. Although recent evidence has emerged that some patients diagnosed as being in PVS may in fact show cortical activity,[2] in what follows I will assume that the diagnosis has been correctly made.

The first and most important case of this sort to be considered by a court in the United Kingdom was that of *Airedale NHS Trust v Bland*.[3] The significance of this case is reflected in the fact that it ultimately reached the most senior civil court in the country – the House of Lords. As is well known, the case concerned a young man – Anthony Bland – who was injured and deprived of oxygen in a football stadium disaster. He was subsequently diagnosed as being in a PVS and the hospital trust, with the support of Anthony's parents and two independent doctors, petitioned the court to authorise removal of the nasogastric nutrition and hydration. The question to be resolved by the various courts which heard this case was whether or not it could ever be lawful to remove this means of survival from a patient. Although ultimately the House of Lords concluded that it would be lawful to withdraw the assisted nutrition and hydration, their Lordships used a variety of routes to reach that decision which are worth considering in some detail.

Lord Keith focused his attention in particular on the argument put forward that assisted nutrition and hydration did not amount to medical treatment, but was rather 'simply feeding indistinguishable from feeding by normal means'.[4] This, however, he found unpersuasive. Rather, he concluded, we should look at the entire regime that was keeping Anthony Bland alive, which included, but was not confined to, assisted nutrition and hydration (ANH). While accepting that it would normally be unacceptable for healthcare professionals to fail to provide nutrition and hydration, in this case there was 'a large body of informed and responsible medical opinion . . . to the effect that no benefit at all would be conferred by continuance'.[5] He concluded, therefore, that the decision about its provision was a matter for the healthcare professionals looking after Anthony.

1   Jennet, B and Plum, F, 'Persistent vegetative state after brain damage: a syndrome in search of a name', *The Lancet*, 1 April 1972, pp 734–737.
2   For a full discussion of PVS see Mason, J K, and Laurie, G T, *Mason and McCall Smith's Law and Medical Ethics*, 7th edn, 2005, Oxford University Press, Chapter 16.
3   (1993) 12 BMLR 64.
4   Ibid. at p 106.
5   Ibid. at p 107.

Lord Goff, while accepting that Anthony was legally alive, nonetheless described his condition as a 'living death'.[6] He noted that, although the principle of the sanctity of life was fundamental, it was not absolute. In this case, he argued, 'there is no absolute rule that the patient's life must be prolonged . . . regardless of the circumstances'.[7] However, he was at pains to draw a distinction between withdrawing treatment and administering a lethal injection. Although the outcome would be the same – the death of the patient – for Lord Goff, the two were different classes of behaviour. The first could lawfully form a part of medical judgement; the latter was always a crime. In order to justify this Lord Goff accepted that withdrawing treatment amounted to an omission, whereas administering a lethal injection was an act. This is an important distinction since it is a general rule that we are culpable for our acts but not our omissions.

However, whatever the debate around this question, it is arguably a distinction without a difference when a duty of care exists between the parties concerned. Thus, it was not sufficient simply to reach a conclusion as to whether or not removing the ANH was an act or an omission; it was also necessary to consider whether or not Anthony's doctors could reasonably be held to owe him a duty to maintain his existence. If such a duty existed, then the 'omission' to continue providing ANH would be of equivalent status to a deliberate act. The decision about whether or not such a duty existed rested substantially on an assessment of what was in the patient's best interests; a test which was described as 'broad and flexible'.[8] However, Lord Goff was also at pains to stress that he was not approaching this question from the perspective that it could be said to be in someone's best interests to die; a caveat which was essential if he was to avoid the conclusion that, if it could be in someone's interest to die, this could also be true in other cases – for example, when someone seeks an assisted death. Thus, he concluded, that in Anthony's case, 'the question is not whether it is in the best interests of the patient that he should die. The question is whether it is in the best interests of the patient that his life should be prolonged . . .'.[9] For Lord Goff this question was answered in the negative. Indeed doubt was expressed about whether or not it would be lawful to *continue* to provide treatment to Anthony in the absence of his consent. Normally, of course, treatment without consent would amount to an assault. However, non-consensual treatment is permissible where consent cannot be obtained and the purpose of the treatment is to prevent deterioration or improve the patient's condition.[10] In the case of a person in PVS there is, of course, no possibility of improvement, but it could certainly be argued that

---

6 Ibid. at p 111.
7 Ibid.
8 Per Lord Goff at p 121.
9 Per Lord Goff at p 115.
10 Using the principle of necessity.

the continued provision of ANH would serve to prevent deterioration in Anthony's condition.

In this case some of their Lordships did not consider this possibility, preferring rather that the test which emanated from the case of *Bolam v Friern Hospital Management Committee*[11] be used to evaluate the clinical behaviour under consideration, and therefore the patient's best interests. The so-called Bolam Test basically holds that where a doctor has acted in a manner which is accepted as reasonable by a responsible body of medical opinion, then s/he will not be negligent. Although this test has been subsequently amended,[12] it remains essentially intact. Basically, the test was designed as a tool to evaluate purely clinical matters, such as the quality of treatment provided, although over the years its use was expanded to include broader matters such as the quantity and quality of information provided to a patient.[13]

Although commending itself to some of their Lordships as a way of evaluating what the patient's interests would be, as the basis for discovering whether or not a duty of care existed, the Bolam Test has been widely criticised, even when its use is confined to what might be called 'standard' negligence cases.[14] How much more problematic is the use of this test to decide on matters of life and death?[15] Indeed, in the *Bland* case, Lord Mustill, while accepting that the Bolam Test was appropriate in matters of 'diagnosis, prognosis and appraisal of the patient's cognitive functions . . .',[16] also concluded that 'there is no reason in logic why on such a decision the opinion of doctors should be decisive'.[17]

Lord Lowry agreed with the analysis of his colleagues and further concluded that withdrawing treatment should be seen as indistinguishable from not providing it in the first place. Failure to accept this, he argued, would be perverse, since

> such a distinction could quite illogically confer on a doctor who had refrained from treatment an immunity which did not benefit a doctor who had embarked on treatment in order to see whether it might help the patient and had abandoned the treatment when it was seen not to do so.[18]

11 [1957] 2 All ER 118.
12 *Bolitho v Hackney Health Authority* (1998) 39 BMLR 1; *Pearce v United Bristol Healthcare NHS Trust* (1999) 48 BMLR 118.
13 *Gold v Haringey Health Authority* [1987] 2 All ER 888.
14 For discussion, see McLean, S A M, *A Patient's Right to Know: Information Disclosure, the Doctor and the Law*, 1989, Aldershot: Dartmouth.
15 For a discussion, see Laurie, G T and Mason, J K, 'Negative treatment of vulnerable patients: euthanasia by any other name?', *Juridical Review*, Part 3, 2000, 159–178.
16 (1993) 12 BMLR 64 at p 143.
17 Ibid.
18 Ibid. at p 121.

Moreover, Lord Lowry expressed the view that:

> Even though the intention to bring about the patient's death is there, there is no proposed guilty act because, if it is not in the interests of an insentient patient to continue the life-supporting care and treatment, the doctor would be acting unlawfully if he continued the care and treatment and would perform no guilty act by discontinuing.[19]

Perhaps the most interesting and thought-provoking judgments came from Lords Browne-Wilkinson and Mustill. Each of them took an arguably broader view of the decision they were being asked to make. Lord Browne-Wilkinson, for example, clearly stated that 'behind the questions of law lie moral, ethical, medical and practical issues of fundamental importance to society'.[20] The decision to be made was, therefore, bigger than a straightforward legal one, engaging as it did with a variety of other social and ethical considerations. Indeed, it was clear that decisions about best interests concerned very much more than a person's best medical interests, thus broadening the kinds of issues which could and should be taken into consideration. In addition, Lord Browne-Wilkinson questioned whether it was for judges or for Parliament to 'reach its decisions on the underlying and practical problems . . .',[21] concluding that it was for Parliament. Nonetheless, he accepted that the House of Lords was obliged to reach a conclusion in the absence of relevant legislation. He also asked how it could be acceptable to dehydrate someone to death when it would not be so to help him die quickly by, for example, administering a lethal injection, particularly since it was clear that 'the whole purpose of stopping artificial feeding is to bring about the death of Anthony Bland'?[22]

Lord Browne-Wilkinson was, however, persuaded that failing to provide continued nutrition and hydration was an omission rather than an act. In fact, he argued that even if the removal of the feeding tube could be considered an act, it could not be regarded as a positive act bringing about death as the 'tube itself, without the food being supplied through it, does nothing'.[23] He also agreed that, if it was not in Anthony's best interests to continue to be fed, then his doctors could not lawfully continue to treat him without his consent. He concluded, therefore, that '[u]nless the doctor has reached the affirmative conclusion that it is in the patient's best interest to continue the invasive care, such care must cease'.[24] Given his concern about the proper role for the courts in such cases, he resorted to existing principles, derived as we have

---

19 Ibid. at p 123.
20 Ibid. at p 124.
21 Ibid.
22 Ibid. at p 127.
23 Ibid. at p 128.
24 Ibid. at p 129.

seen from the case of *Bolam v Friern Hospital Management Committee*,[25] and reached the view that 'the court's only concern will be to be satisfied that the doctor's decision to discontinue is in accordance with a respectable body of medical opinion and that it is reasonable'.[26] It may seem paradoxical that, having started his judgment by noting that the problem was extremely wide and was not simply able to be categorised as a legal or a medical matter, Lord Browne-Wilkinson ultimately rested a significant part of his decision on a test which relies so heavily on medical opinion or practice and which has been so regularly criticised.

Lord Mustill also expressed his concern about the decision the court was being asked to reach, because the 'authority of the state, through the medium of the court, is being invoked to permit one group of its citizens to terminate the life of another'.[27] The case, he declared, raised 'acute problems of ethics',[28] but also was 'exceptionally difficult in point of law . . .'.[29] Interestingly, however, Lord Mustill was not comfortable taking the route which some of his colleagues had adopted; namely, basing his judgment on the distinction between acts and omissions. Indeed, as we have seen, he felt extremely uncomfortable using this alleged distinction because in his view it was not possible ethically to differentiate between them. Nor was he persuaded by the argument that it was not in Anthony Bland's best interests to continue the provision of nutrition and hydration. For Lord Mustill, while what the doctors proposed would alleviate the distress of his parents and caregivers, it made no sense to suggest that Anthony had any interest in this happening. As he said, '[t]he distressing truth which must not be shirked is that the proposed conduct is not in the best interests of Anthony Bland, for he has no best interests of any kind'.[30] The interests being served therefore were not those of Anthony. If so, it could be asked, how could it then be possible to evaluate the doctors' duties if they are so intimately connected to the concept of 'best interests'. Although more critical than the other judges of the question before the court, Lord Mustill was ultimately persuaded as follows:

> Now that the time has come when Anthony Bland has no further interest in being kept alive, the necessity to do so, created by his inability to make a choice, has gone; and the justification for the invasive care and treatment together with the duty to provide it have also gone. Absent a duty, the omission to perform what had previously been a duty will no longer be a breach of the criminal law.[31]

25 [1957] 2 All ER 118. The test derived from this case is referred to as the Bolam Test.
26 (1993) 12 BMLR 64 at p 130.
27 Ibid. at p 131.
28 Ibid.
29 Ibid.
30 Ibid. at p 141.
31 Ibid. at p 142.

From this somewhat lengthy discussion of the House of Lords judgment it is clear that the ultimate conclusion that assisted nutrition and hydration could be withdrawn from Anthony Bland was reached by a variety of routes, not all of them obviously compatible with each other. One thing, however, on which their Lordships were agreed was that subsequent decisions of this sort would require court authority. Only one year later, the courts were again invited to deal with a similar case, although in this case the hospital took advantage of the fact that a feeding tube had become dislodged and the court granted permission not to reconnect it.[32]

In Scotland, the first case to be presented to the courts was *Law Hospital NHS Trust v Lord Advocate*.[33] This case involved a woman, Janet Johnstone, who had lapsed into a PVS following an unsuccessful suicide attempt. In similar vein to the courts in the *Bland* case, the Inner House of the Court of Session concluded that the outcome should rest on the issue of best interests; of whether or not any benefit could be obtained from continuing ANH. However, the Scottish court went further than its English counterpart and indicated that court authority would not inevitably be needed when such decisions are to be taken. Following this, the Lord Advocate (Scotland's senior prosecuting officer) declared that no prosecution would follow if a doctor first obtained the authority of a court before discontinuing treatment, although equally he did not state that prosecution would necessarily follow should such approval not be obtained. This somewhat ambivalent position has been criticised by Mason and Laurie who argue that the 'situation has now arisen where the doctor may be required to second guess the criminal law – a position that is hardly desirable'.[34] Not only is this potentially problematic, it may also run counter to Article 6 of the European Convention of Human Rights which was incorporated into UK law by the Human Rights Act 1998. Article 6 guarantees the right to a fair hearing, and arguably in the absence of the impartial scrutiny of a court, this is denied to patients in PVS in Scotland. Nonetheless, in the leading case in which the human rights issue was raised (albeit that Article 6 was not referred to), the court held that discontinuation of assisted nutrition and hydration was indeed compatible with the terms of the Convention.

In *NHS Trust A v M* and *NHS Trust B v H*,[35] the court was invited to test the lawfulness of withdrawing ANH from two patients in PVS against a number of Convention Articles, specifically Article 2 (the right to life), Article 3 (the prohibition of cruel and inhuman treatment) and Article 8 (the right to respect for private and family life). In this case, the court declined to find that any of these rights had been breached. In respect of Article 2, the judge was of the opinion that 'the phrase "deprivation of life" must import a deliberate act, as

32 *Frenchay Healthcare NHS Trust v S* [1994] 2 All ER 403.
33 1996 SLT 848.
34 Mason and Laurie, op. cit. at p 590, para 16.128.
35 (2001) 58 BMLR 87.

opposed to an omission . . .'.[36] Very much in line with at least some of the judgments in *Bland*, the judge in this case held to the distinction between act and omission. As for Article 3, the judge held that for someone to be subject to cruel and inhuman treatment they must be able to experience it.[37] Clearly, patients in PVS were unable to do so; therefore, their Article 3 right was not breached. In terms of Article 8, the court held that the right to autonomy, which is protected by this Article, would in fact be breached by continuing unconsented to treatment. Mason and Laurie challenge this conclusion, arguing that '[t]he error lies in the failure to appreciate that it is *respect* for the human being that is required, not only (or necessarily) respect for her "right to choose"'.[38]

In a powerful critique of the two main PVS cases, Laurie and Mason describe the routes used to make the decisions as 'arguably hypocritical, dishonest, misleading, illogical and, as a result, questionable in moral and ethical terms'.[39] Whatever one's views about the reasoning which led to the deaths of Anthony Bland, Janet Johnstone and others, there is no doubt that many people would have believed that the right answer was reached, even if doubt surrounds the reasoning. Moreover, arguably the English requirement that cases should always be brought before a court was designed to offer an additional layer of protection for the incapacitated individual. However, subsequent decisions suggest that this has not been the case. Indeed, Mason and Laurie suggest that 'one cannot avoid the impression that the precedents laid down in these cases are being extended to include less well defined conditions than was intended at the time'.[40] While some might argue that this is precisely an example of the 'slippery slope' that they predict would result from legalisation of assisted dying, in fact it is a *result* of the current law, not an example of what might occur were the law to be changed to allow the vindication of competent choice.

Patients in 'near' PVS

The apparent desire to facilitate certain deaths but not others has resulted in the courts – generally on medical advice – taking upon themselves the task of effectively measuring quality of life in situations where the person him- or herself cannot express his or her own views. For example, in the case of *Re G (Adult Incompetent: Withdrawal of Treatment)*,[41] the court was asked

36   Ibid. at p 95.
37   Interestingly, this conclusion was challenged by Mr Justice Munby in the case of *R (on the application of Burke) v General Medical Council* (2004) 79 BMLR 126.
38   Mason and Laurie, op. cit. at p 587, para 16.117.
39   Laurie and Mason (2000), at pp 177–178.
40   Mason and Laurie, op. cit. at p 595, para 16.141.
41   (2001) 65 BMLR 6.

to consider authorising the withdrawal of nutrition and hydration from a woman who had suffered serious anoxic brain damage, was not in PVS, but was said to have no prospect of recovery. Her family wanted her to be allowed to die by removing her ANH and also claimed that she would not want to continue existing in her current circumstances. Despite her inability to express an opinion, Dame Elizabeth Butler-Sloss granted the application authorising removal of sustenance.

Mason and Laurie regard this decision 'with a degree of concern ...'[42] because it depends so heavily on medical opinion rather than on a 'principled approach to individualised human and patients' rights ...'.[43] Yet, as we have seen, dependence on medical opinion is inherent in utilising the Bolam Test to adjudicate on matters of life and death. In other words, using a responsible body of medical opinion to answer the question as to whether or not ANH can lawfully be withdrawn places too much emphasis on doctors' views about the point of continuing a patient's existence and gives insufficient weight to that patient's potential right to life.

On the other hand, in the case of *W Healthcare NHS Trust v H and others*,[44] the family of a woman who had been incapacitated – but not insentient – for many years gave evidence that their belief was that she would not wish the tube that was delivering nutrition and hydration to be reinserted after it had fallen out. Clearly the patient in question could not make her views known, although her family was convinced that she would not wish to be maintained in her current condition. However, her doctors had intended to reinsert the tube and the court was forced to consider whether or not the evidence from her family could reasonably be taken to amount to an advance directive of her wishes. In the Court of Appeal, Brooke LJ declared that the judge in the lower court had been

> ... correct in finding that there was not an advance directive which was sufficiently clear to amount to a direction that she preferred to be deprived of food and drink for a period of time which would lead to her death in all circumstances. There is no evidence that she was aware of the nature of this choice, or the unpleasantness or otherwise of death by starvation, and it would be departing from established principles of English law if one was to hold that there was an advance directive which was established and relevant in the circumstances in the present case, despite the very strong expression of her wishes which came through in the evidence.[45]

---

42   Mason and Laurie, op. cit. at p 587, para 16.120.
43   Ibid.
44   [2004] EWCA Civ 1324.
45   Ibid. at para 21.

On reflection, as examples of decision-making on the best interests of an incompetent patient who has not left clear directions behind, these cases seem to pose as many questions as they answer. However, it is of interest that in the latter case the medical staff caring for the patient wanted the tube reinstated, just as those in *Re G* took the opposite position. It may well be, then, that yet again the decision as to what was in the patient's best interests was dominated by medical opinion.

A number of factors seem to have influenced the courts' decisions in these important cases. Medical opinion clearly plays a significant role as does the interpretation as to what amounts to best interests. However, perhaps the most significant consideration yet again is the distinction drawn between acts and omissions – between killing and letting die, based in part on the idea that 'letting die' is morally neutral because it is just letting nature take over. Yet, as has already been suggested, this is a dubious distinction which rests on arguable foundations. The purported difference between acts and omissions will be returned to later, but for the moment it is worth briefly addressing the argument from 'nature'. The assumption that if something is 'natural' it is desirable or acceptable is surely false. We routinely interfere with 'nature'; indeed, that is the job of medicine. If I visit my doctor with a serious infection, s/he will not simply 'let nature take its course'. Rather, I will be treated with antibiotics. If my appendix ruptures, doctors will not stand by and watch me die from peritonitis; they will operate immediately to save my life. The use of the argument from nature in the case of people in PVS, then, is simply a smokescreen and what it is attempting to disguise is that quality of life decisions are being taken – not by the person whose life it is, but by third parties (doctors or courts) whose qualifications for so doing are clearly moot.

Do not resuscitate orders

It is, in fact, not only in PVS cases that decisions are made about the quality of other people's lives, or – to put it another way – about whether their deaths should be facilitated. One of these situations relates to what are called 'do not resuscitate' (DNR) or 'do not attempt resuscitation' (DNAR) orders. In this situation, a doctor may conclude that cardiopulmonary resuscitation (CPR) should not be attempted should the patient suffer a cardiac incident. This decision may be based on the alleged futility of CPR, either because CPR is itself not particularly successful or because the quality of life which it is anticipated the patient would have following CPR is not thought to be good. Although the first reason might be thought more obviously susceptible of clinical judgement, neither of these reasons is in fact value neutral. In some cases, it may be possible to conclude scientifically that CPR will be unsuccessful, but this will not be true in all cases. Equally, the decision about speculative quality of life is not obviously susceptible to medical judgement. It might, therefore, be expected that – where possible – any decision to place a

DNR order on a patient's medical records would require the agreement of the patient him or her self.

These orders are placed on patients for whom it is thought further resuscitation would be futile or perhaps overly burdensome. Ideally, I have suggested, any such decision should be made by the patient him or herself in discussion with his or her doctors. However, it has been noted that '[a]lthough patients report an interest in discussing DNR issues with their physicians, few report actually having these discussions'.[46] In fact, it has been demonstrated that '[i]n one study, 86 per cent of families but only 22 per cent of patients had participated in discussions about DNR orders'.[47] Moreover, when efforts are made to involve individual patients in DNR decisions, 'they usually occur late in the patient's illness, often after extensive and painful medical interventions have occurred'.[48] Thus, if a discussion ever takes place, it often happens at a time when the patient is least able to make an informed and competent decision.

Additionally, this evidence also suggests that proxies were more commonly asked to make life and death decisions than were the people most directly involved. When this is added to the fact that very often the people whose deaths were being contemplated were not involved in the discussion about their fate at all, there is surely cause for concern. This despite the fact that '[a] timely, caring, and open exchange of information involving the appropriate individuals and taking into account the patient's prognosis, quality of life, and value system is vital to humane DNR decision-making'.[49]

Tassano concludes that '[t]he use of "do not resuscitate" (DNR) orders without the knowledge of either the client or his relatives has become one of the more notorious scandals of the medical industry'.[50] Further, Oratz proposes that:

> Decisions about cardiopulmonary resuscitation are not different in process from other health care decisions. . . . They should be made by competent patients after disclosure of the pertinent medical facts and discussion of relevant issues with health care providers, family members, and significant others. DNR status should reflect the patient's own preferences.[51]

46 Ebell, M H, Doukas, D J and Smith, M A, 'The do-not-resuscitate order: a comparison of physician and patient preferences and decision-making', *The American Journal of Medicine*, Vol 91, (1991) 255–260, at p 255.

47 Ibid. at pp 255–256.

48 Ibid.

49 Ibid. at p 260.

50 Tassano, F, *The Power of Life or Death: A Critique of Medical Tyranny*, 1995, London: Duckworth, at p 126.

51 Oratz, R, 'Commentary', in Cohen, C B, (ed) *Casebook on the Termination of Life-Sustaining Treatment and Care of the Dying*, 1988, Bloomington: Indiana University Press, pp 39–41, at p 39.

This situation has become a matter of real concern for some people 'after several cases in which patients or their relatives have complained that resuscitation orders have been written in notes without their knowledge or consent'.[52] Moreover, it seems to leave open the very real possibility that selection of patients on grounds which may or may not be discriminatory, might occur. Garcia *et al* have noted for example that '[o]lder, white, sicker, or functionally impaired patients receive DNR orders more often than younger, black, healthier, or functionally intact patients do'.[53]

Moreover, while the use of these orders is widely accepted, the arguments of the disability rights lobby against assisted dying must also be relevant here. For example, the US National Council on Disability claims that '[t]he so-called "slippery slope" already operates in regard to individuals with disabilities and decisions to discontinue life-support systems and "Do Not Resuscitate" orders . . .'.[54] The UK Disability Rights Commission (DRC) also speculates on the extent to which discrimination is rife in the attitudes of doctors and others to those who are disabled, claiming that there is 'considerable anecdotal evidence that decisions by medical professionals on whether disabled people live or die, are sometimes being made against a backdrop of negative images and poorly informed assumptions of disabled people's lives'.[55] Moreover, it also argues that '. . . there is compelling evidence from research over a number of years up to the present day that discrimination in general health services exists. This qualitative research has recorded consistent testimony from disabled people and their families about the discriminatory attitudes they face from medical professionals, and poorer services they receive in the NHS'.[56] While this evidence is no more reliable than the opinion evidence rejected by the House of Lords Select Committee on the Assisted Dying for the Terminally Ill Bill, it is generally given great credibility. Nor is the Disability Rights Commission comforted by the existence of guidelines, such as those that already exist in the United Kingdom. For the DRC, not only are some decisions made without guidelines being followed, but also '[g]uidelines themselves risk institutionalising discriminatory attitudes'.[57] Moreover, the DRC highlights a more general concern, namely that:

52 Mayor, S, 'New UK guidance on resuscitation calls for open decision making', *British Medical Journal*, 2001: 322: 509.

53 Garcia, J A, *et al*, 'Sociodemographic factors and the assignment of do-not-resuscitate orders in patients with acute myocardial infarctions', *Medical Care*, 2000 June 38(6): 670–8.

54 National Council on Disability (US), 'Assisted suicide: a disability perspective', available at http://www.ncd.gov/newsroom/publications/1997/suicide.htm (accessed on 16/06/05) at p 14.

55 Disability Rights Commission, 'Policy statement on voluntary euthanasia and assisted suicide', available at http://www.drc-gb.org at pp 6–7, para 1.9.

56 Ibid. at p 18, para 3.21.

57 Ibid. at pp 6–7, para 1.9.

The language used in legal decisions to describe impairment and life with a disability reveal an institutional discomfort with disability. There is a very strong presumption that life with a disability is a lesser life that, even when tolerable, is tragic or regrettable. Legal decisions reinforce the notion that some people are too disabled to merit treatment, or sustain life and rely on explicit 'quality of life' assessments, largely by medical professionals, to determine what that is.[58]

Shakespeare also records the concerns of the disability community that the kinds of assumptions that tend to disvalue people with disability might all too easily influence DNR decisions, although he concludes that 'calm and evidence-based deliberation is usually more useful to disabled people than extreme rhetoric'.[59]

What this discussion shows is that, far from respecting the sanctity of life, in fact decisions are sometimes taken, often without the involvement of the individual, that continued life is not preferable to death. Not only is this a challenge to the law's repeated claims to respect the sanctity of all life, it also denies people the respect to which they should be entitled. For some, however, the question of respect seems to be irrelevant. For example, some commentators are disinclined to accept that people should be involved in such important decisions about their own future. Manisty and Waxman, for example, say:

> Patients increasingly want to participate in decisions about their medical treatment. Although this is appropriate in most circumstances, discussing cardiopulmonary resuscitation with terminally ill patients is not practical, sensible, or in the patient's best interests. In these special situations, patient involvement is tokenism and entirely of negative value.[60]

This assertion seems to suggest that there is something about a DNR decision which precludes patients from having a say. Presumably this is based on the assumption that DNR decisions are always based on a clear decision that CPR would be futile, yet this evidence is unlikely to be available even to the doctors. Equally, why it would not be in the patient's interests to have this discussion is also not clearly explained. Even if the outcome of the discussion is knowledge and foresight concerning one's own impending death, is this not information to which the patient is entitled? Guidelines from the Royal College of Anaesthetists, the Royal College of Physicians of London, the

---

58 Ibid. at p 22, para 3.33.
59 Shakespeare, T, *Disability Rights and Wrongs*, 2006, London: Routledge, at p 121.
60 Manisty, C and Waxman, J, 'Doctors should not discuss resuscitation with terminally ill patients', *British Medical Journal*, 2003: 614–615, at p 614.

Intensive Care Society and the Resuscitation Council recommend that 'all health care institutions should have a resuscitation committee, at least one resuscitation officer, adequate training' and that a DNAR policy 'should be compiled, communicated to relevant members of staff, used and audited regularly'.[61] They also say:

> Where there is no resuscitation plan and the wishes of the patient are unknown, resuscitation should be initiated if cardiopulmonary arrest occurs. However, a decision not to attempt resuscitation may be appropriate when:
>
> - The patient's condition indicates that effective CPR is unlikely to be successful;
> - CPR is not in accord with the recorded, sustained wishes of a mentally competent patient;
> - CPR is not in accord with an applicable advance directive (living will). Such directives are legally binding in England and Wales;
> - Successful CPR is likely to be followed by a length and quality of life that is not in the best interests of the patient.[62]

The guidelines conclude that:

> A decision not to attempt resuscitation applies only to CPR. It should be made clear to the patient, people close to the patient and members of the health care team that it does not imply 'non-treatment' and that all other treatment and care that are appropriate for the patient will continue to be considered and offered.[63]

These guidelines at least seem to accept that the patient should, where possible, be involved in the decision, or at least participate in a discussion and explanation.

Clearly, the terms of these guidelines also amount to an acceptance that a decision for death is sometimes appropriate. On the evidence, this will often occur on the say-so of clinical staff or relatives; not the person him or herself. Battin, for example, suggests that although hospital and other policies in the United States mandate that the patient or his/her legal representative should be consulted before such orders are made, 'such directives are by no means always followed'.[64] This seems to be true also in the United Kingdom.

---

61 *Cardiopulmonary Resuscitation: Standards for Clinical Practice and Training, A Joint Statement from the Royal College of Anaesthetists, The Royal College of Physicians of London, The Intensive Care Society and the Resuscitation Council (UK)*, October 2004, at p 5. Available at http://www.resus.org.uk.

62 Ibid. at pp 16–17.

63 Ibid. at p 17.

64 Battin, MP, *The Least Worst Death*, 1994, Oxford University Press, at p 117.

It is necessary, therefore, to conclude that, despite the rhetoric to the contrary, sometimes death is seen as the 'best' or the 'right' way out. It seems extraordinary that it is apparently permissible or accepted that *others* can decide on this, and even that I may initiate or be involved in the decision not to instigate CPR, yet I may not choose another route which would have the same result – a chosen, assisted death. Of course, it could be said, in cases where a DNR order is likely to be considered the patient will presumably be near death in any case. So too, however, was Diane Pretty. And, of course, it could be argued that not offering treatment – where the outcome will be death – is different from actually killing a patient, but this acts/omissions distinction has already been criticised and largely discounted.

Of course, it is not only adults who might be at risk if decisions about their lives are taken – not by themselves but by others. Very young children may also be vulnerable to such decisions.

Handicapped neonates

When children are born suffering from certain conditions, treatment may either be withheld or withdrawn. While sometimes this may be because the treatment offers no possibility of affecting the health status or life-expectancy of the infant, in other cases it would seem that a more value-laden assessment is being made. A series of cases of this sort has gone through the UK courts and these are worthy of some consideration here. Mason and Laurie note that:

> decisions taken immediately after birth concern human beings who are at the most vulnerable period of their lives – human beings, moreover, who cannot express their feelings for the present or the future and who clearly cannot have indicated their preferences to their surrogates.[65]

Thus, if we are committed to protecting the vulnerable and respecting their right to life, we can reasonably anticipate that the law will place clear and unambiguous barriers around behaviour which brings about their death.

Evaluation of these situations is generally conducted in terms of the civil law. However, in one case a criminal prosecution was brought against the paediatrician in charge of the child's treatment. In the case of *R v Arthur*,[66] the parents of an infant who – so far as they and Dr Arthur were aware – suffered only from Down's Syndrome, indicated that they did not want the child to survive. Dr Arthur prescribed 'nursing care only', which meant that the infant was offered no nourishment and was also prescribed regular doses of a powerful tranquiliser, presumably in order to prevent the child from suffering

---

65   Mason and Laurie, op. cit. at p 543, para 16.13.
66   (1981) 12 BMLR 1.

as he died. Evidence given during the course of the trial showed that the child was much more seriously disabled than had been thought; the charge against Dr Arthur was accordingly reduced from murder to attempted murder, since it was not clear precisely what had been the cause of death. In the event, Dr Arthur was acquitted. It is not, of course, clear what would have been the outcome had the murder charge stood, and the *Arthur* case is not generally regarded as one of jurisprudential significance. What is interesting about the judgment, however, is the furore it caused in medical circles; not, it should be noted because a child was deliberately left to die, but rather about the fact that Dr Arthur had ever been prosecuted. It seems troubling that the evidence of doctors as to standard practice was permitted to be definitive of whether or not a child should live or die, particularly as the decision was made at a time when the child would have been expected to live the normal lifespan of a child with uncomplicated Down's Syndrome. Yet, in evidence, not only did other doctors concede that they would have acted in precisely the way that Dr Arthur did, one eminent physician argued that it could be entirely ethical to let such a child die. Sir Douglas Black, then President of the Royal College of Physicians, said in evidence:

> Where there is an uncomplicated Down's case and the parents did not want the child to live, the child requires normal, healthy care, but I think there are circumstances where it would be ethical to put it upon a course of management that would end in its death. . . . I say that with a child suffering from Down's and with a parental wish that it should not survive, it is ethical to terminate life. . . .[67]

While he also approved the difference between 'allowing to die and killing', he conceded that this 'is somewhat difficult to defend in logic . . .'.[68] Yet, he nonetheless endorsed the positive effort not to maintain life based on the presence of handicap and lack of parental interest in the child's survival; indeed, he specifically referred to termination of life, and not simply allowing to die, as being 'ethical'. This suggests, perhaps, that even those who wish to support the difference between killing and letting die are themselves occasionally confused.

Shortly before Dr Arthur's prosecution, another case had been heard in an English civil court. In the case of *Re B (A Minor)*,[69] the Court of Appeal was asked to adjudicate on whether or not a Down's child, with an intestinal obstruction which would be fatal if not treated, should have the surgery in the face of parental objections. Templeman LJ put the court's position as follows:

---

67 Ibid. at pp 21–22.
68 Ibid. at p 21.
69 *In re B (A Minor) (Wardship: Medical Treatment)* [1981] 1 WLR 1421.

... it devolves on this court ... to decide whether the life of this child is demonstrably going to be so awful that in effect the child must be condemned to die, or whether the life of this child is still so imponderable that it would be wrong for her to be condemned to die. ...[70]

In other words, the court had to make a judgment about the child's quality of life. In the event, the court concluded that the surgery should proceed. What is important, however, is Templeman LJ's clear recognition that *quality* of life was the issue before the court; not *sanctity* of life.

Subsequent cases have relied on this relatively elderly decision. For example, in the case of *Re C*[71] the court authorised a hospital to treat a moribund child in a manner that ensured that her death was peaceful, but not to take aggressive action to save her life. In *Re J*,[72] the child concerned was brain damaged, but not dying. The question was whether or not efforts to rescue the child should be made should he require them. In this case, the court held that 'it would not be in J's best interest to reventilate him in the event of his stopping breathing unless to do so seems appropriate to the doctors caring for him given the prevailing clinical situation'.[73] In another case, *Re J (A Minor) (Wardship: Medical Treatment)*,[74] a mother tried to force doctors to provide treatment for her child, but the court said that it could 'conceive of no situation where it would be proper ... to order a doctor ... to treat a child in the manner contrary to his clinical judgment'.[75]

The dictum in this last case has formed a central plank in cases where there is a dispute between parents/relatives and clinicians, for example in the case of *Re C (A Minor)*.[76] It also shows very clearly the extent to which courts rely on the opinions of healthcare professionals rather than on the sanctity of all life. Two more recent cases can be considered in this context. In the case of *Re Wyatt*, the child was described as having 'chronic respiratory and kidney problems coupled with the most profound brain damage that has left her blind, deaf and incapable of voluntary movement or response'.[77] The question, as described by Hedley, J, was 'in all probability not whether this baby should live or die but how and when she should die'.[78] Her parents were unprepared to accept the glum prognosis of the doctors caring for baby Charlotte, and argued that, should she need it, doctors should be prepared to initiate artificial

70 Ibid. at p 1424.
71 *Re C (A Minor) (Wardship: Medical Treatment)* [1989] 2 All ER 782.
72 *Re J (A Minor) (Wardship: Medical Treatment)* (1992) 6 BMLR 25.
73 Ibid. at p 29.
74 [1992] 4 All ER 614.
75 Balcolme LJ, at p 625.
76 (1997) 40 BMLR 31.
77 *Re Wyatt (A Child) (Medical Treatment: Parents' Consent)* (2004) 84 BMLR 206, at p 207, para 1.
78 Ibid. at p 207, para 1.

ventilation which it seemed more than likely she would at some stage need. The question for the court, therefore, was whether or not doctors should be instructed to begin artificial ventilation if that ever became necessary. The view of the doctors was that Charlotte's quality of life was 'terrible' and that 'the enduring of further aggressive treatment . . . [was] intolerable'.[79]

Interestingly, the judge noted that 'both the quality of life and its tolerability have strong subjective elements to them'.[80] Although the views of the parents and the doctors might be persuasive, therefore, the definitive calculation was for the court. In the event, the judge came down in favour of the doctors' position, saying, however, that

> . . . this relief is only permissive, it does not relieve them of the right or responsibility for advising or giving the treatment that they and the parents think right in the light of the circumstances as they develop. All it does is to authorise them, in the event of disagreement between the parents and themselves, not to send the child for artificial ventilation or similar aggressive treatment.[81]

In January 2005, Hedley, J was invited to vary the order he had made and declined to do so on the basis that no grounds had been provided that would encourage him to change his mind. Charlotte's condition had not become any better. In October 2005, it was decided to remove the order, although this did not mean that the parents could insist on Charlotte receiving assisted ventilation. Merely, it meant that doctors would address Charlotte's treatment from traditional professional ethics, and work out what was in her best interests. In December 2005, Charlotte spent her first Christmas at home with her parents. In February 2006, given that Charlotte's condition had worsened, Hedley, J agreed that doctors could choose not to intubate or resuscitate Charlotte should the need arise. In October 2006, Charlotte celebrated her third birthday; alive despite the expectations of the doctors caring for her.

One further case can be considered. In the case of *An NHS Trust v MB*[82] the child was born in August 2004, and was subsequently diagnosed as suffering from spinal muscular atrophy (SMA). This is a progressive and degenerative condition, and the child in question suffered from the most severe type. His condition was described by Holman, J as being that 'he has now reached a point where, save for the movement of his eyes and possible slight but barely perceptible movement of his eyebrows, corners of his mouth, thumb and toes or feet, he cannot move at all . . .'.[83] Additionally, he suffered from epilepsy.

---

79   Ibid. at p 214, para 30.
80   Ibid.
81   Ibid. at p 217, para 41.
82   [2006] EWHC 507 (Fam) (15 March 2006).
83   Ibid. at p 2, para 6.

Despite these tragic circumstances, which in the judge's view meant that baby M had a 'helpless and sad life',[84] M's parents read to him and played with him and believed that he experienced pleasure as well as discomfort. However, the doctors caring for baby M believed that

> the quality of life for M is now so low and that the burdens of living are now so great that it is unethical (the word 'cruel' has been used) to continue artificially to keep him alive, and that his endo-tracheal tube should be withdrawn.[85]

The purpose of the court was, said Holman, not to consider the ethical issues that arise in these situations but rather to 'decide, and only to decide, where the objective balance of the best interests of M lies'.[86] Indeed, he believed M's case to be different from those which had been considered by courts in the past, saying:

> So far as I am aware, no court has yet been asked to approve that, against the will of the child's parents, life support may be withdrawn or discontinued, with the predictable, inevitable and immediate death of a conscious child with sensory awareness and assumed normal cognition and no reliable evidence of any significant brain damage.[87]

In this case, therefore, the question was not whether or not to offer treatment, but rather whether it was appropriate to remove life-sustaining treatment which was currently in place and whose removal would cause a virtually immediate death. The issue was not, therefore, the same as in the *Wyatt* case where the question was whether or not treatment should be provided or withheld in the future. The judge, however, was minded to regard these as being equivalent; a position with which the Royal College of Paediatrics and Child Health is in agreement, even though it also notes that 'emotionally they are sometimes poles apart'.[88] The position that there is no difference between the two was also recently endorsed by the Nuffield Council on Bioethics, which said that 'there are no good reasons to draw a moral distinction between withholding or withdrawing treatment, provided these actions are motivated in each case by an assessment of the best interests of the baby'.[89] In M's case it was said

---

84 Ibid. at p 17, para 100.
85 Ibid. at p 3, para 10.
86 Ibid. at p 5, para 24.
87 Ibid. at p 3, para 11.
88 *Witholding or Withdrawing Life Sustaining Treatment: A Framework for Practice*, 2nd edn, 2004, London: Royal College of Paediatrics and Child Health, at p 13.
89 *Report on Critical Care Decisions in Fetal and Neonatal Medicine: Ethical Issues*, November 2006, London: Nuffied Council on Bioethics, para 2.33.

that if the intubation were removed '[b]y the use of sedatives, he could have a peaceful, pain free and dignified death, but he would die almost immediately, probably within a few minutes'.[90] In practical terms, this is problematic because the coincidence in time between the actions of the doctors and the death of the child – to the lay person at least – makes it appear that the two are intimately connected. That is, that the doctors' behaviour looks as if it would amount to killing the child. However, for Holman, and despite the fact that continued treatment could keep the child alive, the cause of death would not be the sedatives; rather '[h]e would die from his own inability to breathe'.[91] This was an important finding, since – as was said in the earlier case of *Arthur*:

> There is no special law in this country that places doctors in a separate category and gives them extra protection over the rest of us. It is undoubtedly the case that doctors are, of course, the only profession who have to deal with these terrible problems. But notwithstanding that they are given no special power . . . to commit an act which causes death, which is another way of saying killing. Neither in law is there a special power, facility or licence to kill children who are handicapped or seriously disadvantaged in an irreversible way.[92]

It was imperative, therefore, that the doctors' behaviour could not be categorised as a criminal act if the desired outcome – the so-called painless and dignified death – was to be facilitated. This also permitted the court to address the question from the traditional civil law position. Given that there was no perceived distinction to be drawn between withdrawing and withholding treatment, the appropriate test was that of the child's best interests. This, the judge decreed, could be decided upon in large part by drawing up a list of benefits and burdens. He concluded thus:

> I am not persuaded, even taking into account predicted future deterioration, that it is currently in the best interest of M to discontinue ventilation with the inevitable result that he will immediately die. . . . I actually go further and consider that currently it is positively in his best interests to continue with continuous pressure ventilation and with the nursing and medical care that properly go with it. . . . There are, however, procedures which go beyond maintaining ventilations, which require the positive infliction of pain and which, if required, will, in my view, mean that M has moved naturally towards his death despite the ventilation. If that

90 [2006] EWHC 507 (Fam) at p 3, para 10.
91 Ibid.
92 (1981) 12 BMLR 1, at p 5.

point is reached, it would be in his best interests then to withhold those procedures even though he would then probably die.[93]

However, the judge was also careful to say that his decision was 'very fact specific'[94] and he did not wish to see it being regarded as the foundation of a policy. What seemed to be critical was that M was not (yet) dying. Should that stage be reached, invasive or burdensome treatments would not be imposed on him. In the cases we have considered, then, the courts seem to endorse a position which allows that the sanctity of life can be defeated by other considerations. This was probably best expressed by Lord Donaldson in the case of *Re J (A Minor) (Wardship: Medical Treatment)*:[95]

> There is without doubt a very strong presumption in favour of a course of action which will prolong life, but . . . it is not irrebuttable. . . . Account has to be taken of the pain and suffering and quality of life which the child will experience if life is prolonged. Account has also to be taken of the pain and suffering involved in the proposed treatment itself.[96]

Finally, it has been held that there is no breach of the child's right to life when treatment is withheld or withdrawn. In the case of *A National Health Service Trust v D*,[97] the court had the opportunity to address the practice of allowing some children to die against the backdrop of the European Convention on Human Rights. The child in this case was born with irreversible lung disease and multi-organ failure. The Trust applied for a declaration that it would be lawful not to resuscitate the child if he suffered cardio-respiratory arrest and that only treatment which would allow him to end his life peacefully need be given. The parents opposed this plan, and the court said that, although the parents' views were relevant, they could not 'themselves override the Court's view of the ward's best interests'.[98] Additionally, the court concluded that non-resuscitation did not amount to a breach of the right to life enshrined in Article 2 of the Convention.

In only one case that I am aware of have courts been prepared to prioritise the views of parents over those of doctors. In the case *of Re T (A Minor) (Wardship: Medical Treatment)*,[99] the child in question was born with biliary atresia. Without a liver transplant, the child was unlikely to survive but – although a previous attempt had failed – the overwhelming medical opinion

93 [2006] EWHC 507 (Fam) at p 16, paras 89–91.
94 Ibid. at p 18, para 16.
95 [1990] 3 All ER 930.
96 Ibid. at p 938.
97 (2000) 55 BMLR 19.
98 Ibid. at p 28.
99 (1996) 35 BMLR 63.

was that a future transplant would be likely to be successful. In the face of objections by the parents, the court declined to authorise any future transplantation. The status to be accorded to this case is unclear, since it seems to fly in the face of all previous judgments, but it may be relevant that both parents were described as healthcare professionals and that they had in any case removed the child from the jurisdiction of the court. This case aside, it seems that medical evidence is given priority status in courts, even though courts will reserve to themselves the right to make the final decision.

There are, of course, other cases which have not been referred to here. However, there is no need to rehearse them as essentially they all follow a pattern derived from the *Re B* decision. These cases tell us a number of things. First, that doctors and courts when confronted with these situations are making quality of life and not sanctity of life decisions. Even if this is sometimes denied, the language of the court decisions, and very often the medical opinion that informs it, clearly revolves around quality issues. Even when decisions are couched in terms of 'best interests' we cannot altogether avoid the fact that quality of life issues *are* inherent in this calculation. Second, that courts have been – with only one exception – led to their conclusion by medical evidence about the 'best interests' of the children concerned, even though it could be persuasively argued that doctors are not qualified to be judges of non-medical matters. Best interests are identified by reference to a wider range of considerations than the purely medical, as we have already seen; medical information should, therefore, form only one part of a complex evaluation. The current position translates the values and traditions of medicine into law and profoundly influences the shape of legal principle. In a very real sense, doctors' professional or ethical commitments, for example to the Hippocratic tradition, become determinants of matters which are effectively about human rights. Jackson describes this as 'anachronistic',[100] and indeed one might go further to describe it as fundamentally unacceptable. For some people life is always preferable, yet our courts allow the unwillingness of doctors to treat, and the court's refusal to tell doctors what to do, to end the life of these vulnerable children.

Interestingly, the professional guidelines issued to doctors by the Royal College of Paediatrics and Child Health explicitly declare that '[a]lthough it is necessary and fundamental to practice within the framework of the law', nonetheless it is

> important to define best practice in relation to the interests of the family and the child rather than presenting the minimum legal requirement. We

---

100 Jackson, E, 'Whose death is it anyway?: Euthanasia and the medical profession', in Holder, J, O'Cinneide, C and Freeman, M, (eds), *Current Legal Problems 2004*, Vol 57, 415–442, at p 416.

must look at what is legally permitted and required, but also at what is ethically appropriate, which may exceed the minimum standards set by law.[101]

The relevant guidelines refer to five situations in which it 'may be ethical and legal to consider withholding or withdrawal of life sustaining medical treatment'.[102] These are as follows:

The Brain Dead Child – where treatment is agreed to be futile; the child in a permanent vegetative state; the 'No Chance' situation, which arises when '[t]he child has such severe disease that life-sustaining treatment simply delays death without significant alleviation of suffering';[103] the 'No Purpose' situation, where '[a]lthough the patient may be able to survive with treatment, the degree of physical or mental impairment will be so great that it is unreasonable to expect them to bear it';[104] and the 'Unbearable' situation, where '[t]he child and/or family feel that in the face of progressive and irreversible illness further treatment is more than can be borne'.[105]

Some of the cases which have been considered by courts could be said to fit into the 'No Purpose' category, which seems to support the right of third parties to take the decision for the child that s/he has no quality of life, or at least one that is not sufficiently high. Others seem to fit into the 'No Chance' situation, which is arguably more obviously susceptible of clinical judgement, although it does not seem to fit neatly with the assertion that no one should be deprived of even the last few minutes of life, leading to the conclusion that quality of life is also important even in this category of cases.

A recent report from the Nuffield Council on Bioethics,[106] which was welcomed by the Royal College of Paediatrics and Child Health,[107] made a series of recommendations in the area of neonatal medicine. In particular, they require consideration of a number of factors when deciding whether or not to provide life supporting treatment immediately after the child is born, including likelihood of survival, the presence of any significant abnormalities and taking account of parental views.[108] Where the decision concerns

101 *Witholding or Withdrawing Life Sustaining Treatment in Children: A Framework for Practice*, 2nd edn, May 2004, London: Royal College of Paediatrics and Child Health, at p 19.

102 Ibid. at p 10.

103 Ibid.

104 Ibid. at p 11.

105 Ibid.

106 'Critical care decisions in fetal and neonatal medicine: ethical issues', London: Nuffield Council on Bioethics, 2006, available at http://www.nuffieldbioethics.org/fileLibrary/pdf/CCD_web_version_8_November.pdf (accessed on 23/02/07).

107 Available at http://www.rcpch.ac.uk/publications/recent_publications/press/nuffieldpremature%20babiesnov%2006.pdf (accessed on 23/02/07).

108 Nuffield Council on Bioethics (2006), para 28.

withholding or withdrawing treatment, doctors should consider a number of matters, including whether the treatment would significantly prolong a child's life, whether or not the treatment will be burdensome and what benefits may be anticipated.[109]

Where the baby has what the Council called a 'limited prognosis'[110] decisions about whether to withdraw life-sustaining treatment should take account, inter alia, of what survival time is anticipated and, again, whether or not benefits outweigh burdens of the treatment.[111]

So much, it might be said, for the sanctity of life. Even more critically for this argument, however it is disguised, doctors, courts and august bodies, such as those referred to above, are endorsing – in some cases at least – a positive (even if benevolent) decision that the children in question should die. So, in summary, patients who are unable to express a decision are assisted to die. Even if that assistance is categorised as 'passive' rather than active – and the relevance of this can be and has been disputed – and even if it accords with what doctors believe to be good medical practice, it qualifies in terms of intention, causation and outcome as assisted dying.

Conclusion

Patients in PVS arguably show most clearly the difficulties inherent in maintaining a distinction between acts and omissions – between killing and letting die. Whatever sophistry courts and others use, the inescapable fact is that patients die because of the removal of nutrition and hydration – a fact that is both foreseen and intended by those who remove ANH. Unless we can truly identify a moral difference between act and omission, and are comfortable with characterising behaviour as one or the other, our current legal position simply hangs on to the pretence that death is not the desired outcome. Yet it is difficult to hold to that position in the face of reality or logic. Doctors routinely assist their patients to die; death is not always to be avoided. The examples of handicapped neonates and people in 'near PVS' are yet further examples of the non-consensual and deliberate bringing about of death. Deliberately conflating the decisions for death in each of the examples used in this chapter with medical futility or 'proper medical practice' denies the centrality of the intention to bring about the end of another person's life and falsely distinguishes that from other behaviour which results in the intentional ending of life. But even if that differentiation is valid, and I would argue that it is not, it still does not explain how it is morally 'better' to bring about someone's death slowly and without their agreement than to achieve the same result speedily, with their agreement and following their competent and considered

109 Nuffield Council on Bioethics (2006), para 29.
110 Nuffield Council on Bioethics (2006), para 30.
111 Ibid.

request. The problem is that we seem comfortable with making decisions that another person's death is appropriate, and deeply uncomfortable with accepting that people can make that decision for themselves. Yet, as Freeman has said, '[i]n effect doctors can assist patients to die, even in situations where no such request is made. But, as the law stands, they cannot assist the patient to end his/her own life'.[112] That surely is the ultimate irony.

112 Freeman, M, 'Death, dying, and the Human Rights Act', *Current Legal Problems*, Vol 52, 218–238 (1999) at p 232.

Chapter 5

The United Kingdom position

Although it has been argued that some forms of assisted dying are already regarded as lawful in the United Kingdom, technically, actively assisting in the death of another person is a crime, whether by statute, in England and Wales, or at common law in Scotland. Despite this, it is an interesting fact that when people act to breach the criminal law's prohibition on assisted dying, they are generally treated with remarkable leniency if charged and convicted. Mason and Laurie, for example, say that:

> The great majority of the few who have come to trial in these circumstances on charges of murder, manslaughter or culpable homicide have been accused of no more than using therapeutic drugs in overdose and all the relevant verdicts have indicated the reluctance of British juries to convict a medical practitioner of serious crime when the charge arises from what they see as his considered medical judgment.[1]

Moreover, Dignity in Dying reports that 'Home Office figures show that in 13 per cent of mercy killing cases and 15 per cent of assisting suicide cases, criminal charges are dropped or, on the advice of the Director of Public Prosecutions, never initiated'.[2] Although I have indicated that numbers will not form the basis of my argument, this is more than simply opinion evidence; it is instead based on ascertainable fact. In light of this, it is easy to agree with Braithwaite that '[a]lthough . . . [opinion] surveys have been criticised as too simplistic, the progressive rise in the proportion of positive respondents strongly suggests that public opinion is increasingly in favour of change'.[3] Indeed, it is interesting that there is little, if any, objection when sentencing following conviction is lenient; in such cases 'there is no public outcry that

---

1 Mason, J K and Laurie, G T, *Mason and McCall Smith's Law and Medical Ethics*, 7th edn, 2005, Oxford University Press, p 602, para 17.6.
2 Available at http://www.dignityindying.org.uk (accessed on 13/10/06).
3 Braithwaite, M A, 'Taking the final step: changing the law on euthanasia and physican assisted suicide', *British Medical Journal*, 2005: 331: 681–3, at p 682.

punishment has been inadequate. This contrasts with feelings expressed if the courts are preceived to be unduly lenient to convicted rapists or child molesters'.[4] It would seem, then, that the public at least is able to make a distinction between chosen deaths and truly criminal behaviour, even if our courts are reluctant to follow suit.

In some cases, the law avoids punishing people who have assisted others to die by using the principle of double effect. A number of examples of this can be briefly mentioned. In November 2000, a Dr Moor was acquitted of murder even although he admitted that he had administered a lethal dose of drugs to many patients. Although he claimed that he had only intended to relieve pain – that is he used the principle of double effect – the fact that he was charged at all suggested that the prosecution at least thought that there was more to it than that. In 2002, Annie Lindsell asked the High Court to rule that she could be given increased doses of analgesia when the suffering from her motor neurone disease became too acute. The case was subsequently dropped when she was assured that the principle of double effect would apply in her circumstances.

In other situations, where double effect is not available, it is also the case that leniency seems to be the order of the day. For example, in the case of *R v Carr*,[5] a doctor who injected a massive dose of phenobarbitone into a terminally ill patient was acquitted of the charge of attempted murder. Dr Nigel Cox, who injected a patient with potassium chloride after repeated requests from her for help to die, was given a suspended sentence and was allowed to continue to practise medicine albeit under certain limited restrictions.[6] Dr Cox, unlike Dr Moor, was not able to use the defence of double effect, which the court indicated would have rendered his act lawful:

> If a doctor genuinely believes that a certain course is beneficial to his patient, either therapeutically or analgesically, then even though he recognises that that course carries with it a risk to life, he is fully entitled, nonetheless, to pursue it. If in those circumstances the patient dies, nobody could possibly suggest that in that situation the doctor was guilty of murder or attempted murder.[7]

On the other hand, '[i]f he injected her with potassium chloride with the primary purpose of killing her, of hastening her death, he is guilty of the offence charged'.[8] Since there was no therapeutic rationale for the use of potassium chloride, Dr Cox could only have intended the injection to bring

4   Ibid. p 682.
5   *The Sunday Times* 30 November 1986.
6   *R v Cox* (1992) 12 BMLR 38.
7   Ibid. p 41.
8   Ibid. p 39.

about his patient's death. As the judge said in his summing up to the jury, '[w]hat can never be lawful is the use of drugs with the primary purpose of hastening the moment of death'.[9] Accepting that his action 'was prompted . . . by his personal distress, the distress of Mrs Boyes's family and her own frequently expressed wish to have her journey through this veil of tears brought to an end . . .',[10] the judge – as in law he had to – also directed the jury that this was irrelevant to guilt or innocence, although 'it is highly relevant to any consequences which follow from a verdict of guilty . . .'.[11]

Even when the accused are not doctors, courts tend to act leniently. Bernard Heginbotham, who killed his wife by stabbing her, allegedly based on his concerns about her future welfare, although convicted was given only a 12-month community rehabilitation order by way of sentence.[12] In Scotland, in the case of Mr Brady, who assisted his brother who was suffering from Huntington's Disease to die, he was also convicted but was given only a suspended sentence.[13] In 2005, Brian Blackburn was given a suspended sentence at the Old Bailey after he pleaded guilty to the manslaughter of his terminally ill wife.[14] In October 2006, David March, who tightened the plastic bag around his wife's head and sat with her until she died, was given a suspended sentence and 50 hours of unpaid work at the Sutton and Croydon MS Therapy Centre, where he was already the chairman.[15] Further, when people have chosen to travel overseas for assistance in dying, it had been mooted that those who accompany them might be subject to criminal prosecution on their return to the United Kingdom. Yet again, however, no such prosecution has been undertaken.[16] Equally, when the Voluntary Euthanasia Society published a booklet with practical instructions on how to commit suicide, the court declined to declare this to be a breach of s 2(1) of the Suicide Act 1969 which prohibits assisting a suicide.[17]

These cases show that – whether or not the law claims to treat all killing in the same way – when the killing involved is a 'mercy killing', the prosecution services, courts and juries seem inclined to distinguish them from other examples of killing in terms of both prosecution and sentencing policy. So, not only is it unlikely that a genuine 'mercy killing' will be prosecuted, but it also appears that even where a conviction is secured the apparently benign intention

---

9 Ibid. p 41.
10 Ibid. p 43.
11 Ibid.
12 http://news.bbc.co.uk/1/hi/england/lancashire/3876615.stm (accessed on 26/02/07).
13 For discussion of this unreported case, see Christie, B, 'Man walks free in Scottish euthanasia case', *British Medical Journal*, 1996: 313: 961.
14 http://news.bbc.co.uk/1/hi/england/4174155.stm (accessed on 26/02/07).
15 Available at http://news.bbc.co.uk/1/hi/wales/5377246. stm (accessed on 26/02/07).
16 See, e.g., the case of Paul Bennett, available at http://newsvote.bbc.co.uk (accessed on 12/10/06).
17 *Attorney General v Able and Others* [1984] QB 795.

of the actor will most likely result in a lenient sentence. It must, therefore, be asked what purpose is served by a law which technically criminalises behaviour which it then effectively ignores or forgives? Thus, it is arguable whether a stand-alone crime of assisted dying is necessary. The law of murder would be available in cases where motive was suspect, and would obviously be an appropriate charge. However, in genuine cases of consensual assisted dying, to insist on prosecution or a trial which will result almost certainly in little or no punishment being meted out to the person convicted seems unnecessary and wasteful. It also does little to add to respect for the law.

Of course, current practice may change and a more robust prosecution and sentencing policy may yet emerge. However, whether or not this is likely is debatable given the historical position adopted by the law. In and of itself this is no reason to move towards legalisation of assisted dying, but it is an interesting indication of the law's actual rather than its theoretical approach to assisted dying.

Support for assisted dying

Proponents of assisted dying routinely point to opinion evidence that suggests that a majority – sometimes said to be as high as 82 per cent – of the British public would support legalisation. There are many such polls, all of which seem to show a preference for legalisation, and some of which even suggest that a significant proportion of healthcare professionals would be prepared to participate in assisted dying were it legal – although some other polls would refute this. Nonetheless, the House of Lords Select Committee on the Assisted Dying for the Terminally Ill Bill was critical of much of the opinion evidence adduced to show public support for assisted dying, believing that in some cases the questions asked were insufficiently subtle or nuanced to elicit a dependable response.[18] As my argument does not hinge on public opinion, I make no further reference to their comments, nor indeed to the polls themselves, beyond saying that I believe the House of Lords argument to be debatable. However, if assisted dying is to be legalised, it must be grounded in more than samples of public opinion; indeed, even were there robust evidence of public and professional support, this would not in and of itself be sufficient justification for legal change, although in a House of Lords debate in May 2006, Viscount Craigavon suggested that 'we should be taking more account of public opinion. However much some inconvenient opinion polls are discounted, it seems to me to be clear that a convincing majority of the public are in favour of some change in the law'.[19]

18 House of Lords Select Committee on the Assisted Dying for the Terminally Ill Bill, *Report of the House of Lords Select Committee on the Assisted Dying for the Terminally Ill Bill*, HL Paper 86-1, London, HMSO, 2005. See particularly pp 75 *et seq.*
19 *Hansard*, HL Deb, Vol 681, Col 1219, 12 May 2006.

Whatever weight we are to give to public opinion, there is hard evidence that – for some people at least – there are virtually no lengths to which they will not go to attain a chosen death. Recently, for example, British people – and others – seeking access to assisted dying have found an alternative route to allow them to achieve their goal. Rather than risking the prosecution that might arise in the United Kingdom, even given the relative leniency demonstrated by British courts, they have chosen to travel to Switzerland where assisted dying is only a crime if the person committing it is acting in his or her own interests rather than in the interests of the other individual.[20] The first British person to obtain an assisted suicide in Switzerland was Reg Crew, who suffered from motor neurone disease and was assisted to die in 2003.[21] It was estimated in 2006 that 'the number of Britons having help to commit suicide in Switzerland has now surged past fifty . . .',[22] and demand for the service provided by Dignitas seems likely to continue.[23] Although Dignitas is the organisation most frequently referred to, there are now several other Swiss clinics helping foreigners to die. For people such as Mr Crew, death in a foreign country is the only option available to them, given that medical assistance in ending their lives in the United Kingdom is not legally permissible, even if it does happen. As we have seen, on occasion, family or friends will travel with the person seeking assisted dying to Switzerland in order that at least they have some close and loving company in the final moments of their lives. In 2004, in a case known as the Z case, the English prosecution services seriously considered whether or not a man who wanted to take his chronically sick wife to Switzerland for an assisted suicide might be charged with a breach of s 2 of the Suicide Act 1961. In the event, the High Court lifted an injunction banning him from doing this and Mrs Z died some time later in Switzerland.[24] More recently, a retired doctor, Dr Ann Turner, made the decision to travel to Switzerland for an assisted death. She explained her decision in this way:

> In order to ensure that I am able to swallow the medication that will kill me, I have to go to Switzerland before I am totally incapacitated and unable to travel. If I knew that when things got so bad I would be able to request assisted suicide in Britain, then I would not have to die before I am completely ready to do so.[25]

20 Swiss Penal Code, articles 114 and 115.
21 Available at http://news.bbc.co.uk/1/hi/england/2688843.stm (accessed on 26/02/07).
22 Available at http://www.dignityindying.org.uk/news/news.asp?id=208 (accessed on 03/04/07).
23 Doward, J, 'UK demand rises for Swiss suicide clinics', 20/03/05 available at http://observer.guardian.co.uk/print/0,3858,5152339-102285,00.html (accessed on 21/03/05).
24 [2005] 1 FLR 740.
25 O'Neill, S, 'Why a retired GP chose to end her life seven years before time', 25/01/06 TimesOnLine, available at http://www.timesonline.co.uk/article/0,,2-2008855,00.html (accessed on 29/06/06).

Dr Turner was accompanied to Switzerland by her children. In a poignant statement, her son Edward described how the family had made efforts to change Dr Turner's mind and described their feelings as follows – 'Our immediate reaction was a combination of enormous grief at the prospect of losing our mother, as we are a very close family, but also of logical acceptance of her course of action.'[26] Like many of the patients who have sought assisted dying in Switzerland, Dr Turner suffered from a degenerative neurological disease; in her case, the condition is known as progressive supranuclear palsy. In a recent survey of 790 people, commissioned by the Voluntary Euthanasia Society (now Dignity in Dying), it became clear that Mr Crew and Dr Turner were by no means unusual. Fifty per cent of those asked said that they would consider going abroad for assistance to die if they were 'suffering unbearably from a terminal illness'.[27] Even if we treat opinion evidence with caution, the fact that people are *in fact* driven to travel overseas, and even to die before they need to, provides hard evidence (and not just speculation) that, for them at least, there are powerful reasons to die at a time and in a manner of their own choosing.

Legislative activity in the United Kingdom

Although assisted dying remains illegal in the United Kingdom, this does not mean that there has not been a certain amount of legal and political activity around the subject; both for and against legalisation. For example, in 2000 the Medical Treatment (Prevention of Euthanasia) Bill was introduced to the UK Parliament. This Bill was described as 'A Bill to prohibit the withdrawal or withholding of medical treatment, or the withdrawal or withholding of sustenance, with the purpose of causing the death of the patient . . .'. The Bill would have made it unlawful for any person 'responsible for the care of a patient to withdraw or withhold from the patient medical treatment or sustenance if his purpose or one of his purposes in doing so is to hasten or otherwise cause the death of the patient'. This Bill was initially introduced in December 1999 by Ann Winterton MP, and was almost certainly a direct result of the *Bland* judgement, which has already been discussed. Morris described the Bill as 'confused and unhelpful, failing in its aim of developing the law in a way that would be of assistance or reassurance to vulnerable patients, or to those caring for them'.[28] In any case, the Bill progressed no further.

---

26   Available at http://news.bbc.co.uk/1/hi/health/4761143.stm (accessed on 03/04/07).
27   'Swiss group "helped 22 Brits die"', available at http://news.bbc.co.uk/1/hi/health/3623874. stm (accessed on 11/04/2005).
28   Morris, A, 'Easing the passing: end of life decisions and the Medical Treatment (Prevention of Euthanasia) Bill', *Medical Law Review*, 8 Autumn 2000, 300–315, at p 314.

In 2002–03, the Patients' Protection Bill was introduced to the House of Lords. This Bill would also have made it 'unlawful for any person responsible for the care of a patient to withdraw or withhold sustenance from the patient if the purpose in doing so is to hasten or otherwise cause the death of the patient'. As might be expected, these various Bills generated intense and impassioned debate. Two examples will suffice to show the major differences between commentators. In the House of Lords debate on 6 May 1998, for example, Lord Taverne said

> ... in a civilised society one should respect the wishes of those who wish to avoid horrible suffering at the end of their lives and who want to die in dignity and do not wish to go on living. ... In my view the Dutch have shown how society can become more, not less, compassionate. In their approach to, and rules on, voluntary euthanasia they have shown a greater, and not a lesser, respect for the value of human life.[29]

In that same debate, the Lord Bishop of Oxford said:

> I respect the fact that in the Netherlands the approach to euthanasia has been conscientious and responsible. Nevertheless, it is fundamentally misconceived, a wrong turning which history will, I hope, quickly judge to be a cul-de-sac. I believe that in allowing people, in increasing numbers, to focus on the question of when and in under what circumstances they might ask for euthanasia, distracts society from its proper concern, which is how to improve palliative care and how to bring good palliative care to everybody in society. The request to die indicates that something is wrong. Let us concentrate on identifying on what is wrong and doing all we can to make it right.[30]

More recently we have seen the progress through the House of Lords of a series of Bills introduced by the distinguished human rights lawyer, Lord Joffe.[31] The Patient (Assisted Dying) Bill was first introduced into Parliament in 2003, but did not proceed beyond a second reading. A revised version, The Assisted Dying for the Terminally Ill Bill, was then introduced into the House of Lords in March 2004. This Bill would have allowed both physician-assisted suicide and voluntary euthanasia. After its second reading, the Bill was referred to a specially established Select Committee of the House of Lords, which reported in 2005, and made a number of recommendations. A debate on the Bill was held in October 2005, but no vote was taken at that time. This Bill ran out of

---

29   *Hansard*, HL Deb, Vol 589, Cols 713–714, 6 May 1998.
30   Ibid. Col 716.
31   For an account of the history of the Bill, see http://dignityindying.nvisage.uk.com/information/assisteddying.asp?id=103 (accessed on 13/10/06).

time and was reintroduced in November 2005. A debate on this Bill was held in May 2006. Before briefly considering this debate, it is worth looking at the report of the Select Committee.

The House of Lords Select Committee on the Assisted Dying for the Terminally Ill Bill[32]

The Select Committee heard evidence from a range of individuals and organisations as to the terms of Lord Joffe's Bill. Its report is a comprehensive account of the principal arguments raised, and concludes by making a number of recommendations. Perhaps the most significant was that any future Bill should take account of the difference between euthanasia and assisted suicide. Although throughout this narrative I have referred to assisted dying, intending to include both of these, the Select Committee felt it to be important that there was

> an opportunity to consider carefully these two courses of action, and the different considerations which apply to them, and to reach a conclusion on whether, if such a bill is to proceed, it should be limited to the one or the other or both.[33]

This recommendation was based on the visits the Committee members made to Oregon, where only assisted suicide is permitted, and the Netherlands, where both assisted suicide and voluntary euthanasia are permissible, and on the evidence they identified from practice in each jurisdiction. In Oregon, 'less than 1 in 700 deaths is currently attributable to assisted suicide', whereas in the Netherlands 'the figure is more than 1 in 40, less than 10 per cent of which are from assisted suicide while over 90 per cent are as a result of voluntary euthanasia'.[34] These figures suggested to the Select Committee that there is 'a strong linkage between the inclusion of voluntary euthanasia in assisted dying law and a significantly higher rate of take-up'.[35]

Implicit in this conclusion seems to be the view that, even if the arguments in favour of legalisation are accepted, the fewer deaths that result from what is legalised the better. The Committee noted that:

> In Oregon, in 2003, one in 714 deaths resulted from assisted suicide. In the Netherlands in the same year one in 38 of those who died did so via either assisted suicide or voluntary euthanasia, mainly the latter

---

32 *Report of the House of Lords Select Committee on the Assisted Dying for the Terminally Ill Bill.*

33 Ibid. at p 91, para 269 (c)(i).

34 Ibid. at p 83, para 243.

35 Ibid.

(the figure is 1 in 32 if cases of euthanasia without explicit request are included).[36]

Thus, where the legalised activity requires the patient to take the final act, it seems that fewer people avail themselves of it; where doctors are authorised to make the final step – as in voluntary euthanasia – then the numbers are higher. Therefore, the Select Committee concluded that 'the demand for assisted suicide or voluntary euthanasia, if measured in terms of the numbers of applicants, will vary according to what the law permits'.[37] This reflects the findings of the report already referred to which demonstrated that, if asked whether or not people would prefer to legalise assisted suicide or voluntary euthanasia, by a margin of 2:1 the public preferred legalisation of the latter, while the healthcare professionals who responded would prefer to see the former legalised, by the same margin.[38] Mason and Laurie conclude that on the basis of this evidence, 'in this very sensitive situation, most people would wish to pass the ultimate responsibility to others'.[39] While there are obviously practical consequences that follow whichever form of assisted dying is legalised, it is not clear why these should be held to be important in a debate based in principle. Nonetheless, perhaps in the interests of moving forward, Lord Joffe took the Select Committee's commentary very seriously in this – and in other – areas and produced an amended Bill which is very much more restrictive than the original, limiting itself to the legalisation of physician-assisted suicide only. Interestingly, some commentators have expressed concern that limiting legalisation to physician-assisted suicide only might have negative rather than positive consequences. Emanuel, Daniels and Fairclough, for example, suggest that:

> While laws permitting PAS but prohibiting euthanasia may have appeal by providing a barrier to the 'slippery slope', there may be serious practical problems. Despite significant education through public debate, media attention, and many articles in both medical journals and the lay press, physicians and others may not accurately distinguish PAS from euthanasia. . . .[40]

36   Ibid. at p 49, para 131.
37   Ibid. at p 49, para 132.
38   McLean, S A M and Britton, A, *Sometimes a Small Victory*, 1996, Glasgow: Institute of Law and Ethics in Medicine.
39   Mason and Laurie, op. cit. at p 615, para 17.39.
40   Emanuel, E J, Daniels, R, Fairclough, D L, Clarridge, B R, 'The practice of euthanasia and physician-assisted suicide in the United States: adherence to proposed safeguards and effects on physicians', *Journal of the American Medical Association*, Vol 280(6), 12 August 1998, 507–513 available at http://gateway.uk.ovid.com/gwl/ovidweb.cgi (accessed on 11/08/06), at p 9.

However, they also note that this should be treated merely as a caution, because 'additional instructional efforts may successfully educate physicians about the differences between PAS and euthanasia'.[41] Apparently, this 'caution' was not considered by the Select Committee in what can be characterised as its encouragement to Lord Joffe to restrict the form of assisted dying to be legalised. There are, however, rather obviously, other reasons to doubt the value of limiting legalised assisted dying in this way.

If it is accepted that assisted suicide alone should be legalised, only those with the psychological and physical capacity to perform it themselves would be able to benefit, despite the fact that their reasons, intentions and aspirations will almost certainly be the same as those who fall outside the scope of the law. Equally, if patients are required to act themselves, this may result in people committing suicide earlier than necessary because they will need to be physically able to ingest the medication. Just this situation arose in the Canadian case of *Rodriguez v Attorney-General of British Columbia*.[42] The applicant in this case was a woman in her early 40s suffering from a degenerative condition – amyotropic lateral sclerosis – which would result in her deterioration to the point at which, although mentally alert, she would be unable to move or breathe on her own. Although aware of the fact that she could lawfully commit suicide before reaching that stage, Mrs Rodriguez wanted to spend as much time with her family as she could. This meant, in her view, that only when her life became intolerable would she want to be helped to die, but unfortunately for her that stage was unlikely to be reached before she was unable to kill herself. She argued that a number of the articles in the Canadian Charter of Rights and Freedoms could be prayed in aid of her request to make it lawful for a doctor to assist her at that stage. By the narrowest of margins (5:4) she lost her case. In the event, she was able to find – with the help of a Canadian parliamentarian – a doctor prepared to assist her.[43] The doctor remained anonymous and no prosecution was ever brought. Although Mrs Rodriguez was unsuccessful in convincing the court of the merits of her claim, the dissenting judgments were powerful and their reasoning may yet be given more heed in a future case; in particular those that argued for the importance of autonomy. For example, Cory, J made a powerful plea to respect individual choice, saying:

> The life of an individual must include dying. Dying is the final act in the drama of life. . . . It follows that the right to die with dignity should be as well protected as is any other aspect of the right to life. State

41   Ibid.
42   (1993) 50 BMLR 1.
43   For further discussion of this case, see Lemmens, T, Dickens, B, 'Canadian law on euthanasia: contrasts and comparisons' *European Journal of Health Law* 8: 135–155: 2001.

prohibitions that would force a dreadful, painful death on a rational but incapacitated terminally ill patient are an affront to human dignity.[44]

In the United Kingdom, the House of Lords Select Committee on the Assisted Dying for the Terminally Ill Bill recognised that this was indeed one of the major arguments in favour of legalisation. Nonetheless, in its view 'patient autonomy cannot be absolute and ... there must be some limits set, in the interests of the wider community, to what a patient can require his or her doctor to do ...', noting however that '[t]here is not consensus ... on where those limits should be'.[45] It is, nonetheless, unclear why patient autonomy should not be absolute in this case, particularly since it clearly is given primacy when patients are allowed effectively to commit suicide by rejecting life-sustaining treatment. It is also unclear what 'interests of the wider community' are served by preventing people from obtaining assistance in dying. It may, and this is arguable, be in society's interests that doctors are not involved in assisted dying, but they already are. If this is what the Select Committee has in mind, then it should surely have instigated a debate on those practices which are currently permitted in law and in ethics, or they should have decontextualised assisted dying from the medical arena. On the other hand, if the Select Committee's concern was that doctors should not be forced to act against their conscience, this is taken account of in the conscience clause contained in the Bill.

The Select Committee also addressed the question of the alleged difference between withholding and withdrawing treatment. In an echo of the report from the House of Lords Select Committee on Medical Ethics, while conceding that '[i]t might perhaps be argued that the case of withholding or withdrawing treatment is more open to question because the patient's consent to such action is not required if the treatment is deemed futile or burdensome',[46] the recent Select Committee was nonetheless apparently persuaded by the evidence of most of the medical practitioners – and of course some others questioned – that they 'saw a clear difference between withholding or discontinuing life-prolonging treatment considered to be futile – and often burdensome to the patient – and taking action specifically to end his or her life'.[47]

Recognising that patients might not see a difference between assisted dying and refusing life-sustaining treatment, yet again the Select Committee was at pains to reinforce what they identified as being the 'medical' view:

> ... we recognise ... that there is a clear difference between the two situations from the point of view of the physician, mainly because the

44 (1993) 50 BMLR 1 at p 63.
45 *Report of the House of Lords Select Committee on the Assisted Dying for the Terminally Ill Bill*, op. cit. at p 26, para 62.
46 Ibid. at p 23.
47 Ibid.

intention in the former case is not to bring about the death of the patient, whereas that is indisputably the intent in the case of assisted suicide ... there is consensus among us that, in the last analysis, the acceptability or otherwise of the Bill is a matter for society as a whole. Having said that, we recognise also the crucial role which doctors would have to play in the implementation of the Bill, were it to become law, and that the views of the medical and nursing professions must be considered very seriously.[48]

That doctors would play a significant role in terms of Lord Joffe's proposal is indisputable, although – as will be discussed later – this is not the only possible route to, or consequence of, legalisation. Equally, however, the Select Committee can be challenged for taking account only, or primarily, of the views of those doctors who are opposed to or uncomfortable about involvement in assisted dying. There is ample evidence to suggest that not every doctor holds this position. In the United Kingdom opinion amongst doctors, and other healthcare professionals, is by no means uniform and doctors do on occasion admit to having assisted their patients to die. Indeed, even in the relatively conservative country of France, 2,000 healthcare professionals, including doctors and nurses, recently signed a petition admitting to having assisted the deaths of some terminally ill patients during their careers and calling for an immediate change to the law to decriminalise assisted dying.[49] The Select Committee's critique of the opinion evidence, which suggests that a majority of the public supports assisted dying, should surely equally be applied to the 'evidence' the Select Committee believes to exist about doctors' attitudes.

Given its view that assisted dying was a matter for society as a whole, the Select Committee also proposed that the way forward would be to find a balance between those terminally ill people who want assistance in dying and those who do not.[50] For the Select Committee, a cost/benefit analysis required to be undertaken and

> ... the balance of advantage needs to take into account the different weightings on each side of the scales. In this case it is necessary to know, for example, how many people are being deprived of benefit on the one side of the equation and how many others might be endangered on the other side. We need also to take a view of the size of the benefits to the one group as against the magnitude of the damage to the other.[51]

48   Ibid., at p 27, para 64.
49   Spurgeon, B, 'Two thousand health staff sign petition calling for euthanasia to be decriminalised', *British Medical Journal*, 2007; 334: 555; available at http://www.nouvelobs.com (accessed on 04/04/07).
50   *Report of the House of Lords Select Committee on the Assisted Dying for the Terminally Ill Bill*, op. cit. at pp 27–28, para 67.
51   Ibid.

This conclusion can, of course, be criticised as in part suggesting that a calculation on principle can be reached by counting those who will and will not benefit. Moreover, this assertion seems to assume that those who want assisted dying and those who do not are necessarily in some kind of opposition to each other. This is an unwarranted assumption. Those who want assistance in dying do not seek to suggest that those who do not should be subjected to it. Equally, in this portion of the Select Committee's argument, it appears that they have – deliberately or inadvertently – conceded that the slippery slope works; in other words the presumption underpinning this statement is that legalisation would pose dangers to one group, even if it brings benefits to another. As we have seen, the slippery slope is, however, a weak – albeit pervasive – argument. Despite this, the Select Committee, apparently uncritically, uses a version of this argument. As the Report says:

> The essence of the concern here is that, if assisted suicide and voluntary euthanasia should be legalised and if implementation of the law were to be carried out within the health care system, these procedures will of necessity become a therapeutic option; that over time there will be drift from regarding the death of a patient as an unavoidable necessity to regarding it as a morally acceptable form of therapy; and that pressure will grow as a result for euthanasia to be applied more widely – for example, to incompetent people or to minors – as a morally acceptable form of medical therapy which is considered to be in the patient's best interests.[52]

There are two obvious problems with this assertion. First, if there is nothing inherently 'bad' about assisted dying, then there is no reason to be concerned should it become a therapeutic option; indeed, that is precisely what proponents would wish to see happening. Second, it is mere speculation that pressure to extend the categories for whom assisted dying is available would either appear or not be capable of being resisted. Certainly, in the Netherlands it seems that the categories of those for whom assisted dying is permissible have been expanded. This is not necessarily bad, of course, but this is as likely as not a feature of the basis for legalisation, which allows doctors to decide that a conflict of duties exists, rather than being founded in support for the assertion and vindication of patients' rights.

The Select Committee then returned to a consideration of the views of the medical professions. Given the view that alternatives to assisted dying are preferable, the Committee recommended that 'high priority should be given to the development and availability of palliative care services across the country and we hope that the efforts which are being made in this direction will be

---

52 Ibid. at p 40, para 102.

intensified'.[53] This is unobjectionable, but what is less so is the consideration given – yet again – to the views of healthcare professionals. Without exploring the quality of the survey on which they based their analysis of medical opinion – which, as I have said, the Committee was at pains to do with public opinion surveys – the Select Committee noted that:

> We were . . . given the results of a survey carried out by the Association of Palliative Medicine (APM). We were told that in the APM survey of its members, which attracted an 84 per cent response rate, 72 per cent . . . of respondents had said that they would not be prepared to participate in a process of patient assessment which formed part of an application for assisted suicide or voluntary euthanasia.[54]

It seems scarcely surprising that this would be the result of any such survey, but why it should be deemed so important, and apparently to be relied upon, is unclear. Indeed, if this is the attitude of this group of professionals, a more interesting comment on it would be to ask why it is that these particular doctors are so unwilling to respect what their patients actually want? It is also not clear why, given its enthusiastic criticism of opinion evidence, this survey – and not others – was apparently taken at face value by the Select Committee.

Finally, the Select Committee addressed itself to a number of essentially practical – albeit relevant – issues. For example, Lord Joffe's Bill requires the existence of a terminal illness before a patient qualifies for assisted dying, yet as the Committee noted, '[t]he evidence which we have taken from medical practitioners suggests that the prognosis of a terminal illness is far from being an exact science'.[55] Equally, the Committee was warned of the problems associated with predicting the behaviour of degenerative diseases and malignancies.[56] Additionally:

> There was a general consensus among our expert witnesses on one point – that the attending and consulting physicians who are envisaged as being effectively the 'gatekeepers' in regard to applications for assisted dying could not be expected to spot impairment of judgement in all cases.[57]

Practical to an extent these concerns may be, but they are not unimportant. However, they arise more because of the shortcomings of the Bill itself than from a principled debate about assisted dying. In other words, if we conclude

53   Ibid. at p 36, para 90.
54   Ibid. at p 44, para 116.
55   Ibid. at p 44, para 118.
56   Ibid. at p 45, para 120.
57   Ibid. at p 47, para 126.

that assisted dying should be legalised then, as will be discussed in the final chapter, the problems with Lord Joffe's Bill are consequent primarily on the extent to which he has been persuaded, or forced, to place such limitations in it. Indeed, these very problems might speak in favour of a liberalisation of the availability of assisted dying. In any case, and despite these issues, having taken account of the Select Committee's comments, Lord Joffe introduced an amended version of his Bill, the terms of which will now be considered.

The Assisted Dying for the Terminally Ill Bill 2005

Following the October 2005 debate, The Assisted Dying for the Terminally Ill Bill was reintroduced to the House of Lords on 9 November 2005. The short title describes it as a Bill which would enable 'an adult who has capacity and who is suffering unbearably as a result of a terminal illness to receive medical assistance to die at his own considered and persistent request; and for connected purposes'.

The Bill would allow a doctor to assist a 'qualifying patient' to die by prescribing medication and, if the patient is unable to ingest it, to provide a means whereby this would become possible.[58] For a patient to qualify for assistance s/he must have made and signed a declaration requesting assistance in dying[59] and the doctor must be satisfied as to the patient's capacity following an examination of the patient and his/her medical records.[60] The doctor must also conclude that the patient is suffering from a terminal illness[61] and that s/he is suffering unbearably as a result of the illness.[62] The patient must have been told of his/her diagnosis,[63] the prognosis,[64] the process of being assisted to die[65] and 'the alternatives to assisted dying, including, but not limited to, palliative care, care in a hospice and the control of pain . . .'.[66]

The doctor must also have 'ensured that a specialist in palliative care, who shall be a physician or a nurse, has attended the patient to inform the patient of the benefits of the various forms of palliative care',[67] and 'recommended to the patient that the patient notifies his next of kin of his request for assistance to die'.[68] Should the patient persist in his/her request, the doctor must

---

58 The Assisted Dying for the Terminally Ill Bill, s 1.
59 Ibid. s 2(2)(a).
60 Ibid. s 2(2)(b).
61 Ibid. s 2(2)(c).
62 Ibid. s 2(2)(d).
63 Ibid. s 2(2)(e)(i).
64 Ibid. s 2(2)(e)(ii).
65 Ibid. s 2(2)(e)(iii).
66 Ibid. s 2(2)(e)(iv).
67 Ibid. s 2(2)(f).
68 Ibid. s 2(2)(g).

satisfy him- or herself that the request is voluntary and informed[69] and refer the patient to a consulting physician.[70] The doctor must also be sure that the person making the request is competent to do so. A person will be deemed to lack capacity for these purposes 'if at the material time he is unable to make a decision for himself in relation to that matter because of an impairment of, or a disturbance in the functioning of, the mind or brain resulting from any disability or disorder of the mind or brain'.[71] If there is any doubt about the question of capacity, the doctor must refer the patient to a 'consultant psychiatrist, or a psychologist, who shall be independent of the attending and consulting physicians, for an opinion as to the patient's capacity'.[72] No assistance can be given unless the patient is deemed to have capacity.[73] This provision takes account of the concerns expressed by some commentators on the law in the state of Oregon. For example, Emanuel, Daniels, Fairclough and Clarridge note that '[t]he data suggest that laws like Oregon's, which permit PAS but do not mandate a psychiatric evaluation, may not lead to adequate detection and care of mental illness among patients requesting PAS'.[74]

Once the patient has been adjudged as 'qualifying', s/he must make a declaration of his/her wish to die, which must be witnessed by two people, of whom one must be a solicitor or public notary[75] and must be able to verify both the identity of the patient, that the request was made voluntarily by a person of sound mind and that the patient understands the effect of the declaration.[76] Fourteen days must elapse before the assisting physician takes any action to carry out the request.[77] Before taking any action, the doctor must also ensure that the patient knows that the declaration can be revoked and that the patient still holds to it.[78] The declaration can be revoked verbally or in any other way, irrespective of the physical or mental condition of the patient.[79]

The Bill also includes a so-called conscience clause which provides that nobody has any duty to be involved in any part of the process,[80] but there is a requirement that where such an objection exists, 'the physician who has a conscientious objection shall immediately, on receipt of a request to do so, transfer the patient's medical records to the new physician'.[81]

---

69   Ibid. s 2(2)(h).
70   Ibid. s 2(2)(i).
71   Ibid. s 2(4).
72   Ibid. s 3(1).
73   Ibid. s 3(2).
74   Emanuel, *et al* (1998), p 10.
75   The Assisted Dying for the Terminally Ill Bill, op. cit. s 4(1) and (2).
76   Ibid. s 3(a)–(c).
77   Ibid. s 5(2).
78   Ibid. s 5(3)(a) and (b).
79   Ibid. s 6(1).
80   Ibid. s 7(1).
81   Ibid. s 7(6).

Finally, if a doctor helps someone to die, providing that the terms of the Bill have been complied with s/he will not be guilty of a criminal offence.[82] In order to ensure safe and appropriate practice, the Bill also proposes the creation of a monitoring commission, or commissions, which are designed to 'review the operation of this Act and to hold and monitor records maintained pursuant to this Act'.[83] Finally, an illness is deemed terminal if it –

in the opinion of both the attending and the consulting physician –

(a) is inevitably progressive,
(b) cannot be reversed by treatment (although treatment may be successful in relieving symptoms temporarily), and
(c) will be likely to result in the patient's death within six months.[84]

The concept of unbearable suffering is described as 'suffering whether by reason of pain, distress or otherwise which the patient finds so severe as to be unacceptable'.[85] The test, therefore, is objective as to the terminal nature of the condition and subjective as to the suffering entailed by it. The patient who wishes to have assistance in dying, therefore, would have to clear a number of hurdles before that desire could be given effect under the terms of this Bill. It is perhaps unsurprising that this is so, as clearly the Bill faces an uphill battle. Presumably, the thinking behind the terms of the revised Bill was that the narrower and more difficult the criteria for eligibility, the more likely it would be to succeed.

The debate

In the final debate on The Assisted Dying for the Terminally Ill Bill in May 2006, Lord Joffe explained the rationale for introducing the Bill as follows:

The current law has the following defects. It results in unnecessary suffering by a significant number of terminally ill patients who are denied the right to end their suffering by ending their lives and the right, as they see it, to die with dignity. It is ignored by some caring doctors who, from time to time, moved by compassion, accede to persistent requests by suffering patients to end their lives. That results in grave risks to those doctors' careers, reputations and possibly freedom. It is also ignored by loved ones who face a terrible emotional burden when helping with such a request. It places patients at risk of making spontaneous and ill

82 Ibid. s 8(1).
83 Ibid. s 12(1).
84 Ibid. s 13.
85 Ibid.

formed decisions to end their lives. It influences patients with progressive physical diseases to end their lives earlier than they need to, such
as Dr Turner, because they fear that at a later stage they may not be
physically able to do that.[86]

In the same debate, Baroness Jay of Paddington argued that '[h]owever
much we may respect the opposition in principle to this Bill from those with
religious faith and those of us who have a spiritual concern that perhaps may
not be a formal religious faith, we live today in a diverse and predominantly
secular society where the importance of individual human rights is increasingly
valued'.[87] Reinforcing the faith-based nature of much of this debate, the
Archbishop of Canterbury contrasted the 'abstract principle of the sanctity
of life' with 'a conviction, rather, about the possibilities of life'.[88] He also
referred to the possibility that 'even experiences of pain and helplessness can
be passed through in a way that is meaningful and that communicates dignity
and assurance'.[89]

Interestingly, however, Lord Prior had a different interpretation of the
religious view, arguing, that [s]urely any Christian doctrine has to accept that
there are people who suffer deeply, for whom the Lord would take the view
that they should be helped, and that there is no point in causing people to
suffer the indignities that go with such diseases and which have nothing to do
with the sanctity of life.[90]

Baroness Thomas of Walliswood argued that 'we live in a secular society
within which individuals may express their own belief in the way they live
their individual lives ...', and expressed her concern about the 'so-called
Christian campaigns against the Bill.'[91] In any event, she concluded that 'this
issue is surely one for society as a whole to determine, not doctors or divines
acting on our behalf.[92]

Noting the power of the religious lobby in this debate, Lord Desai claimed
that 'we have not seen so many Bishops here since the debate on Sunday
trading'.[93] In a clear attack on this infleuence, he continued:

Religion relies on fear and the religious love suffering. I am an atheist
and I have no fear, certainly no fear of God or the afterlife. I value my

---

86 *Hansard*, HL Deb, Lord Joffe, Vol 681, Col 1184, 12 May 2006.
87 Ibid. Col 1194.
88 Ibid. Col 1196.
89 Ibid.
90 Ibid. Col 1209.
91 Ibid. Col 1232.
92 Ibid.
93 Ibid. Col 1258.

life, but I value it for the pleasure it gives me, and as soon as I cannot derive any pleasure, I want to be rid of it. I have always liked the Bill because it gives me autonomy.[94]

Further, the Earl of Sandwich argued that it was inappropriate to impugn 'the genuine humanitarian motives of those who wish to relieve suffering . . .', suggesting that '[b]y using such language, they alienate those of a reforming tendency who still occupy the middle ground.'[95] Lord Pearson of Rannoch also expressed a concern that will resonate with many. As he said:

I find it perplexing that our humanists, who presumably do not believe much in an afterlife, should support this Bill, whereas my Christian friends, who trust that death leads to the salvation of the soul and eternal bliss, should oppose the death proposed by the Bill. I should have thought that the humanists would be more likely to hang on to life like grim death rather than the Christians, but it appears to be the other way round.[96]

His comments point to yet another inconsistent facet of the faith-based opposition to legalisation, as well as reinforcing my claim that those who value suffering at an existential level, or believe that life is a non-returnable gift from God, are limiting the options available to others. Additionally, as Lord Goodhart said, '[w]e do not wish to use this Bill to force you to do anything that you do not wish to do; but we ask you also to respect our views and not to deny us access to an option that we would like to have at hand, even though we hope that we will never need to use it'.[97] Baroness Warnock took this thought forward saying:

The whole purpose of my noble friend's Bill is to define a small category of person for whom the general law against assisted suicide should not apply. It is to be presumed that these people, who choose suicide when facing the suffering that will lead to their death, do not think it morally wrong to do so. It is not contrary to their moral principles, or, perhaps, those of their family. Is it just, then, that they should be governed by moral principles, whether of the clergy or the medical profession, in which they do not believe? I do not argue that they should disregard the law simply because they do not agree with it; only that the law should be changed in such a way that they, in their extreme circumstances,

94   Ibid.
95   Ibid. Col 1263.
96   Ibid. Col 1215.
97   Ibid. Col 1206.

should be allowed to follow the morality in which they do believe, not another which would compel them to live against their wish.[98]

Some of the Peers who spoke also addressed the issue of palliative care. As we have seen, the argument that good palliative care would remove the need for assisted dying has considerable resonance. However, as Baroness Greengross pointed out, while this may be true for many people, it is not true for everyone. For those who do not benefit from palliative care, 'this Bill, were it an Act, would bring a sense of security and the knowledge that, if necessary, they can call on help. For most people, that knowledge is all they need. It is a form of insurance policy'.[99] In any case, as Lord Lipsey noted, 'palliative care and assisted suicide are not alternatives. They are complementary; we need both'.[100] Indeed, he concluded, '[i]f the proponents of palliative care are honest, and I know that they are, they will admit that there are some conditions, particularly neurological conditions, where palliative care really cannot prevent unbearable suffering'.[101]

This snapshot of the debate in the House of Lords obviously omits many of those who spoke in opposition to the Bill, primarily because their arguments have already been well-rehearsed, but most importantly the selected comments demonstrate the extent to which the arguments against legalisation in reality hinge on faith-based arguments, which apply only to those who believe in them. In any case, Jackson suggests that the regular involvement of doctors in decisions and actions which result in the death of their patients might lead to the conclusion that 'God's monopoly on determining the moment of death has already been substantially undermined . . .'.[102] In the event, and despite the support of many Peers, the Bill was stalled by a vote of 148 to 100. This meant that the Bill could not complete its passage in that Parliamentary Session. However, Lord Joffe has indicated that he intends to reintroduce it.

Responses to the Bill

Predictably, and importantly, the Disability Rights Commission (DRC) has commented extensively on Lord Joffe's Bill. Equally predictably, it has grave concerns about what would be its impact, particularly on those with disability. In a policy statement issued in January 2006 the DRC raised a number of

98 Ibid. Col 1221.
99 Ibid. Col 1240.
100 Ibid. Col 1274.
101 Ibid.
102 Jackson, E, 'Whose death is it anyway?: Euthanasia and the medical profession', in Holder, J, O'Cinneide, C and Freeman, M, (eds), *Current Legal Problems* 2004, Vol 57, 415–442, at p 420.

specific concerns.[103] First, it said, legalisation of assisted dying 'would set disability rights back and be a negative step'. This position is entirely in line with the DRC's concern that assisted dying would become, for society, an easy way out. Rather than investing in care for people with disability, or shaping a society that accommodates disability, it would be easier and cheaper to allow their despair at marginalisation to lead to a 'chosen' death. This is obviously an intelligible position to take. As we have already seen, the reality of discrimination against disabled people cannot be disputed. However, it also, in my view, overstates the case. There is no necessary link between the compassion that militates for a competently chosen assisted death and the callousness that would target people for death involuntarily or nonvoluntarily. In any case, similar scrutiny of the decisions of people such as Ms B – whose disability was the cause of her request to die – is not currently required – beyond, of course, assessing her capacity. Now, it might be said, perhaps it should be. However, making this a requirement would fly in the face of the rights that people have to reject medical treatment; it would turn both ethics and the law on their head.

Second, the DRC was concerned that the Bill provides neither sufficient safeguards nor adequate scrutiny and analysis of practice. Moreover, even although the Bill contains provisions directed to ensuring that patients are aware of the alternatives, particularly the availability of palliative care, the DRC also objects that '[t]his does not account for the patchy existence of palliative care services across the country. . . . Nor does it account for the fact demand for the service currently outstrips supply'. This 'patchy' provision might, of course, be remedied were Baroness Finlay's Palliative Care Bill to become law, at least in England and Wales.[104] The DRC believes – and it is difficult to argue with this position – that if the option of palliative care is to be a real alternative for people contemplating assisted suicide it must *in fact* be available. The Palliative Care Bill would require health authorities to 'ensure the provision of palliative care to every person with a terminal illness to such extent as is necessary to meet all such persons' reasonable requirements'.[105] For the moment, however, the DRC argues – almost certainly correctly – that this level of palliative care is not currently on offer, saying:

> Given who the Bill is targeted at, being offered palliative care is not a 'real' option if there is a six-month waiting list for treatment. To legalise

103 *Disability Rights Commission, Assisted Dying Policy Statement, 20/01/2006,* available at http://www.drc-gb.org/library/policy/health_and_independent_living/assisted_dying_policy_statement.aspx (accessed on 29/08/06).
104 This Bill was introduced into the House of Lords on 16/11/06, and had an unopposed second reading in the House of Lords on 23/02/07; for further information, see http://www.carenotkilling.org.uk/?show=393 (accessed on 03/04/07).
105 Palliative Care Bill, s 1(1).

assisted dying before the service is available nationally and to the same standards could create a postcode lottery false choice between palliative care and assisted dying – and would undermine current Government initiatives to roll-out coverage and double palliative care staff by 2015, as well as introducing another layer of health inequality.

The DRC explains its broad position in this way:

The DRC believes it is fundamental to create a society in which disabled people can participate fully as equal citizens. We believe there are a number of steps that need to be taken before assisted dying legislation is progressed further. The most important items are:

- Abolishing discriminatory guidelines and practice on withholding and/or withdrawing life-saving treatment for disabled people;
- Producing demonstrable reductions in discrimination and inequalities in health services;
- Improving the quality and capacity of palliative care provision equally across the country and ensuring supply does not lag behind demand (as is currently the case);
- Implementing effective rights to independent advocacy and communication support; and
- Implementing rights to independent living to create a society where all disabled people are able to participate fully as equal citizens.

These are undoubtedly laudable aims, and will be supported by both proponents and opponents of legalising assisted dying. What is not clear, however, is that they refute the right of people to make a choice for death. At best, they point to the need to remove from the equation the possibility that such choices are not truly voluntary or autonomous. For this reason, presumably, the DRC does not support legalisation for the moment, but does not rule it out in the future should its demands be met. As Shakespeare points out, '[d]isability rights-based objections to disabled people's exercise of autonomy at the end of life are procedural, not substantial'.[106] He also critiques the overall approach of the disability rights movement to legalisation since 'the basis of independent living philosophy is support for the rights and choices of disabled people to have control over their own lives. It seems to me to be inconsistent to support autonomy for disabled people in all matters except at the end of life'.[107] He concludes, therefore, that '[w]ith suitable safeguards and regulation, assisted suicide legislation should be supported by those who support choices and

---

106 Tom Shakespeare, submission to the Select Committee on the Assisted Dying for the Terminally Ill Bill, para 8.1.
107 Shakespeare, op. cit. para 1.4.

rights for disabled people'.[108] This support for closely regulated assisted dying, coming from a leading commentator on disability rights, further reinforces my argument that it is both wrong and unhelpful to characterise the debate as being disabled people versus the rest. Just as doctors, patients, nurses and citizens have different views, so too will those with disability and those speaking for them. Although I have conceded earlier that the disability rights lobby's concerns are the strongest of the arguments against legalisation, even they are by no means homogeneous, nor do they ultimately defeat a principled argument in favour of legalisation.

One additional argument merits consideration. Yuill argues that a negative consequence of Lord Joffe's Bill would be that it would in fact restrict doctors' ability to help out suffering patients, saying:

> During my last days, if I am spared a sudden death, I want to be able to look my doctor in the eyes and know that he or she will do the right thing. I want to know that, if I am in pain but fading fast, the doctor will give me enough morphine to alleviate pain and to stop my breathing. Ironically, it is this last act of kindness that is jeopardised if the UK Assisted Dying for the Terminally Ill Bill is ever passed.[109]

Leaving aside the question of whether or not morphine would have this effect, in an interesting, and arguably somewhat startling, critique of the Bill, Yuill argues against some of the potentially strong reasons for legalisation. For example, he says:

> The relentless drive towards making things 'transparent' and 'recognising the needs' of a small minority of patients opens a veritable Pandora's box. The concept of the patient as first and foremost an individual will be replaced by a generic 'patient' whose even more generic 'quality of life' is determined not by individual qualities and relationships but by a flow chart. Instead of dying surrounded by friends and family, we will be surrounded by paper – and lawyers.[110]

Quite how this conclusion is reached is not clear. Certainly, proponents of legalisation are often keen to use the transparency argument to support their position; indeed, transparency is commonly viewed as a good thing. What Yuill seems to be saying is that once we achieve transparency, doctors will not be able to help patients in the ways that they can at the moment. However, if what doctors currently do is lawful, the passing of the Bill will not affect

108 Shakespeare, op. cit. para 8.2.
109 Yuill, K, 'Killing trust between doctors and patients' 3 October 2005, available at http://www.spiked-online.com/Printable/0000000CAD88.htm (accessed on 14/10/05).
110 Ibid.

them; if it is not, then surely it is preferable that these practices are 'outed'? Indeed, this does seem to be precisely the thrust of Yuill's complaint; that is, that '[t]he real effect of the Bill becoming law will be the regrettable formalisation of something that has occurred for many years informally, and mostly unproblematically'.[111]

In fact, of course, this is a highly dubious proposition. Quite why it should be 'regrettable' that life and death decisions should become subject to the rigours of legal scrutiny is unclear. Certainly, as we have seen, the principle of double effect is accepted by our law and doctors who can establish that they have used this principle to guide their behaviour will escape legal consequences. However, there is nothing in Lord Joffe's Bill that would have any effect on the use of the double effect principle; Yuill's fears, therefore, seem at best rather contrived. Moreover, it seems a somewhat bizarre argument that proposes it to be better that practices which involve life and death decisions should continue to be carried out in a clandestine manner without the scrutiny which a legalised regime would offer. At present, doctors can – if they are prepared to – operate entirely without their motives being explored (unless they are found out), surely rendering patients more rather than less vulnerable.

Assisted dying and the courts revisited

Alongside all of this attempted legislative activity sit the courts of law. In the absence of law reform – at least for the present – their interpretation of what rights, if any, people may have in terms of assisted dying are of paramount importance. Of course, the courts are constrained by the terms of the Suicide Act 1961, at least in England and Wales. However, much hinges on the extent to which the courts can – or are willing to – find a way to circumvent the apparently incontrovertible terms of the 1961 Act. Thus, for example, if the courts can find a way, or wish to find a way, to permit chosen deaths to occur in some circumstances, then, as we have seen in the previous chapter, they will achieve this. We have also seen that courts and juries are reluctant either to convict or to punish severely those who have engaged in assisted dying out of compassion. Further, we have already seen in the case of *Airedale NHS Trust v Bland* [112] that a number of the judges in the House of Lords were considerably exercised by, and unhappy about, the distinction which they were forced to draw between actively and passively bringing about a death; both Lord Browne-Wilkinson and Lord Mustill seemed to a great extent unconvinced by the distinction.

The problems associated with drawing this distinction have also led courts to struggle to find justifications for acts which are clearly designed to result

---

111 Ibid.
112 (1993) 12 BMLR 64.

in death, but which are thought to be preferable, even desirable. For example, in the case of *Re A (Children) (Conjoined Twins: Surgical Separation)*, Ward LJ stated that:

> It should not need stating that the court cannot approve of a course of action which may be unlawful. The stark fact has to be faced in this case that to operate to separate the twins *may* be to murder Mary. It seems to me, however, that the question of what is in the best interests of the child is a discrete question from whether what is proposed to be done is unlawful. A patient in terminal decline, racked with pain which treatment may not be able fully to alleviate, may beg to die and it may be said – at least by some – that it is in his best interests that he should be allowed so to do, but that would not justify unlawfully killing him.[113]

Like Battin, then, this court seemed to draw a distinction between killing on the one hand and *unlawful* killing on the other. However satisfactorily, the court in this case was able to find a way of circumventing the very clear fact remains that the decision to separate the twins inevitably, immediately and knowingly would result in the death of Mary in order to offer Jodie – the second twin – a real opportunity of life. However this was dressed up, it was a decision to cause the death of Mary. In this case, the courts attempted to justify an outcome which they believed to be 'right', by utilising legal devices which are at best disingenuous and at worst completely opaque.

Conclusion

Lord Joffe's attempts to change the law in respect of assisted dying may never come to fruition, not least because of the resistance of some members of the medical professions and a number of Parliamentarians. Equally, the Select Committee's Report shows that resistance to change exists at the highest level, albeit with a significant number of exceptions. As I said at the beginning of this book, it is unlikely that these positions will ever be reconciled. Fundamentally, the objectors base their position on faith, fear of the slippery slope and on identifying a difference between acts and omissions. For them, even if it needs terminal sedation, all suffering can be managed; therefore there is no need to legalise assisted dying. Moreover, as the Select Committee on Medical Ethics said:

> Belief in the special worth of human life is at the heart of civilised society. It is the most fundamental value on which all others are based,

113 (2000) 57 BMLR 1 at p 43.

and is the foundation of both law and medical practice. The intentional taking of human life is therefore the offence which society condemns most strongly.[114]

This, however, is somewhat a poor critique of what actually happens and what proponents of legalisation are proposing. Those who support the case for legalisation do not disrespect human life. Rather, unlike opponents of legalisation, they believe that we can maintain that respect while still allowing individuals to decide *for themselves* that their own life has reached a point where it no longer has value, or that the quality of the life they can anticipate is insufficient. To be sure, the intentional killing of another person is generally conceived of as wrong, but its wrongness lies not in how it is achieved – actively or passively, for example – or simply because it results in death, but rather in the intentional deprivation of a life which the individual wants to continue. Doctors already kill patients; that the law condones this speaks to its inconsistency.

It is, of course, the case that consent is not a defence to the crime of murder. Legalising assisted dying would, therefore, require a recasting of the role of consent in this area of the criminal law. This, however, is not an argument against legalisation; many behaviours which were once criminal – for example suicide – have been decriminalised. There is no reason that the same could not happen when death is chosen but requires assistance. At present in the United Kingdom, some of those most intimately affected by the legal position are forced into early suicide, in order to obtain assistance far removed from family and home or they are reduced to experiencing the very death they wish to avoid. It is not that death will not occur in any event; merely, they wish to accelerate the process. We do not reduce the number of deaths by outlawing assisted dying – we simply delay their occurrence in the face of the clear, unequivocal and informed wishes of the people concerned and add to the sum of human suffering. Moreover, the shortcomings of the current legal position, based as they are on arguable presumptions, surely suggest that some kind of reassessment is required. In the final chapter, consideration will be given to the form that might take, as well as to a re-evaluation of the arguments for and against law reform. First, however, it is necessary to address the question as to whether or not appropriate legislation can be designed that would facilitate autonomy, yet at the same time take account of the fears of opponents.

114 House of Lords Select Committee on Medical Ethics, *Report of the House of Lords Select Committee on Medical Ethics*, HL Paper 21-1, 1994, p 13, para 34.

Chapter 6

Is there a way forward?

If we can agree that the arguments against legalisation of assisted dying are flawed to the extent that they can be, or have been, defeated then the next question must be how, if at all, we should proceed. Should we simply continue to tolerate behaviour which is otherwise unlawful by either failing to prosecute or by handing down only very lenient sentences, or should we legislate to clarify that assisting someone to die is no longer a criminal offence? Even more importantly, should we place tight regulation in the way of such acts or simply leave it to the private decisions of individuals in conjunction with anyone who is prepared to offer the help needed?

In the United Kingdom, as we have seen, the closest we have come to legalisation has been through the Bills drafted by Lord Joffe and presented to the House of Lords. For the moment, the most recent Bill has stalled and even if reintroduced, it may well suffer the same fate as his earlier efforts. In any case, even if he were to achieve success in the House of Lords, it seems more than unlikely that the Bill would survive debate in the House of Commons. In large part this is probably because of a general concern that we cannot put in place mechanisms that are sufficiently robust to ensure that the law will not be abused. Those who oppose legalisation point to the experience in other jurisdictions where full or partial legalisation of assisted has occurred, claiming that they show how impossible it would be to provide a safe environment in which decisions are always free and uncoerced by, for example, mental disorders or family pressures. It is worth, therefore, briefly considering some of these jurisdictions and their experiences before concluding on the appropriate way forward in the United Kingdom. Although Belgium legalised voluntary euthanasia – but, oddly, not assisted suicide – in 2002 and other countries such as Switzerland do not 'regulate assistance with suicide other than to prescribe that such action should not be self-serving',[1] in what

---

1   House of Lords Select Committee on the Assisted Dying for the Terminally Ill Bill, *Report of House of Lords Select Committee on the Assisted Dying for the Terminally Ill Bill*, 2005, HL Paper 86-1, at p 69, para 195.

follows the focus will initially be on probably the two most widely publicised and discussed jurisdictions where legalisation, in one form or another, has taken place.

The Netherlands

There is a huge volume of literature on the experience in the Netherlands, which has progressed from tolerance of assisted dying providing certain conditions have been met to outright legalisation. The current legal regime can be found in The Termination of Life on Request and Assisted Suicide (Review Procedures) Act 2002. The legislation requires that the doctor 'holds the conviction that the request by the patient was voluntary and well-considered . . .'.[2] S/he must also satisfy the following conditions; namely that s/he:

b   holds the conviction that the patient's suffering was lasting and unbearable,

c   has informed the patient about the situation he was in and about his prospects,

d   and the patient holds the conviction that there was no other reasonable solution for the situation he was in,

e   has consulted at least one other, independent physician who has seen the patient and has given his written opinion on the requirements of due care, referred to in parts a–d, and

f   has terminated a life or assisted in a suicide with due care.

For assisted dying to be lawful, the patient must be suffering from 'unbearable and unremitting pain, with no prospect of improvement'.[3] The request must be sustained and competent, and all other options must have been offered.[4] As the House of Lords Select Committee on the Assisted Dying for the Terminally Ill Bill noted, '[t]he 2002 law is not limited to adults. Nor does an applicant for euthanasia have to be terminally ill'.[5] Regional Review Committees have been established, whose function is to review notifications of cases where an assisted death has been brought about.

The Dutch model has been widely commented on and it is not intended to reiterate much of that commentary here. However, some salient points are worthy of note. Since there is no requirement that the person asking for an

2   The Termination of Life on Request and Assisted Suicide (Review Procedures) Act 2002, article 2, 1, a.

3   Cohen-Almagor, R, *Euthanasia in the Netherlands: The Policy and Practice of Mercy Killing*, 2004, Dordrecht: Kluwer Academic Publishers, at p 37.

4   Ibid. at p 38.

5   *Report of House of Lords Select Committee on the Assisted Dying for the Terminally Ill Bill*, op. cit. at p 61, para 170.

assisted death is terminally ill, the terms of the Dutch legislation have left it open to expand the categories of those who seek to gain, and sometimes obtain, access to it. Most recently, a Dr Sutorius assisted an 86-year-old man, Edward Brongersma, to commit suicide. In a discussion of this case, Huxtable and Möller describe Mr Brongersma's condition as 'life fatigue' or 'existential suffering'.[6] In other words, he was tired of living, but suffered from no physical or psychiatric illness. Although there seemed to be no doubt that Mr Brongersma wanted to die – satisfying the autonomy requirement – Dr Sutorius nonetheless was accused of having acted unlawfully, as he failed to satisfy himself that Mr Brongersma's suffering was 'unbearable' as is required by the concept of 'due care'. Initially acquitted, the case was appealed and referred by the Court of Appeal for expert consideration. The experts concluded that 'a doctor's role in euthanasia should be limited to matters within the medical domain'.[7] Ultimately, Dr Sutorius was culpable because he had failed to consider alternatives, although he escaped punishment.

While opponents of legalisation point to this case as a paradigmatic example of the much feared 'slippery slope' in action, in that the categories of those for whom assisted dying might become lawful will continue to expand, others would argue that this is in fact a suitable case for assisted dying. For example, it has been asked why 'unbearable suffering' should be required for an assisted death, or indeed why availability of assisted dying should be constrained by medical notions of what suffering amounts to. Varelius, for example, argues that

> ... it is implausible that only persons who are suffering because they have a severe illness or injury can be willing to die. There are persons who have asked for euthanasia, or committed suicide, because they are tired of living, consider their existence as meaningless, and can find no value in anything that their lives have to offer them, etc.[8]

Thus, he asks, 'why should voluntary euthanasia require that the person who wants to be euthanised is suffering'?[9] This question has already been briefly touched upon; just how, and why, are we to set limits on who may and who may not have an assisted death? Although for many people extending the categories of eligible people beyond those who are in any event dying is anathema it is legitimate to ask which of the principles identified as supporting legalisation is offended by allowing any person to make such a choice? In fact,

6 Huxtable, R and Möller, M, '"Setting a principled boundary?" Euthanasia as a response to "life fatigue"', *Bioethics*, No 3, 2007, 117–126, at p 118.
7 Ibid. at p 118.
8 Varelius, J, 'Illness, suffering and voluntary euthanasia', *Bioethics*, No 2, 2007, 75–83, at p 76.
9 Ibid. at p 77.

the values that underpin the claim that people should be free to seek and obtain an assisted death rest only tenuously, if at all, on concepts such as medically defined suffering or terminal illness. Nor do they rely on the fact that death is in any case imminent. Indeed, it could be argued that the further off natural death is the more urgent is the freedom to choose an assisted death when life has lost meaning for the person him or herself. Of course, some – if not many – people in this situation will take their own lives thus avoiding the thorny question of third party involvement, but for others this will not be a viable or acceptable option.

A second major criticism of the Dutch position is a variation on the first; that is, that the slippery slope will lead inevitably not only to large numbers of people being killed by doctors, but to a tolerance for killing that will also add to the number of illicit assisted deaths. However, evidence from the Netherlands suggests on the contrary that requests for assisted dying, far from being thoughtlessly accepted, in fact are routinely denied. The House of Lords Select Committee on the Assisted Dying for the Terminally Ill Bill was told that there were 9,700 requests for euthanasia annually in the Netherlands, of which 3,800 were successful – 300 of these being assisted suicides.[10] So, about two-thirds of requests were not agreed to. Despite this, Griffiths, Bood and Weyers note that, although the practice of euthanasia in the Netherlands has some support, critics fear that 'it is not, and cannot be, adequately controlled, so that its dangers outweigh its benefits'.[11] Thus, the argument would run that even if every case that is formally approved meets the legal criteria, there is concern that some, if not many, more are carried out that do not. Keown, for example, points to the number of cases in which patients' lives were ended in the Netherlands without their explicit consent as a sure sign that legalising voluntary euthanasia creates an atmosphere in which tolerance becomes, or can become, coercion; that is, once we legalise voluntary euthanasia, it is a short step to the practice of non-voluntary or involuntary assisted dying.[12] The strength of this argument has already been challenged, but it is indisputable that some deaths *are* brought about in the Netherlands without the patient's explicit request. Onwuteaka-Philipsen *et al* note, however, that '[t]he proportion of physicians who were ever engaged in the ending of life without a patient's explicit request decreased from 27 per cent in 1990 to 23 per cent in

10 *Report of House of Lords Select Committee on the Assisted Dying for the Terminally Ill Bill*, op. cit. at p 62, para 171.

11 Griffiths, J, Bood, A, Weyers, H, *Euthanasia and Law in the Netherlands*, 1998, Amsterdam University Press, at p 24.

12 See, for e.g., Keown, J, 'Defending the Council of Europe's opposition to euthanasia', in McLean, S A M (ed), *First Do No Harm: Law, Ethics and Healthcare*, 2006, Aldershot: Ashgate, pp 479–494.

1995, and further to 13 per cent in 2001'.[13] Of course, these figures pre-date the new legislation, but the real question is whether or not this is unusual or unique to the Netherlands.

In a recent study in the United Kingdom, Seale identified that voluntary euthanasia accounted for only 0.16 per cent of the studied deaths, PAS accounted for 0 per cent, alleviation of symptoms with possibly life-shortening effect 32.8 per cent and non-treatment decisions 30.3 per cent.[14] He concludes that '[t]he proportion of UK deaths involving all three forms of doctor-assisted dying (voluntary euthanasia, physician-assisted suicide and ending life without an explicit request from the patient) was extremely low'.[15] Thus, he concludes that UK clinical practice is informed by 'a palliative care philosophy . . .'[16] because of the number of cases which involved non-treatment rather than active killing. Whether this is of benefit to patients is not clear, however, and certainly the relatively high numbers where it is possible that the patient was not involved does not appear to be an improvement on the Dutch situation. While Seale argues that the fact that numbers are relatively low gives the lie to those who argue that keeping these practices secret – such as in the United Kingdom – is problematic, it is equally plausible that his sample – like all such evidence – shows us only a microcosm of what is happening.

In an effort to discover whether or not prohibition or legalisation affected the behaviour of doctors, Kuhse, *et al* conducted a survey of 800 doctors in Australia, where assisted deaths are precluded by law.[17] Their findings have been widely used to suggest that Seale's view is arguable; that is, that assisted dying is every bit as common – if not more so – when no legalisation has taken place. Their findings were as follows:

> The medical end-of-life decisions reported by the 800 doctors were as follows: 26 doctors (3.2%) reported euthanasia; 51 doctors (6.4%) reported ending the patient's life without the patient's explicit request; 289 doctors (36.1%) reported making a decision not to treat, of which 55 doctors (19%) reported no intention to hasten death, and 234 doctors (81%) reported an explicit intention to hasten death; and 434 doctors (54.2%) reported alleviating the patient's pain with opioids in large doses,

13 Onwuteaka-Philipsen, B, *et al*, 'Euthanasia and other end-of-life decisions in the Netherlands in 1990, 1995, and 2001' *The Lancet*, published online 17 June 2003. Available at http://image.thelancet.com/extras/03art3297web.pdf (accessed on 08/03/07).

14 Seale, C, 'National survey of end-of-life decisions made by UK medical practitioners', *Palliative Medicine* 2006: 20: 3–19.

15 Ibid. at p 6.

16 Ibid. at p 8.

17 Kuhse, H, Singer, P, Baume, M, Clark, M, Rickard, M, 'End-of-life decisions in Australian medical practice', 166 *Medical Journal of Australia* 191–196 (1997) available at http://www.mja.com.au/public/issues/feb17/kuhse/kuhse.html (accessed on 22/02/07).

of which 335 doctors (77.2%) reported no intention to hasten death, and 99 doctors (22.8%) reported a partial intention to hasten death.[18]

These results, they claim, suggest that Australia's rate of intentional but non-consensual ending of life was 'significantly higher' than in the Netherlands.[19] Thus, they say,

> ... our study undermines suggestions that the rate at which doctors intentionally end patients' lives without an explicit request is higher in a country where euthanasia is practised openly (the Netherlands) than in a comparable country which has not allowed euthanasia to be practised openly, such as Australia.[20]

Bagaric, however, suggests that these results do not *in fact* undermine the slippery slope argument.[21] Rather, he argues, doctors in Australia were effectively in the same position as those in the Netherlands, so that the apparent difference between the legal regimes is ephemeral. Using Kuhse's analysis, he estimates that in the period that she and her colleagues were conducting their research there were 125,771 deaths in Australia. On their argument, he argues, this would mean that there would have been 6,700 cases of voluntary and non-voluntary euthanasia, yet not one single prosecution was brought against a doctor. Quite simply, he says, the law is not enforced, thus effectively equiparating the position in Australia and the Netherlands and defeating the significance of the Australian findings.

If detection and punishment are absent, he continues, then there is no deterrent from unlawful behaviour and he argues that 'the only cogent evidence . . . shows that in a climate where voluntary euthanasia is condoned, there are also a large number of cases of non-voluntary euthanasia'.[22] Two things need to be said in response, however. First, it is overly simplistic to maintain that people only obey the law when they believe that failure to do so will result in punishment. There are many more reasons for obedience than this. To give a simple example: I am an otherwise upright citizen with no criminal record, but a good knowledge of forensic science, who decides to murder a stranger. The chances of my act being followed by apprehension or punishment are extremely remote as there would be no reason to suspect me and I know how to avoid leaving incriminating evidence behind. I have neither a history of violence – or indeed any criminal behaviour – nor any

---

18   Ibid. transcript at pp 4–5.
19   Ibid. at p 6.
20   Ibid. at p 7.
21   Bagaric, M, 'The Kuhse-Singer euthanasia survey: why it fails to undermine the slippery slope argument – comparing apples and apples', *European Journal of Health Law*, 9, 229–241, 2002.
22   Ibid. at p 233.

link to the person who has been killed. Therefore, I have virtually no fear of being punished. Yet, I still would not do this for a variety of ethical, social and political reasons. Thus, the Australian and the Dutch doctors do not operate in the same climate and their positions are not the same. Second, it may well be that where voluntary assisted dying is condoned there will be examples of non-voluntary assisted deaths, but this, as we have seen, is true *whether or not* the law overtly condones assisted dying.

In the case of the Netherlands it may also be argued that the number of non-consensual killings apparently brought about might plausibly suggest that, even where assisted dying has been legalised, the boundaries have been drawn too tightly, forcing or encouraging people to act outside of these constraints, possibly for perfectly benign reasons. Equally, the statistical evidence from the Netherlands does not show what was the pattern before legalisation; Lewis, for example, argues that '[t]here is no evidence from the Netherlands that the legalisation of voluntary euthanasia caused an increase in the rate of non-voluntary euthanasia'.[23] Despite this, as we have seen, many have used the slippery slope argument in interpreting the Dutch situation, with, as Lewis notes, 'little attempt to evaluate the data robustly or to consider the effect on such arguments of the vastly different social context'.[24] Further, Griffiths, Bood and Weyers suggest that the application of the slippery slope argument to the Netherlands is erroneous because it gets 'the direction of legal developments backwards. It assumes a tendency towards relaxing legal control over medical behaviour, whereas what is going on is a quite massive *increase* of control'.[25] In fact, it has been suggested that the rate of requests has stabilised and 'physicians seem to have become somewhat more restrictive in their use'.[26] In any case, as we have already discussed, slippery slope arguments are inherently 'extremely problematic'.[27] As an example of how it is possible to put adequate safeguards in place, Hilliard points to the State of Oregon where 'so far abuses have not occurred'.[28]

Oregon

The State of Oregon remains the only one in the United States where assisted dying is legalised. Challenges to the laws in New York[29] and Washington[30]

23 Lewis, P, 'The Empirical Slippery Slope from Voluntary to Non-Voluntary Euthanasia', *Journal of Law, Medicine and Ethics*, Spring 2007, 197–210, at p 205.
24 Ibid.
25 Griffiths, Bood, Weyers, op. cit. at p 302.
26 Onwuteaka-Philipsen *et al* (2003) at p 4.
27 Hilliard, B, *The US Supreme Court and Medical Ethics*, 2004, St Paul Mn: Paragon, at p 331.
28 Ibid.
29 *Vacco and others v Quill and others* (1997) 50 BMLR 119.
30 *Washington and another v Glucksberg and others* (1997) 50 BMLR 65.

which prohibit assisted dying were not successful, with the US Supreme Court holding in both cases that the prohibition did not breach the Equal Protection Clause of the 14th Amendment to the United States Constitution. In Oregon, however, as the result of a citizen's initiative, physician assisted suicide – but not voluntary euthanasia – was legalised by the 1994 Death With Dignity Act (DWDA). This initiative survived an initial challenge which delayed its implementation and was recently upheld by the US Supreme Court.[31]

As we have seen, the Act only permits physician-assisted suicide. To be eligible for assistance, a patient must be over 18 years of age, legally competent, suffering from a terminal disease and a resident of Oregon.[32] In order to obtain a prescription

> . . . to end his or her life in a humane and dignified manner, a qualified patient shall have made an oral request and a written request, and reiterate the oral request to his or her attending physician no less than fifteen (15) days after making the initial oral request. At the time the qualified patient makes his or her second oral request, the attending physician shall offer the patient an opportunity to rescind the request.[33]

The request can be rescinded 'at any time and in any manner without regard to his or her mental state'.[34] Finally, no prescription can be written until 48 hours has passed from the patient's final, written request.[35]

As in the Netherlands, the prospect of legalisation resulted in anxiety about the kinds of people who would seek to take advantage of the law. For example, some predicted that 'the patients most likely to avail themselves of PAS would be the poor, the ill-educated, and the uninsured who are without access to adequate hospice care'.[36] In addition, the disability lobby expressed its usual concerns about the vulnerability of people with disabilities. So, have these fears been realised?

The Oregon Department of Human Services has produced a report every year on the practice and demographics of physician-assisted suicide. Unlike the speculative arguments of the opponents of legalisation, these reports produce hard data, not mere guesswork as to practice,[37] and, it is argued, show

---

31 For discussion see 'US judges back assisted suicide', available at http://news.bbc.co.uk/1/hi/world/Americas/4621328.stm (accessed on 18/01/06).
32 DWDA 1994, §2.01.
33 DWDA 1994, §3.06.
34 DWDA 1994, §3.07.
35 DWDA 1994, §3.08.
36 Dahl, E and Levy, N, 'The case for physician assisted suicide: how can it possibly be proven?', *Journal of Medical Ethics*, 2006: 32: 335–338, at p 335.
37 For further discussion, see Rothschild, A, 'Oregon: does physician-assisted suicide work?', (2004) 12 *Journal of Legal Medicine* 217.

that 'a previously illegal activity such as physician-assisted suicide could be legislated for without it spiralling out of control . . .'.[38] In its eighth report, the Department offers the following picture:[39]

> In 2005, 39 physicians wrote a total of 64 prescriptions for lethal doses of medication. In 1998, 24 prescriptions were written, followed by 33 in 1999, 39 in 2000, 44 in 2001, 58 in 2002, 68 in 2003, and 60 in 2004.[40]

There is, from these figures, no evidence that legalisation of physician-assisted suicide in Oregon has led to a wholesale slaughter of the weak and the vulnerable as some opponents bleakly hypothesised would happen, nor has there apparently been a rush to seek or provide prescriptions to bring about death. Indeed, in this report the Department calculated that only about 1 in 800 deaths among Oregonians was brought about by assisted suicide.[41] Nor do the characteristics of those availing themselves of assisted suicide match what was feared by some opponents. The report indicates as follows:

> Males and females have been equally likely to take advantage of the DWDA. Divorced and never-married persons were more likely to use PAS than married and widowed residents. A higher level of education has been strongly associated with the use of PAS; Oregonians with a baccalaureate degree or higher were 7.9 times more likely to use PAS than those without a high school diploma. Conversely, several groups have emerged as being less likely to use PAS. These include people age 85 or older, people who did not graduate from high school, people who are married or widowed, and Oregon residents living east of the Cascade Range.[42]

Interestingly, it was found that although over 65 per cent of people using assisted suicide were over the age of 65, the rates of participation actually decreased with age.[43] Nor were patients seeking or using assisted suicide in the absence of alternative support mechanisms or as the result of a financial inability to access other medical treatment. For example, in 2005, everyone using assisted suicide had some form of health insurance – presumably therefore minimising

---

38 Ibid. at p 219.
39 'Eighth Annual Report on Oregon's Death with Dignity Act', Oregon Department of Human Services, 9 March 2006 available at http://egov.oregon.gov/DHS/ph/pas/docs/year8.pdf (accessed on 09/03/07).
40 Ibid. at p 4.
41 Ibid. at p 5.
42 Ibid. at p 12.
43 Ibid. at p 5.

fears about financial pressures leading to a request for death. In addition, 92 per cent of these patients 'were enrolled in hospice care',[44] suggesting that the claims of the palliative care movement in the United Kingdom, which we have already discussed, are ill-founded – at least in Oregon. Based on discussion between the prescribing doctors and their patients, and in support of other evidence, the most frequently cited reasons for seeking an assisted death were 'a decreasing ability to participate in activities that make life enjoyable (89%), loss of dignity (89%), and losing autonomy (79%)'.[45]

One final finding of interest is that not everyone actually uses the prescription they are given, lending weight to the theory that some people want the reassurance that they have the means to control their deaths without necessarily needing or intending to use them immediately – or indeed ever. The report provides the following data:

> Thirty-two of the 2005 prescription recipients died after ingesting the medication. Of the 32 recipients who did not ingest the prescribed medication in 2005, 15 died from their illnesses, and 17 were alive on December 31, 2005. In addition, six patients who received prescriptions during 2004 died in 2005 as a result of ingesting their medication, giving a total of 38 PAS deaths during 2005.[46]

In March 2007, the Department produced its ninth report,[47] which – unlike the earlier reports – appears in abbreviated form. However, it provides comparable information to the eighth report, which was considered in some detail because of its fullness. The report notes that since the law came into effect in 1997, 292 patients have died using the legislation. It also records that:

> During 2006, 65 prescriptions for lethal medications under the provisions of the DWDA were written. . . . Of these, 35 patients took the medications, 19 died of their underlying disease, and 11 were alive at the end of 2006. In addition, 11 patients with earlier prescriptions died from taking the medications, resulting in a total of 46 DWDA deaths during 2006. This corresponds to an estimated 14.7 DWDA deaths per 10,000 total deaths.[48]

Moreover, '[a]ll patients, except one, had some form of health insurance: 64 per cent had private insurance and 33 per cent had Medicare or Medicaid'.[49]

---

44 Ibid. at p 12.
45 Ibid. at p 14.
46 Ibid. at p 11.
47 http://egov.oregon.gov/DHS/ph/pas/docs/year9.pdf (accessed on 09/03/07).
48 Ibid. at p 1.
49 Ibid. at p 2.

The concerns expressed by patients which led them to seeking an assisted death were virtually identical to those recorded in the previous report, and 'participants were more likely to have cancer (87%), and have more formal education (41% had at least a baccalaureate degree) than other Oregonians who died'.[50]

In other words, the position in Oregon has remained relatively stable over the years since the law was changed. A small number of people choose to ask for a prescription to help them die, albeit that not all of them use it. They are typically people who are accustomed to control over their lives, and who apparently wish to attain that same control over their deaths. They are not poor, uneducated or obviously socially vulnerable. Indeed, Rothschild claims that:

> The figures provided by the Oregon Department of Human Services . . . provide evidence that the safeguards and regulations provided by the Act are working and that only those for whom the Act was intended are making use of it. That a previously illegal activity such as physician-assisted suicide could be legislated for without it spiralling out of control seems to have been demonstrated. . . .[51]

What then of the arguments from the disability lobby? As ever, these must be taken seriously, but they can also be challenged. Mayo and Gunderson, for example, argue that, while taking these concerns seriously, evidence from Oregon does not show 'any *additional* risks to patients who may already opt to cut short a fate they view as worse than death'.[52] In fact, as they point out, the safeguards built into the Oregon law are '*more stringent* than those that apply to cases in which terminal patients routinely elect to forgo life-prolonging therapies . . .'[53] (original emphasis).

Certainly, criticisms of the Oregon law have been more muted than those levelled at the Dutch situation. Perhaps this is because of its narrow scope. As we have already seen, the House of Lords Select Committee on the Assisted Dying for the Terminally Ill Bill seemed gently to nudge Lord Joffe in the direction of omitting voluntary euthanasia from his revised Bill, which in fact he did. However, it must be asked whether or not this is either desirable or necessary. Restricting availability to physician-assisted suicide only will limit the number of people who are eligible for an assisted death if the figures from

---

50   Ibid.
51   Rothschild, A, 'Oregon: does physician-assisted suicide work?', (2004) 12 *Journal of Legal Medicine* 217, at p 219.
52   Mayo, D and Gunderson, M, 'Vitalism revitalized: vulnerable populations, prejudice, and physician-assisted death', *Hastings Center Report*, July–August 2002, 14–21, at p 18.
53   Ibid.

the Netherlands and Oregon are to be believed. For opponents, even this is unacceptable; for those on the fence, it may seem that a good outcome is one which allows for some assisted deaths but keeps their numbers small. However, this will not satisfy those who wish to see full legalisation of assisted dying. So, we must ask, would it be feasible – or desirable – to legislate to permit assisted death in both of its forms? If the principles which support legalisation, such as autonomy and respect for persons, are to be vindicated, is there any logic in facilitating them only where people are willing and able to take a lethal prescription, but not where – because of temperament or circumstance – they are unable or unwilling to do so?

The ProLife submission to the House of Lords Select Committee seemed to discount the temperament issue, saying '[o]nly a very tiny number of patients could not commit suicide if they wished to do so'.[54] This somewhat harsh assessment led them to conclude that it was illegitimate to satisfy the needs of this 'small number' 'at the expense of frightening many thousands of vulnerable disabled or ill people . . .'.[55] Their argument, however, ignores the fact that many of those who seek access to assisted dying may have conditions which physically prevent them from committing suicide, either because of their situation, in hospital or hospice, for example, or because they suffer from a degenerative condition that prevents them from taking medication by themselves. In Oregon, '[t]he ratio of DWDA deaths to all deaths resulting from the same underlying illness was highest for three conditions: amyotrophic lateral sclerosis (ALS) (269.5 per 10,000), HIV/AIDS (218.3), and malignant neoplasms (39.9)'.[56]

Second, it must be said that the ProLife submission makes rather large – and untested – assumptions about the number of people who would benefit from legalisation. Although the number of assisted deaths is small in Oregon, evidence from the Netherlands suggests that relaxing the law to allow also for voluntary euthanasia will result in a larger number of people seeking assistance. If respect for autonomy lies at the heart of this debate then there can be no principled objection to this. In any case, numbers are not the issue; it is the suffering of these people that counts. Finally, the assertion that many people would be frightened were assisted dying to be legalised is also made without evidence. We do not know whether this assertion is accurate; it certainly is not obviously logical, and even if we did know this to be the case, that in itself need not mandate denying some people the right to act on their own conscience.

54   ProLife submission to Select Committee, 22 February 2005, available at http://www.prolife.org.uk (accessed on 22/2/05).
55   Ibid.
56   Eighth Report, op. cit. at p 12.

A place for legislation?

As we have seen, efforts at law reform has been made recently in the United Kingdom. However, the adequacy of the proposed legislation can be criticised. Although legislation would be necessary to place the lawfulness of assisted dying beyond doubt, the terms of the Assisted Dying for the Terminally Ill Bill are open to criticism from a variety of perspectives, both from opponents and proponents of legalisation. First, of course, from the opponents' perspective, they are unacceptable because they would allow some people to choose an assisted death. This objection has already been canvassed, and requires no restatement here. There are, however, other concerns that need reflection.

Who should be eligible?

As we have seen, the House of Lords Select Committee on the Assisted Dying for the Terminally Ill Bill seemed to prefer that, if law reform were to occur, assisted suicide rather than voluntary euthanasia should be considered as appropriate for legalisation, and Lord Joffe's most recent attempt at legislation reflects that position. It will be remembered that a qualifying patient would, under the terms of the Bill, be entitled to receive assistance in dying from a medical practitioner under certain conditions. These have already been discussed, but for present purposes the critical ones are that the patient has a terminal illness from which s/he is 'suffering unbearably'.[57]

In evidence to the Select Committee, a number of medical experts gave evidence that it is not always possible to decide clearly when an illness has reached the terminal stage and some also expressed doubts about how unbearable suffering was to be measured. The first of these is potentially problematic, although it seems clear that doctors do indeed make such judgements reasonably regularly. The fact that this is not always a clear-cut decision does not, as opponents of the Bill would argue, mean that it is unworkable; merely it means that doctors will require to be satisfied with the reliability of their prognosis. Arguably, this is no different from the current position where doctors not uncommonly tell patients that their condition is terminal. The second caveat is, I would have thought, relatively straightforward to resolve. Surely, it is for the individual to decide when their suffering is unbearable? No one else is either required or able to 'measure' it. People will tolerate pain and discomfort in different ways and will have personal views as to how much of either they are prepared to accept and what amounts to suffering.

There are other reasons for critiquing these provisions. If the basis for legalisation of assisted dying rests primarily in respect for autonomy, then it is unclear why such tight constraints should be built around its exercise.

---

57 Assisted Dying for the Terminally Ill Bill, HL Bill 36 54/1, s 2(2)(c) and (d).

As Brazier says, if this *is* the primary argument for legalisation, then the law 'need do no more than ensure a means of obtaining unequivocal evidence of the individual's free and informed choice and that appropriate, human mechanisms exist to effect that choice'.[58] The implications of this would seem to be that there is no need to impose the kinds of constraints that would result from the Joffe Bill in its most recent form. In other words, logic would dictate that any person who wishes an assisted death should be entitled to seek one, providing that they are competent to do so, and that their choice can be given effect to. For those who oppose legalisation even in its narrowest form, this would obviously be anathema and it is seldom argued for even by supporters of legalisation. Yet it is a logical conclusion of an argument based solely or primarily on autonomy.

Although no country in the world – even those which have legalised one or more forms of assisted dying – has been prepared to take that step, although Switzerland is very close, arguably it must be considered if the autonomy/respect for persons arguments truly underpin the demand for law reform. As we have already seen, there are reasons to question why, for example, the clinical condition of the person seeking an assisted death should be relevant to their autonomy rights. People who seek assisted dying will doubtless regard themselves as 'suffering', but that need may have nothing to do either with a clinical diagnosis that their illness is terminal, nor indeed with illness itself. If the aim of legalisation is to demonstrate respect for the wishes of the individual, then basing entitlement on the views of doctors as to diagnosis and prognosis seems set to undermine the very reason for legislating in the first place. It can be argued, therefore, that the seeds of discontent, even abuse, lie not in legalisation itself but rather in the determination to build its legitimacy on a medical model. This, as Magnusson says, presents a challenge for those who want to change the law but are aware of the politics which inevitably lurk behind arguments in this area.[59] If they accept the supremacy of autonomy based arguments, but do not face up to the consequences, they are left desperately floundering; trying to find reasons to draw lines in the sand which will essentially be arbitrary. More worrying for proponents of legalisation is the fact that just as the current regime effectively blocks the exercise of autonomy for some people, so too would any reform which incorporates limitations; which attempts to limit the availability of assisted dying, for example to assisted suicide rather than voluntary euthanasia, or to people with a terminal illness.

There are pretty obvious reasons why *opponents* would want to limit the availability of assisted dying, assuming that they cannot sustain the arguments against any legalisation at all. Entirely consistently, they would want to ensure

58   Brazier, M, 'Euthanasia and the law', *British Medical Bulletin*, 1996: 52 (No 2): 317–325, at p 322.
59   Magnusson, R S, *Angels of Death: Exploring the Euthanasia Underground*, 2002, Yale University Press, at p 213.

that assisted dying would not be widely available to people who are just fed up with life, but it would surely be inconsistent were *proponents* of law reform to accept this.

In fact, it is somewhat strange that the requirement of 'unbearable suffering' is generally – in one form or another – specifically referred to in legislation; after all, which competent person would seek assisted dying on a whim? Moreover, suffering or 'unbearable' suffering is a personal and subjective consideration – requiring evidence of its existence is both cosmetic and futile. Surely, patients will simply announce themselves to be suffering 'unbearably' if they wish to access an assisted death, and nobody can refute this. Alternatively, suffering that is tolerable to some may be 'unbearable' to others. There is no instrument that can measure the 'unbearableness' of suffering and we must rely on what the individual him- or herself claims to be experiencing. Of course, as I have suggested, there are political reasons to support such limitations on autonomous choice, and these reasons may explain why even organisations such as Dignity in Dying have thrown their support behind the Joffe Bill.[60] The moral outrage that would accompany a more liberal Bill would surely spell its immediate rejection. Thus, while logic dictates that *all* autonomous requests for assisted dying should be respected, albeit that this does not preclude attempts to change people's mind nor the offer of alternatives, pragmatic considerations seem to have resulted in denial of that logic and the refusal to certain people of respect for their choices. Most notably, the eligibility constraints imposed where assisted dying has been legalised depend heavily on the judgement of healthcare professionals – generally doctors. Interestingly, this so-called medical model is criticised even by one of the strongest opponents of assisted dying, who points out that '[a]ny permission of euthanasia, voluntary or involuntary, will obviously be a huge accession of power to physicians and healthcare personnel'.[61] This presents one further reason for reconsidering the limitations currently in place elsewhere, or proposed in the United Kingdom. The argument from autonomy is about gathering power to the individual, not awarding it to healthcare professionals. Resting the question of access to assisted dying on clinical considerations still results in disempowering those who, for their own reasons, wish an assisted death. While I have argued that the involvement of doctors, for example in providing the prescription or a lethal injection, does not in itself medicalise the issue, making doctors the gatekeepers obviously does. While it is common to limit lawfulness in this way, it is, as I have argued, not by any means essential to do so and indeed it may be more respectful of the autonomy argument that underpins the claim for legalisation that we consider separating clinical considerations from issues about eligibility.

60 For further information, see http://www.dignityindying.org.uk (accessed on 13/04/07).
61 Finnis, J, 'Euthanasia, morality, and law', (1998) *Loyola of Los Angeles Law Review*, Vol. 31: 1123–1146, at p 1139.

That aside, there are other questions that need to be asked about legalisation. Assuming for the moment that proponents of legalisation win the day, many – even among them – would still want reassurance that it is possible to build a legislative regime which contains sufficient safeguards to prevent abuse.

Is it possible to build robust regulation?

For opponents of legalisation, the answer to this is clearly 'no'. The Disability Rights Commission, for example, contends that there is no jurisdiction that has succeeded in building a law which protects vulnerable people from the possibility of pressure to seek assisted dying.[62] Equally, the Amici Curiae Brief of Not Dead Yet and American Disabled for Attendant Programs Today in Support of Petitioners, in the case of *Vacco, et al v Quill, et al*, maintains that

> ... no system of safeguards can control conduct which results in the death of the primary witness to any wrongdoing or duress. The only 'safeguard' that offers some protection against abuse is that assisted suicide remain illegal and socially condemned for all citizens equally.[63]

And, of course, because legislation almost inevitably places boundaries on those who are entitled to obtain an assisted death, an important question is 'whether it is possible to draft a statute that will cover all and only the justifiable cases'.[64] This is an important question if we want, in addition to legalisation, to ensure that the law is respected – although, of course, the current law is not even in those countries where assisted dying is outlawed. Magnusson suggests that even if we did legalise assisted dying, this would not 'do away entirely with demand for illicit euthanasia in cases not satisfying statutory criteria. Any legalised euthanasia regime will also carry its own share of risks, as opponents of legalisation are swift to point to (and inflate).'[65] Of course, this concern is inflated, not least because it assumes that the fact that there may be examples of disrespect for the law is a *consequence* of legalisation, rather than an already existing fact of life. What we would need to show, if this were to be an effective critique of legalisation, is that law reform would

62   Disability Rights Commission, Briefing and Reports, available at http://www.drc-gb.org at para. 2.3 (accessed on 13/03/07).
63   Amici Curiae Brief of Not Dead Yet and American Disabled for Attendant Programs Today in Support of Petitioners, in the case of *Vacco, et al v Quill, et al*, No 95–1858, Supreme Court of the US, October Term 1995, at http://www.notdeadyet.org (accessed on 18/06/03).
64   Steinbock, B, 'The case for physician assisted suicide: not (yet) proven', (2005) 31 *Journal of Medical Ethics*, 235–241, at p 237.
65   Magnusson, op. cit. at p 247.

result in a worse situation than that which currently exists. For some, it is self-evident that things would be worse in a legalised regime. For example, the Disability Rights Commission sees a clear link between legalisation of voluntary assisted death and pressure or coercion on people with disabilities to end their lives. This slippery slope argument has already been considered and rejected, but its constant repetition particularly by the disability rights community means that it certainly reflects a real fear. What this suggests, however, is not that we cannot find a way of reassuring; merely that we need to be sure that requests are in fact voluntary and, of course, that we build a society in which people with disabilities are enabled to live their lives to their full potential. In any case, despite the Disability Rights Commission's claim that no regulatory structure has been shown to avoid abuse, it is arguable that the Dutch experience has done just that. More significant, perhaps, is the Oregon experience which, as we have seen, shows no sign of being abused or of targeting the disabled or any other potentially vulnerable group. Emanuel argues that '[t]he pressure to legalize euthanasia and PAS comes from relatively educated, well-off, politically vocal people'.[66] While this comment is probably intended to provide a reason for not legalising assisted dying, the experience in Oregon in particular suggests that these are also the people who choose to take advantage of it. It is not, therefore, the 'vulnerable' who are pushed into choosing death; rather, people who have valued choice in life have applied that control to their deaths.

There is apparently a widespread view that legislation requires 'detailed procedures',[67] such presumably as those which Oregon has imposed. Whether or not abuse would occur in the absence of these procedures is, however, moot. Certainly – if this can be called abuse – we know that the current law is ignored on occasion. This, some would suggest, means that:

> a strong argument can be made that the best way to ameliorate slippery slope concerns is to bring euthanasia out in the open by legalising it and hence providing the environment in which proper safeguards can be implemented to prevent abuses.[68]

However, it is also claimed that because '[i]ssues of life and death do not lend themselves to clear definition' it follows that 'it would be impossible to ensure that it would be possible to frame adequate safeguards against non-voluntary euthanasia were voluntary euthanasia to be legalised'.[69]

---

66 Emanuel, E J, 'What is the great benefit of legalizing euthanasia or physician-assisted suicide?' *Ethics* 109 (April 1999), 629–642, at p 641.
67 Cohen-Almagor, op. cit. at p 187.
68 Bagaric, (2002), at p 230.
69 Ibid. at p 234.

This may be so. However, it is not self-evidently so, nor universally accepted. Dieterle, for example, supports legalisation because '[i]f the practice is legal and out in the open, it is easier to put safeguards in place and make sure they are followed'.[70] In any case, Frey argues that '[m]erely to fear the failure of safeguards is not itself to show the failure of any particular one'.[71] It may, of course, be that no law – including, therefore, the current one – is able to withstand the possibility that it will on occasion be circumvented. However, as Jackson argues, '[i]t is important to remember that the fact that it is difficult to regulate a particular practice does not make that practice morally wrong'.[72] She concludes that '. . . hypothetical speculation about an as yet unwritten law's possible future inefficacy does not offer adequate justification for a refusal to contemplate thinking about how we might attempt to regulate euthanasia effectively'.[73] In any case, as has been said,

> . . . every social policy has the *potential* for abuse. When other important rights are at stake, we cannot let the mere potential for abuse of the law keep us from enacting said law. We have to try to foresee those possible abuses and put controls in place so that the abuses rarely, if ever, occur.[74]

The question, therefore, might be not so much whether we should legalise assisted dying, but rather 'whether the practice should proceed underground and unregulated, or openly and regulated to protect patients, regularize access, and accommodate legitimate state interests'.[75] Whether the law is capable of achieving this, however, has been of considerable interest for the anti-legalisation lobby. However, if it is agreed that respect for autonomy underpins the primary support for legalisation, it has been suggested here that logically all competent requests for assisted death should be respected. If so, then concerns about the possibility of abuse effectively disappear as there is no need to frame laws which contain narrow or prescriptive terms. Merely, the law should be concerned with the competence and voluntariness of the request.

70 Dieterle, J M, 'Physician assisted suicide: a new look at the arguments', *Bioethics*, Vol 21, No 3, 2007, 127–139, at p 130.
71 Frey, R G, 'The fear of a "slippery slope"' in Dworkin, G, Frey, R G, Bok, S, *Euthanasia and Physician-Assisted Suicide: For and Against*, 1998, Cambridge University Press, pp 43–63, at p 47.
72 Jackson, E, 'Whose death is it anyway?: Euthanasia and the medical profession', in Holder, J, O'Cinneide, C and Freeman, M, (eds), *Current Legal Problems 2004*, Vol 57, 415–442, at p 418.
73 Ibid. at p 432.
74 Dieterle, (2007), at p 132.
75 Tucker, K L, 'The death with dignity movement: protecting rights and expanding options after *Glucksberg* and *Quill*', *Minnesota Law Review*, Vol 82: 923–938, 1998, at p 924.

Finally, some commentators have even questioned whether or not the law is in fact the best, or the only, vehicle for ensuring that abuse does not occur. Griffiths, Bood and Weyers, for example, suggest that:

> We can safely assume that doctors generally experience far more and more pressing social control from their professional surroundings than from the law and that this applies as much to euthanasia as to other aspects of their practice. We can also safely assume that this professional control is sufficient – especially when taken together with general social norms and control – to ensure that the behaviour of most doctors is socially acceptable most of the time.[76]

However, even if the provision of an assisted death is confined to the discrete area of medical practice, resting the ethics of assisted dying on medical or professional ethics is surely less robust than resting it on autonomy. In any case, it is not essential that doctors are involved, and an ethic would need to be built for non-healthcare professionals if that is so. Respect for autonomy, yet again, seems sufficient. However, one final consideration for this discussion must be precisely the role that doctors would be likely to play under a legalised regime along the lines proposed by Lord Joffe and in place in some other jurisdictions.

Are we giving too much power to doctors?

We have already touched on the possibility that legalisation amounts to medicalisation, but it merits brief reconsideration here. A legal regime based on respect for autonomy implies that it is the person him- or herself who is the actor, even if they need assistance to complete the act. However, because the test for eligibility is generally set in the medical context, the US National Council on Disability suggests that '. . . the more stringent and encompassing one seeks to make procedural safeguards in this context, the more intrusive they become, and the greater the extent to which doctors and psychiatrists become the gatekeepers'.[77] This, it argues, means that the effect of the safeguards and controls is not that people are liberated to act autonomously, but rather that 'the individual's privacy and control of the situation fly out the window, and the medical model runs rampant'.[78] This critique of the so-called medical model is common in disability rights literature, although it is not

---

76 Griffiths, Bood and Weyers, op. cit. at p 259.
77 The National Council on Disability (US), 'Assisted suicide: a disability perspective', available at http://www.ncd.gov/newsroom/publications/1997/suicide.htm (accessed on 16/06/05), at p 13.
78 Ibid.

universally accepted.[79] It has also, of course, been argued here that the fact that medical assistance is presumed to be required to give effect to the individual's expressed wish does not in and of itself 'medicalise' end-of-life decisions. Even in a regime which did not require doctors to be the providers of assisted death, some may choose to become involved. This does not make assisted dying a 'medical' matter, however. Equally in a situation where doctors are the only ones with authority to offer assistance in dying, while this may allow doctors to exercise their conscience and refuse to participate thereby delaying the patient's ability to act on their wishes, this does not mean that doctors are in control rather than the people themselves. In any case, this concern could be simply defeated by removing the gatekeeping function from doctors and leaving it where it should be – in the hands of the individual.

Still others argue that an unfortunate and undesirable outcome of legalisation would be that more lawyers would become involved. Brazier, for example, argues that legalisation 'when a significant number of professionals and laypersons deplore such a move' would mean that the law 'will interfere more not less'.[80] This, it is argued, would result in the current behaviour of doctors, who already ease the passing of some of their patients, being formalised. Yet it must be asked why increased legal intervention is necessarily undesirable. Presumably, it would not be unreasonable to welcome the involvement of the law, whether to ensure that the constraints of the legislation are followed or, more radically, merely to evaluate the competence of the person making the decision.

Conclusion

Concerns about legalisation come from a variety of different sources. On the one hand, it is said, legislation can never be adequately framed to prevent abuse; on the other, legislation gets in the way of doctors doing what is best for their patients by unreasonably forcing this into the public domain. Or, it is said, there is no need to legislate. Only a small number of people want access to assisted dying in any case, so legislating to make it lawful is disproportionate, and even if we could identify some cases where assisted dying could be justified, this does not in and of itself justify legalisation. Steinbock, for example, argues that because legislation is 'inherently general', this means that it 'must be drafted to cover many cases' and cannot therefore identify those which are justifiable and those which are not.[81] This, of course, rests on the assumption that there are ethically unjustifiable cases, an argument that seems indecently paternalistic. If it is for the person him- or herself autonomously

---

79   See, e.g., Shakespeare, T, *Disability Rights and Wrongs*, 2006, Abingdon: Routledge.
80   Brazier, (1996), at p 324.
81   Steinbock, (2005), at p 237.

and competently to conclude on whether they wish an assisted death, who has the right, the knowledge or the authority to decide that this is illegitimate or not justified? Moreover, as Dworkin asks:

> Is it fair that even a small number of patients suffer greatly because we cannot design an institution that will not at the same time cause others to be exposed to pressures of various kinds, or that others will abuse such a permission?[82]

The fear of possible abuse seems to lie at the very heart of the argument here. The likelihood of abuse occurring is highly speculative, of course, which leads some commentators to suggest that unless and until we have obtained evidence it would be folly to proceed to legalisation. The drive to identify empirical evidence is primarily generated by those who oppose legalisation and serves two purposes. First, it suggests that, for example by looking at regimes in other parts of the world and counting the emerging statistical information, we will somehow gain a better picture of what might happen here. I have deliberately tried to avoid 'number crunching' in this narrative, but the collection of empirical evidence of this sort is argued by some to be important. However, the problem is that, as the debate on the Dutch situation in particular shows, numbers can and will be interpreted differently even assuming that solid evidence became available. As Jackson has said, any collected data would 'interpreted through the partisan lens of the opponent or the supporter of legalisation'.[83] The value of such data, then, is in doubt even although it sounds at first sight reasonable that empirical evidence is collected. Coggon also questions the value of empirical evidence on the grounds that the debate on assisted suicide is 'unavoidably partisan and that the protagonists will therefore receive data differently, necessarily because of their moral and philosophical convictions'.[84]

A second consequence of the claim that we should wait until evidence is available on the likelihood and/or scale of abuse, is 'to objectify individuals in the name of a particular moral view about killing'.[85] Rather, Parker suggests, '*individual* rights are often much more efficiently secured through allegiance to abstract principle'.[86] Finally, he argues that the seemingly innocuous demand for more information is little more than a device to delay the decision

---

82 Dworkin, G, 'Public policy and physician-assisted suicide', in Dworkin, Frey and Bok, op. cit. 64–80, at p 77.

83 Jackson, (2004), at p 431.

84 Coggon, J, 'Arguing about physician-assisted suicide: a response to Steinbock', *Journal of Medical Ethics*, 2006: 32: 339–341, at p 339.

85 Parker, M, 'End games: euthanasia under interminable scrutiny', *Bioethics*, Vol 19, Nos 5–6 2005, 523–536, at p 536.

86 Ibid.

'since as long as there are more data to be discovered, it can be claimed that resolution is premature'.[87]

There are, then, many and varied ways to resist law reform in this area based primarily either on the alleged difficulties of legislating safely or in the speculative harm that would allegedly flow from any such legislation. Of course, were it the case that immense harm would follow legalisation, then we would have reason for caution, but despite the best efforts of opponents, no such evidence exists. Frey correctly says that '[t]he mere possibility that such consequences might occur . . . does not constitute evidence'.[88] Further, Dworkin suggests, '[a]t the very least one should assign the *onus probandi* to those who propose to deny the legalization of such a moral claim on the basis of predicted abuses'.[89]

Of course, much of the debate about legislation and consequentially legalisation centres on two critical factors. One is the argument that autonomy, the dominant value in modern biomedical ethics, should be the benchmark against which we judge what is and is not permissible. If autonomous people, no matter how many or how few, want to take control of their deaths as well as their lives, then we should respect that. If it is possible to reach such a decision competently, and we have no reason to believe that it is not, then third parties – including the state and the law – have no justification for interfering; indeed, they may have an obligation to respect such choices, without imposing additional constraints, just as happens when someone refuses life-sustaining treatment.

Second is the concern about safeguards. Although this takes up a considerable amount of the literature in this area, I have suggested that it is essentially an artefact rather than a true obstacle to legalisation. The fact is that although virtually every country that has legalised assisted dying has gone down the path of defining eligibility – however broadly or narrowly – this is by no means a necessary component of radical law reform. A prime example of the radical view is that of Switzerland where – although, as in all jurisdictions it is a crime to take someone else's life – consensual killing is permitted unless it is carried out for 'self-serving ends'. Self-serving ends have been defined as encapsulating a desire 'to satisfy his own material or emotional needs . . . the possibility of eliminating some major problem for the family, or other motives such as gaining an inheritance, relieving himself of the burden of supporting the individual. . . . Or eliminating a person he hated'.[90] Assisted dying is not confined to doctors, and as we have seen, a number of voluntary organisations

---

87 Ibid. at p 524.
88 Frey, in Dworkin, Fey and Bok, op. cit. at p 63.
89 Op. cit. at p 80.
90 Response from the Swiss Federal Ministry of Justice to the *House of Lords Select Committee on the Assisted Suicide for the Terminally Ill Bill*, quoted in the Committee's Report, op. cit. at p 69, para 195.

have sprung up which are willing to assist people to die – even those travelling from overseas. Nor is it linked specifically to evidence of a clinical or terminal condition. The focus, in my view correctly, when classifying behaviour as criminal or not, is not on the *reason* for the request but on the *state of mind* of the actor. Where that state of mind is negative or inherently criminal, then any death resulting from it will be a crime, as seems entirely reasonable. Otherwise, people can expect to be able to exercise their autonomy free from the relatively arbitrary constraints which characterise the law in other jurisdictions whether or not assisted dying occurs *de facto* or *de jure*.

Although the schemes in place in Oregon and the Netherlands are those most usually the subject of debate, the Swiss model seems to provide an alternative worthy of serious consideration. It defeats the charge of medicalisation, it imports no unnecessary limitations on access thereby eliminating the discrimination evident in other regimes, it avoids concerns (whether real or exaggerated) about interpretation of statute and it places the law's focus where it usually is, and in my view should be; that is, on the intention of the actor, rather than on the characteristics of the requestor. Most importantly, it recognises that '[i]f autonomy is a highly valued principle it is logical that patients, especially, and possibly families should have the right to participate in all end-of-life decisions'.[91] The current legal position in the United Kingdom is every bit as regrettable as some would have us believe is true in countries where assisted dying in one form or another is legal. Indeed, in its recent review of the law of murder, the Law Commission (England and Wales) recommended a separate inquiry into 'mercy killings',[92] saying:

> Although they are intentional killings, and thus in principle fall in the top tier of the law of homicide, they commonly share a distinctive quality. A 'mercy' killing involves an intention to prevent the continuation of one kind of harm (extreme pain and suffering) to a person by doing another kind of harm (killing) to the very same person.[93]

Because of the complexity of this subject and the shortage of time available to it, the Law Commission believes that this should be subject to separate consultation, although it devotes one chapter of its report to the subject. We can only await the initiation of any such consultation and its outcome.

---

91 Fraser, S I and Walters, J W, 'Death – whose decision? Euthanasia and the terminally ill', *Journal of Medical Ethics*, 2006: 26: 121–125, at p 123.
92 Murder, Manslaughter and Infanticide (LC 304) (2006). This report is available at http://www.lawcom.gov.uk/docs/lc304.pdf (accessed on 13/03/07).
93 Ibid. at p 155.

Chapter 7

Conclusion

> It is hard to die in America. A process that should shield patients as they disengage from life instead leads with increasing frequency to conflict and media attention and provides an opportunity for third parties with political or self-serving agendas to feather their particular ideological and personal nests.[1]

It is hard to die in the United Kingdom as well, and for similar reasons. As we have seen, ideological and political pressures are brought to bear on those who want to choose an assisted death. A powerful taboo still surrounds even talking about death, far less choosing it, resulting in lack of consistency and clarity in both law and practice. Fletcher, for example, says '[w]hat it comes down to is that most people, including the courts, want the end – death – in certain tragic situations, but the taboo forbids the means'.[2]

Death is, of course, the 'final frontier' from which we will never return. For that reason, many of us fear both the process of dying and the fact of death. Doubtless, we would all wish to live for as long and as healthily as we can. However, not even the miracles of modern medicine can postpone the inevitable and in many cases all that they achieve is an extension of a life which, for the person experiencing it, is characterised by pain, indignity, suffering and distress.[3] While some people will experience spiritual comfort throughout the dying process and regard the enduring of suffering as a high moral calling, others will regard this process with acute dismay. While some believe that life is a non-returnable gift from God, others believe that life is for them to control. As I said at the beginning of this narrative, these positions are

---

1   Dubler, N N, 'Conflict and consensus at the end of life', Improving end of life care: why has it been so difficult? *Hastings Center Report Special Report*, 35, No 6, S19–S25, at S19.
2   Fletcher, J, 'The courts and euthanasia', *Law, Medicine & Health Care*, 1987/88, Vol 15: 4, Winter, 223, at p 226.
3   Callahan, D, *The Troubled Dream of Life: In Search of a Peaceful Death*, 2000, Washington, DC: Georgetown University Press.

essentially impossible to reconcile. At best, we can respect each other's views, but it is unlikely that we will persuade each other of the rightness of our own position. The primary consequence of this is that we must try to identify how we can best accommodate the views of each side in this debate – and those somewhere in the middle. At the same time, I have argued that we must strive to minimise harm and maximise liberty.

Before attempting to explore how we might do this, it is worth briefly restating the major arguments in this area. At a theoretical level, one of the principal arguments against legalising assisted dying is that it disrespects the ethical principle that all human life is sacred. On closer inspection, however, this argument fails to amount to a convincing case against legalisation – except for those who hold it as a tenet of faith, when it ceases to be subject to rational argument and becomes instead a matter of personal conscience. On the other hand, the reduction of the importance of religion in society results in 'the view that each individual controls his or her own life. This autonomy-based view of human life places the burdens of continued existence squarely on the shoulders of the individual, rather than society'.[4]

In any case, even if one believes that all human life is sacred that imposes only an obligation to demonstrate that respect – at least in the secular version – is shown for the lives of others – not that continued existence is an *obligation*. One can, therefore, respect human life – both practically and existentially – yet concede that some people no longer wish to be alive and place no obstacles in the way of their free exercise of that choice. Legally, the sanctity of life is widely referred to as a paramount principle, but, as has been said in a number of cases, it will be superseded by the value of respect for autonomy. Thus, although law and society must pay serious attention to the sanctity of life, when autonomy enters the equation the individual wields the ultimate power. This has been clearly stated in a number of cases, perhaps most clearly in the case of *Re T*,[5] where Lord Donaldson said:

> The patient's interest consists of his right to self-determination – his right to live his own life how he wishes, even if it will damage his health or lead to his premature death. Society's interest is in upholding the concept that all human life is sacred and that it should be preserved if at all possible. It is well established that in the ultimate the right of the individual is paramount.[6]

4   Thomasma, D C, 'An analysis of arguments for and against euthanasia and assisted suicide: Part one', *Cambridge Quarterly of Healthcare Ethics*, (1996), 5, 62–76, at p 69.
5   *Re T (Adult: Refusal of Medical Treatment)* (1992) 9 BMLR 46.
6   Ibid. at p 59.

Since I have adopted the classic libertarian approach to this argument, the primacy of free choice will be defeated only if it can be shown that harm to third parties would be prevented by limiting autonomy. So, the first question we must ask is whether or not there is evidence or reasonable likelihood that harm would indeed follow the legalisation of assisted dying. Were evidence available then it would, even in the liberal tradition, justify a reconsideration of the extent to which autonomy should prevail. It has been argued here, however, that no such evidence exists; indeed, it is arguably impossible to find it. To be sure, people who oppose legalisation of assisted dying may feel offended were their views not to predominate (as they currently do) but this is surely a much lesser 'evil' than the denial of what, for many people, is the only route to liberation from the chains of illness, despair, distress and discomfort. Despite advances in palliative medicine, and even were it widely and equally available, there is evidence that it will not in all cases be sufficient to distract people from their competent and resolute desire for assistance in their death. Indeed, it is plausible to argue that the current situation is itself a direct cause of harm. Cassel and Meier, for example, illustrate the disbenefits that can result from prohibition on the exercise of an autonomous choice for death:

> The fear and anxiety that many people feel when contemplating chronic and terminal debilitating illness is rooted, at least in part, in the fear that their suffering will be prolonged by medical technology and that they will have little or no control over its application. In this context, the medical profession's repeated and firm rejection of any participation by physicians in assisted suicide begins to appear self-serving in its emphasis on a professional scrupulosity that seems blind to the expressed needs of the patients.[7]

This harm is not speculative; we know that it exists and that it can be crippling. The efforts of people such as Diane Pretty show just how important and distressing fear of the way we die can be. As we all die, we all have an interest in doing so in the best possible way and for some people this is not resignation to the suffering we will endure, but rather in a confident, peaceful and personally directed way. A 'good' death, then can be described as 'one that is fitting and appropriate for the person whose life is being brought to a close, for the community of those intimately concerned with the dying person, and for society as a whole'.[8] As Miller argues, this definition of a 'good' death must allow for the encapsulation of assisted dying.

---

7 Cassel, C K and Meier, D E, 'Morals and moralism in the debate over euthanasia and assisted suicide', *New England Journal of Medicine*, (1990), Vol 323, No 11, 750–752, at p 751.
8 Miller, F G, 'A communitarian approach to physician-assisted death', *Cambridge Quarterly of Healthcare Ethics*, (1997) 6, 78–87, at p 86.

Of course, it could be said that if people wish to die, they can do so by killing themselves; that is, that suicide – which is not a crime – is available to the convinced and the determined. This, however, is not only an obfuscation of the concerns at the heart of this debate it is also a misrepresentation of reality. Some people can and do take their own lives; for others this is extremely difficult. For example, some people may be psychologically incapable of suicide, particularly as the means for self-killing are becoming more diffi-cult to attain. Whereas in the past dangerous drugs which could bring about a speedy death were widely available, control of medicinal substances has become increasingly tight making it more difficult to choose this option and successfully bring about a suicide. Equally, some may be precluded from suicide either because they are being carefully watched by medical staff in a hospital setting or because their physical condition prevents them from acting alone. For these people, then, suicide is not an option; help is needed if they are to achieve the 'good' death they desire. Unless we are prepared to continue to inflict suffering on these groups of people, it is necessary to reconsider the prohibition on assisted dying.

Conversely, of course, it might be argued that reconsideration is unneces-sary. After all, the deliberate killing of another is a crime and has been since time immemorial. Since assisted dying – at least in one of its forms – entails the direct and deliberate killing of a third party, it is murder pure and simple. However, it can also be argued that 'it is not that killing a person is wrong *simpliciter*, it is wrong in the absence of a compelling reason'.[9] Therefore, Haber concludes, 'this does not mean that we ought never to kill. What we ought never to do is to kill in the absence of a compelling reason'.[10] The competent wish of someone to die is surely one such compelling reason.

One of the fears of opponents of legalisation is the so-called slippery slope argument which has been extensively discussed in previous chapters. This all too popular argument postulates that the result of legalisation will inevitably be that those who do not request assisted dying, or who do not do so competently, will become victims of a society which will increasingly lose its moral tone and will tolerate, or at least not object to, increasing levels of encroachment on the sanctity of life. The worst-case scenario, often used by those who endorse the slippery slope, is that the horrors of regimes such as the Nazis will be revisited upon us under a liberalised assisted dying system. However, not only is the Nazi analogy overused and fundamentally flawed in this context, there is no reason to believe that the slippery slope argument actually works. We are quite capable of drawing appropriate boundaries – indeed we do so all of the time. Moreover, if autonomy is at the heart of permissibility, then it simply makes no sense to propose that allowing competent choice will inevitably result in

---

9   Haber, J G, 'Should physicians assist the reaper?', *Cambridge Quarterly of Healthcare Ethics*, (1996) 5, 44–49, at p 45.
10 Ibid. at p 46.

non-consensual decisions being made. The search for a 'dignified' death is a quest for self-governance and, as Coggon says, 'each individual would be at liberty to exclude from his definition of dignity the notion of a duty to die'.[11] Although some people point to the experience of countries and states where assisted dying in one form or another has been legalised and raise anxieties about what they see as the slippery slope in action, the figures on which they base their claims are open to wide and differing interpretation. Proponents of legalised assisted dying will use the same information to show that the slippery slope is in fact a fantasy. In any case, it is possible that permitting assisted dying 'rather than weakening the value we place on life, actually strengthens it by ensuring that the *life* of the individual is not despoiled by its finishing in a degrading manner and by respecting the opinions of the individual'.[12]

It should also, of course, be noted that we already do permit, in law and apparently in ethics, the termination of some lives – whether chosen or not. Patients who have life-sustaining treatment that they can refuse are legally empowered to do so, even when it is clear that they are choosing death over life. Healthcare professionals are legally required to respect this decision, irrespective of whether they like it or not. Equally, people can, by making an advance statement or directive, decide in advance of incompetence that life in certain conditions is unacceptable. Where such directives are competently made and applicable to the circumstances healthcare professionals are legally obliged to follow them. In addition, it is not only the individual's own choice that might result in their death being brought about knowingly. As we have seen, patients in a permanent vegetative state (PVS), handicapped neonates and people who have a Do Not Resuscitate Order (DNR) placed in their medical charts – whether or not they are aware of this – will find themselves assisted to die either by the failure to continue life-sustaining treatment or the failure to offer it.

Those who oppose legalisation of assisted dying, but who find these latter examples broadly acceptable, try to distinguish between them and an assisted death based on the pernicious principle of acts/omissions. This principle holds roughly that killing is unacceptable whereas letting die is not. That is, it is both ethical and lawful to remove the means of survival from an individual – based either on their own request or on the judgements of third parties – but it can never be either ethical or legally acceptable to accede to a competent request for active assistance in dying. Leaving aside the argument as to whether or not, for example removing assisted nutrition and hydration is an act or an omission, it surely beggars belief that such a purported distinction can be conceded. In fact, any such distinction, while it may appeal to (some) healthcare

---

11   Coggon, J, 'Could the right to die with dignity represent a new right to die in English law?', *Medical Law Review*, 14, Summer 2006, 219–237, at p 229.

12   Shand, J, 'A reply to some standard objections to euthanasia', *Journal of Applied Philosophy*, Vol 14, No 1, 1997, 43–47, at p 45.

professionals, is unlikely to commend itself to the person who wants an assisted death. Indeed, it probably does not commend itself in all logic to many others. In fact, as Orentlicher points out, '[w]hen we parse the usual arguments for a moral difference between treatment withdrawal and assisted suicide, we will see that none of the arguments really justify the law's rejection of a right to assisted suicide'.[13]

The problem is that the alleged distinction has served courts well in the past, even if some of our most distinguished judges have commented on its fundamental flaws. Adhering to the concept allows fine, sometimes virtually invisible, lines to be drawn so that some deaths can be allowed and others not. It is not clear why this effort should be made, unless it is an attempt to reinforce the religious view of the sanctity of life. On the other hand, this would be somewhat strange given that courts, as we have seen, in fact generally use the secular version of this principle thereby allowing autonomy to trump sanctity. It seems more likely that the distinction has commended itself to opponents of legalised assisted dying because it reflects the views of the healthcare professionals who would (usually) be presumed to have responsibility for being the primary actors in assisted dying.

That doctors and their patients may view assisted dying differently from each other is probably unsurprising. Doctors' views are generally taken seriously because it is generally anticipated that they would be given the responsibility of providing the means to the person who seeks death or actively to carry out euthanasia.[14] Doctors may be able to convince themselves that in withholding or withdrawing treatment they merely let nature take its course, avoiding value judgements and a moral quagmire. However, this is an intellectual or moral sleight of hand. For example, the aim, the intention and the outcome of removing assisted nutrition and hydration (ANH) from a patient in PVS are quite clearly to bring about the death of the patient; this is conceded even by many judges. The primary difference here then is not between acting and omitting to act but between the intuitions, morality or preferences of (some) healthcare professionals and the desires or needs of (some of) their patients.

Some commentators have suggested that legalising assisted dying, far from handing authority to the patient, in fact gives increased power and authority to doctors although, as will be seen, '[i]t is not self-evident that the medical profession should be in a position to end the life of a patient just because it is held that human life is under the autonomous control of the patient'.[15] Others claim that 'legalized aid in dying will give physicians – not patients

13   Orentlicher, D, *Matters of Life and Death: Making Moral Theory Work in Medical Ethics and the Law*, 2001, Princeton and Oxford: Princeton University Press, at p 20.

14   For further discussion, see Louhiala, P and Hilden, H-M, 'Attitudes of Finnish doctors towards euthanasia in 1993 and 2003', *Journal of Medical Ethics*, 2006: 32: 627–628.

15   Ten Have, H, 'Euthanasia: moral paradoxes', *Palliative Medicine* 2001: 15: 505–511, at p 508.

– the increased powers to make choices'.[16] However, it is clear rather that it is the current legal position that does this. Patients will have their competent requests for death denied – unless their doctor is prepared to act outside of the law – but doctors can decide when a life should end irrespective of the actual or presumed wishes of the person him- or herself. Were assisted dying legalised, even although doctors might be involved (of which more later), the decision is that of the patient, and who is in a better position to decide on the quality of their own life? It is decision-making authority that people seek when they argue for legalisation; how this is facilitated is of secondary, not primary, concern.

The opacity of the current situation mandates reconsideration of the law. Doctors do engage in assisting their patients to die and the law allows this in certain circumstances. It is time that this is recognised, not least because it can help us to focus on the truly important issues. At present, patients seek active assistance but, almost without exception, they do not receive it. The question then is not what are the sensitivities of the healthcare professions – or some of them – but what are the interests of the individuals themselves? The current law in the United Kingdom results in sophistry and dishonesty at an intellectual level – which in itself could be described as unethical; more importantly, perhaps, it leaves people to suffer or forces them to abandon home, and sometimes family, in order to seek an assisted death elsewhere.

So what are we to make of this. Should the perception that assisted dying is inimical to the tradition and ethics of medicine, and runs counter to the moral positions of some doctors, be sufficient to justify maintaining the status quo? Two points need to be made here. First, although many UK doctors would purport to subscribe to the Hippocratic tradition, which specifically prohibits the provision of deadly potions to patients, in fact the Hippocratic Oath is widely ignored. Few, if any, doctors nowadays would, for example, swear allegiance to a bunch of obscure Greek gods and goddesses as required by the Oath, and many will participate in pregnancy terminations. The claim that the Hippocratic tradition prevents them from ethically participating in assisted dying is cherry-picking at its worst.

Second, there is no good reason why the sensitivities of doctors and other healthcare professionals should underpin either the ethical or the legal position. They are only members of the public; just like you and I. While they might be thought likely to be more intimately involved in assisted dying than I, this objection – if it is a true one – is not unassailable. First, this is so because we could, in theory at least, take the responsibility for assisting out of the hands of healthcare professionals and hand it to some other group – pharmacists for example, or voluntary organisations such as Dignitas in Switzerland. Doing so would meet the question posed by Finlay (herself a doctor), who says:

16 Woodman, S, *Last Rights: The Struggle over the Right to Die*, 1998, New York and London: Plenum Trade, at p 217.

If the law on intentional killing is altered to allow physician-assisted suicide/euthanasia, every clinician looking after sick patients will inevitably be involved at some time. Would you be willing to administer the lethal injection? If not, don't expect others to.[17]

Second, the fact that a conscience clause is always available to healthcare professionals means that those who object to involvement need not participate. Their sensitivities therefore are only of peripheral interest to the debate on principle. What is important is the interest that their patients may have in avoiding an unpleasant death. As Dworkin says, the reasons to favour legalisation

> consist mainly of the interests that dying patients have in the process of dying being as painless and dignified as possible. They also rely on the interest of patients in determining the time and manner of their death. Autonomy and relief of suffering are values that we can all agree to be important.[18]

Further, and following from this, if medicalisation is a charge that needs to be taken seriously, we can avoid it also by removing assisted dying from healthcare professionals. In any case, as I have already argued, the fact that doctors might be involved in assisted dying does not hand authority to them unless we specifically build in a gatekeeping role. Ten Have proposes that this is just what has happened, arguing that 'medical power has increased because physicians decide whether the suffering is so unbearable that the request for euthanasia can be granted'.[19] He concludes that without this gatekeeping by doctors, 'there would be ten times the number of euthanasia cases than occurring presently'.[20] While some may therefore regard the role played by doctors as being a good thing as it may stem the number of assisted deaths, others regret the power that most regimes which have legalised assisted dying give to them. Unfortunately, the scenario described by Ten Have is precisely what would be the outcome of Lord Joffe's Bill and it is also the case in Oregon, Belgium and the Netherlands. It is not inappropriate, therefore, to reconsider what should trigger a lawful request for assisted dying and who should carry it out.

Hinging lawfulness on clinical criteria such as diagnosis of terminal illness, or a medical evaluation of life-expectancy, does place assisted dying firmly within the medical domain; in fact, it does this more than does the mere

---

17 Finlay, I, '"Assisted suicide": is this what we really want?', *British Journal of General Practice*, September 2005, 720–721, at p 721.

18 Dworkin, G, 'Introduction', in Dworkin, G, Frey, R G and Bok, S, *Euthanasia and Physician-Assisted Suicide: For and Against*, 1998, Cambridge University Press, at p 3.

19 Ten Have, (2001), at p 509.

20 Ibid. at p 510.

involvement of doctors in procuring the death itself. Yet, it must be asked why such constraints should be placed on assisted dying. Clinical condition may have little to do with why people commit suicide. Many terminally ill people will hang on to every moment of life, while people who are not ill may choose to reject it by committing suicide. To insist on clinical indications for the provision of assistance is to ignore the kind of suffering experienced by Mr Brongersma, for example; to devalue its impact on our lives and to downplay the misery and degradation that can accompany conditions which have no clinical diagnosis. Of course, opponents would say that the answer is not to give in to this but rather to find ways of alleviating that suffering, and this is unobjectionable. Thus, Lee argues that rather than 'sitting around moralizing' we should find a way to respond to 'suffering individuals in a loving, caring manner . . .'.[21] If we can achieve this, it is argued, 'physician-assisted suicide would be an option rarely, if ever, chosen'.[22] We do not, of course, know this but we can surely agree that if we can help people to choose life, we should. If someone's pain and/or suffering can be relieved, then as a society we should strive to do so. However, this is not always feasible and it is long past time we accepted this; indeed, it is time to accept that, even if a mechanism did exist to ameliorate all of the problems often associated with the dying process, some people might prefer not to accept it. In any case, Davies questions whether the successes, for example of the hospice movement, mean that there is no longer any need to concern ourselves with assisted dying because of 'increasing skill in coping with many of the distresses of dying'.[23]

The next question, then, is who should be allowed to have an assisted death? Some opponents of legalisation see this question as their trump card. If autonomy is the guiding principle in the legalisation argument then this must presumably mean that anyone who wishes exercise his or her autonomous desire for an assisted death should be entitled to have one. Surely, they ask, it cannot be acceptable that anyone, irrespective of their medical condition, should be allowed to seek and obtain an assisted death?[24] However, the question can be thrown back at them; why not? If that same person had the emotional or physical capacity to commit suicide their choice would not be second-guessed and they would commit no crime. If, on the other hand, they prefer to seek (assisted) suicide in a way which may, for example, be less messy than shooting themselves or throwing themselves under a train, or more likely to succeed, such as by taking a measured dose of pills provided by an

21 Lee, D E, 'Physician-assisted suicide: a conservative critique of intervention', *Hastings Center Report* 33 No 1, (2003) 17–19, at p 19.

22 Ibid.

23 Davies, J, 'The case for legalising voluntary euthanasia', in Keown, J, (ed), *Euthanasia Examined: Ethical, Clinical and Legal Perspectives*, 1995 (reprinted 1999), Cambridge University Press, at p 88.

24 See, e.g., Finnis, J, 'Euthanasia, morality, and law', *Loyola of Los Angeles Law Review*, 1998, Vol 31, pp 1123–1146.

expert, then what is there to say that they should not be permitted to do so? If autonomy is the source of the right to an assisted death, then, we have to concede that medical condition is not the sole indication for seeking access to one, nor can it be the triggering event for its lawfulness. This conclusion may be unpopular even amongst some proponents of legalisation but it is nonetheless the logical conclusion of basing the argument in autonomy, even if, as was discussed earlier, autonomy is taken to be relational rather than atomistic. Associated with the right of autonomy is

> respect for the dignity of the individual human being: our belief that quite irrespective of what the person concerned may think about it, it is wrong for someone to be humiliated or treated without respect for his value as a person.[25]

Taken together, these principles support self-governance irrespective of clinical condition or the nature of experienced suffering.

Given the basic argument in this book about the need to prioritise the liberty of the individual unless harm can be shown to result from allowing its exercise, it would seem that opponents of legalisation have failed to meet the burden of proof and therefore to make their case. We may speculate on the possible outcomes of legalisation, but we do not know for sure what the consequences will be. We may intuitively resist the idea of assisted dying, but that is our moral position. The question is whether or not it should be imposed on others. This leads to one further problem. The status quo achieves precisely this; that is, the choices of some people are defeated by the current law which accords weight to the views of opponents of assisted dying, even though there seems to be a groundswell of support for law reform. The opinions – even the morality – of those seeking legalisation are eclipsed by the (presumed) moral consensus. Yet, not only is it not clear that such a consensus actually exists, this is no way for a liberal society to behave. Thomasma says that once we accept an 'autonomy-centered view of human life'[26] then it is easy to build arguments for legalisation of assisted death. Legalisation on this view is a 'futherance . . . of the rights of individuals over and against repressive social conventions and laws, not to mention ancient religious values incorporated in a culture that is increasingly pluralistic'.[27] Thus, '[a] modern, secular Western state measures its progress through increasingly sophisticated protection of the privacy rights of its citizens'.[28] As this is the approach adopted in this

---

25 *Airedale NHS Trust v Bland* (1993) 12 BMLR 64, per Lord Hoffmann at p 96.
26 Thomasma, D C, 'An analysis of arguments for and against euthanasia and assisted suicide: Part one', *Cambridge Quarterly of Healthcare Ethics* (1996), 5, 62–76, at p 73.
27 Ibid.
28 Ibid.

narrative, such protection is to be welcomed and encouraged. Moreover, in the absence of harm, it is for the 'nay-sayers' to establish their case, yet this they manifestly fail to do. Political cowardice or apathy has resulted in a competent – even if small – group of people being denied the relief they seek, and when combined with the power of certain anti-legalisation groups the result is a society which falls prey to ideological bias or crude majoritarianism. Liberty to decide for oneself frees people from the 'tyranny of pluralism'.[29]

The final question, then, is what are we to do? Leaving things as they are is not, on a liberal account, an option, for both theoretical and practical reasons. If so, then we must strive for a resolution which causes no harm but vindicates individual rights. Arguably, this can only – and best – be done not by cumbersome legislation which hands over gatekeeping authority to doctors, but rather by taking the bull by the horns, respecting free and competent choice and essentially deregulating in this area. The Swiss model, therefore, has much to commend it, and despite the shibboleths of the opponents of legalisation, the Swiss are not being assisted to die in large numbers, nor has society in Switzerland ground to a halt. The predicted apocalypse simply has not happened and shows no sign of being on the horizon, near or far.

This conclusion does not in any way run counter to the argument that we should strive to alleviate suffering – physical, mental or existential – but it does accept that there may be some for whom this is either unwanted or impossible to achieve. Whereas opponents seem to think that legalisation, on this or any other basis, will result in massive numbers of chosen deaths, common sense and experience tell us that this is unlikely. If they are right that we do not need to legalise assisted dying because suicide is always an option, then those who are suicidal will not grow in numbers simply because those who are precluded at present from taking this option are now given help. Certainly, the total number of deaths will rise if those who are currently denied assistance are able to obtain it under a new legal regime, but even opponents of legalisation accept that death is not in and of itself always a 'bad' thing. Arguably, this is especially true when it is competently chosen for reasons which are satisfactory to the individual him- or herself.

There is much in our society which could be improved, and which might make the choice for death less important or desirable for some people. Effective palliation may remove the desire of some – but not all – people for an assisted death, and building a society which accommodates disability properly and which cares for its elderly and vulnerable well may further reduce the impetus for choosing death, but there are some for whom an assisted death will always be the preferred way to end life and this may include the elderly and those with disability. In fact, the House of Lords Select Committee on the Assisted Dying for the Terminally Ill Bill noted that '[d]isabled people . . . appear to believe

---

29 Safranek, J P and Safranek, S J, 'Assisted suicide: the state versus the people', *Seattle University Law Review*, Vol 21: 261–279 (1997), at p 265.

slightly more strongly than others that the law currently discriminates against terminally ill disabled people who wish to commit suicide but need assistance to do so'.[30]

That some people will still prefer an assisted death, even should successful alternatives be available, is evidenced not just by the support which apparently exists for legalisation but also by the fact that people such as Ms B competently choose not to live in the circumstances in which they find themselves and that Diane Pretty – and others like her – was prepared to spend the last months of her life fighting for a right which she believed we should all have. This is an issue about autonomy and equality; autonomy for those who currently are prevented from acting in a manner consistent with their own deeply held views and equality between them and those who currently can choose an assisted death within the narrow terms of the law. None of the devices used by the law to differentiate between these deaths is any more than ideologically, even legally, flawed. Certainly, they scarcely represent more than the morality of some people, albeit by no means everyone. The responsibility of the state, through the law, is to decide which view of morality should guide the community. Adopting the liberal position suggests that, whatever one's personal morality, the state should adopt a stance which respects and enforces a morality which maximises freedom, assuming the absence of harm to others. This mandates law reform, but not simply by way of handing over to doctors the power to decide who will qualify for an assisted death. Rather it means giving to individuals the right to make their own choices about death without being second-guessed or limited by medical or legal authority.

---

30   House of Lords Select Committee on the Assisted Dying for the Terminally Ill Bill, *Report of the House of Lords Select Committee on the Assisted Dying for the Terminally Ill Bill*, 2005, at p 130.

Index

acts and omissions distinction 92, 94, 96–107, 109, 138, 195–6; *Airedale NHS Trust v Bland* 111–12, 117, 119, 120; causation and 110–11; 'deprivation of life' 122–4; intention and outcome 96, 102, 103, 107; 'near' permanent vegetative state 122–4; pressure to choose death and pressure to refuse treatment 101

advance directives 84–7, 101, 123, 128, 195; *see also* refusal of life-sustaining treatment

age factor 175; *see also* elderly

Airedale NHS Trust v Bland 109, 111–12, 113, 116–22, 164

Allmark, P 70

allowing to die *see* letting die

altruism 54

Amarasekara, K 41–2, 49, 52–3, 67

Amici Curiae Brief of Not Dead Yet and American Disabled for Attendant Programs Today in Support of Petitioners 182

amyotrophic lateral sclerosis (ALS) 150, 178

Archbishop of Canterbury 158

Arthur, Dr 129–30, 134

assisted dying: advance directives and 87; equivalent to withholding or withdrawing treatment 113; refusal of treatment and 84; requests for 87–92; use of term 12, 52, 148

Assisted Dying for the Terminally Ill Bill 3, 147, 155–7; debate on 51, 157–60; further criticism of 179–86; responses to 160–4; *see also* House of Lords Select Committee on the Assisted Dying for the Terminally Ill Bill

assisted nutrition and hydration (ANH) 90, 116–21, 196; *see also* permanent vegetative state (PVS)

assisted suicide 10, 12, 103, 148; physician-assisted suicide (PAS) 12, 149–50, 171, 174–8; *see also* assisted dying; suicide

Association of Palliative Medicine (APM) 154; *see also* palliative care

attitudes of healthcare professionals *see* views of healthcare professionals

Australia 95, 171–2

autonomy 19–20, 31–43, 105–6, 112, 159, 200, 202; advance directives and 84, 86; competence and 39–41; differing views of 72–3; disability community and 63, 64, 162; dominant value in law and ethics 76, 100, 188; limiting the exercise of 39–42, 151, 179–80; permanent vegetative state and 122; questioning the autonomy of 'assisted' dying 36–8; refusing medical treatment and 81–2; relief of suffering and 48; slippery slope argument and 50–1; social considerations and 32–6; supersedes sanctity of life 30, 82, 85, 98, 113, 192; versus sanctity of life 5; *see also* control